THE ELECTRIC MIRROR

Politics in an Age of Television

The Electric Mirror

POLITICS IN AN AGE OF TELEVISION

SIG MICKELSON

ILLUSTRATED WITH PHOTOGRAPHS

DODD, MEAD & COMPANY

NEW YORK

ISBN: 0-396-06363-2

Library of Congress Catalog Card Number: 74-39223
Printed in the United States of America
by The Cornwall Press, Inc., Cornwall, N.Y.

INTRODUCTION

On a windy, rainy early June evening in 1952 in the prairie town of Abilene, Kansas, a retired General of the Armies of the United States mounted a rough plank platform set up in a public park. He was there to offer himself to the United States public as a candidate for the Republican nomination for the presidency.

There was nothing unusual about a former general running for the presidential nomination or about picking his old home town as a point from which to launch his campaign.

What was unusual was that two television networks had spent some one hundred thousand dollars (an expenditure of major proportions for a single program at that stage in television development) to contract with American Telephone and Telegraph Company to build a temporary microwave relay out to Abilene from Kansas City and to truck in remote television pickup equipment and crews from Omaha and Kansas City.

The speech itself was something less than a success. A rain-soaked General Eisenhower lost some of the remembered poise of a jaunty leader in a military uniform. He seemed uneasy in these strange circumstances and the audience in the park was apparently too water-logged to respond warmly. If it hadn't been for the CBS crew muscling its way into a press conference the next morning, from which television was supposed to have been decisively barred, the whole Abilene maneuver might have gone down in history as a disaster for Eisenhower's presidential aspirations and for the aspirations of the strong-willed moderate Republicans who supported him.

Aided by the television-oriented advertising agency, Young and Rubicam, and directed by campaign managers who saw in television an opportunity to crack the tight grip the supporters of Senator Robert Taft held on the party machinery, the Eisenhower strategists set out to wrest the nomination away from the man to whom the press referred as "Mr. Republican." In the subsequent election television played a starring roll. For the first time the voting public saw filmed commercials lavishly used in support of a candidate accompanied by filmed documentaries and a final-night televised transcontinental spectacular.

Sideline experts, including politicians, sociologists, public opinion specialists and television executives began to speculate on the meaning of the new phenomenon to determine, if they could, what changes in the American political and electoral processes would be brought about as a result of the experience of the summer and fall of 1952. It seemed then, that a revolution with far-reaching implications had begun, that politics would never be the same again, that the television camera would dominate the action and the television tube the voter response.

Now we're not so sure. We thought then that a candidate had to have television charisma. Campaigns would be shorter. Travel would be drastically reduced. Front porch campaigns might again come into style. Voters would be more knowledgeable and more sophisticated and more understanding of basic issues. With their greater understanding they could be addressed in more serious terms. There would be more interest in the whole political process, including legislation as well as elections. More citizens than ever before would vote. Television's x-ray capability would unmask and destroy the charlatans. The grip of the local machine would be relaxed because the candidate could go over the precinct boss's head directly to the voters. Greater voter sophistication would lead to a greater interest in issues. National political conventions would be streamlined and much of the extraneous nonsense cut away.

Now we're not so sure. We are quite certain that charisma helps, whatever charisma is, but President Nixon is the first person to admit that he simply doesn't have it. We have evidence that campaigns are no shorter, as a matter of fact they may even be longer. It's no exaggeration to say that John F. Kennedy, for example, began campaigning for election to the presidency in 1960 the day after he lost the vice-presidential nomination in August of 1956. This was four years and two months before his ultimate election in November of 1960.

It might be possible to be elected without going through an intensive campaign starting with the New Hampshire filings in January of election year, but the only serious candidate since 1952 who tried it is Senator Robert F. Kennedy and his assassination prevented us from seeing whether the shorter campaign could yield results.

The fact is that many of the glib generalizations of 1952 have been shaken by subsequent events. Our faith in television as the dominant force in the political process has likewise been shaken. We know that television has had a profound effect but perhaps it's had more effect in shaping the campaign and altering the style of politics than it has had on the voter himself. Perhaps the form has been changed more than the substance. We expected revolution but we got evolution. How much further will the evolution go? And what will be the end result?

We're certain that television has left an impact on the voter. But is it an impact which is characterized by immediate and recognizable response to a single stimulus? Or is it rather a gradual modification of views shaped by reaction to all media, including word of mouth? Does television ever induce the voter to switch abruptly from one position to another regarding a candidate or a piece of legislation? Or do the media, with television playing a very large role, reinforce previously held views rather than change them? If so what is the source of the original view?

Critics, in varying degrees of vehemence, have charged that television is shifting all emphasis to the glib tongue, the attractive smile, the well-tailored suit, the well-modulated voice and that elusive attribute, charisma. Critics also charge that the premium is now being put on lighting, camera angles, make-up, stage sets and good direction and production, rather than on the message; that candidates are being packaged for public distribution like boxes of detergents. All of this, critics argue, takes the focus from the hard meaningful issues and places it on external values which bear no resemblance to what competences a candidate would need to exercise after winning public office.

And this costs money, money far beyond what was ever dreamt of in those comfortable pre-television years. Vice-President Humphrey nearly missed getting his campaign in motion at all in 1968 because the Democratic purse was empty. As a matter of fact, as late as the autumn of 1971 the party still owed in excess of $8,000,000 as a result of that losing campaign. It would be a tragedy if elections were frequently to go by default because an able candidate couldn't raise the funds to compete.

Then there's the advantage held by the executive who won the election and sits where he can command the media to serve him. The out-party always complains. The in-party always argues that use of media, including television, is an integral part of leadership. But critics wonder, isn't perhaps the Nixon administration too skilled in its use of television? Doesn't this give the Administration too much power? Isn't it trying to further increase its power by bulldozing the media, particularly television, by such devices as Vice-President Agnew's November 1969 Des Moines speech? Isn't there a danger that the natural checks and balances of interparty politics will erode away and thus deprive the public of its functions as a braking mechanism against a runaway Administration?

Television obviously isn't the only medium playing a part in the political process. But it's the newest, the most expensive, the most intimate, the most widely followed and probably has the sharpest impact. Likewise, it's the most controversial and that's reason enough for a thorough examination.

Moreover, the impact of television on the electoral process hasn't been confined to the United States alone. As television receiver density grew in the other democratic countries of the world, political practitioners began to emulate the processes and techniques tested on the political battlefield by their counterparts in the U.S. Now, there is a very sophisticated use of the medium by the Germans, the Swedes, the English, the Japanese, the Italians, the Filipinos and even the French where General de Gaulle until recently kept a firm hand on the controls.

The history of television in politics is a short one. Really only twenty years, as this is written. But it has been filled with excitement, glamour, thrills, successes and failures, elation and heartbreak, and the bitterest of charges and counter-charges. The pioneers who tested the techniques, experimented with the technology and set the patterns on both sides of the camera are still in large measure active and not at all reluctant to describe their participation.

There is evidence, although circumstantial, that John F. Kennedy won the presidency in 1960 because he more successfully mastered the requirements of television than his opponent, Richard M. Nixon. It is also argued, with considerable evidence in support, that the same Richard Nixon won over Hubert Humphrey in 1968 because he and his supporters demonstrated greater skill in concealing the negative aspects of the Nixon personality and giving maximum display to the candidate's strength.

The availability of financial support of the candidate has become a major element of controversy because of the enormous

appetite of television for expenditures of money far exceeding
the budgets of pre-television campaigns. It is possible that it
was not the campaign skills of the Nixon supporters and the
candidate's own inherent capabilities and attractiveness that won
the 1968 election, but rather the impoverished state of the
Democratic treasury, and the disarray of the Democratic party
resulting from a chaotic nominating convention.

What is true of national campaigns at the top of the ticket,
is equally true of state and local campaigns. Television, finances,
image and showmanship may be crucial factors in winning
elections all the way down to the state legislature and alder-
manic levels.

Not only in the mechanical process of getting elected has
television intruded violently into the public view, but the
entire process of communication between the governors and
the governed has been profoundly affected by the sharp impact
of television's moving image. In many cases the most successful
administrators and law makers have been those who have been
most adept at winning support by mastering the techniques
of effective television presentation or, conversely, by mastering
the art of bluster and threatening a crackdown on television's
freedom to report as it sees fit.

Out-party representatives complain that television is too responsive to pressure from in-party officials, which would put
too much power to communicate over television in the hands of
those who regulate the medium.

Television has become an integral if not a dominant element
in the whole process of government, not only in the United
States but in most of the free world. Effective control by an
administration in power could lead to the destruction of the
democratic process. Irresponsible direction of the medium by
its owners and operators could bring about chaos which would
destroy the system.

So far the countries of the free world have succeeded in
maintaining a precarious balance, a balance that is sustained
by a variety of differing regulatory systems. But the balance is

a delicate one, the instrument volatile, and the consequences of misuse, either by government or television managers, could be disastrous.

Two decades have now passed since the electric mirror began to reflect government and political candidates to the people and the people to government and candidates. The television growth rate has been phenomenal. But where will it go next and what has been its record of achievement? Is it a capricious monster which must be harnessed, a spreading cancer which will consume democratic processes, or an incomparably effective tool for making electoral and governmental processes more responsive to the people and more efficient in meeting the increasing complexities in modern society? Whatever the case may be, the medium deserves a thorough examination.

CONTENTS

TELEVISION DISCOVERS
THE PUBLIC ISSUE

Television suddenly burst upon the American public consciousness in mid-summer of 1952 as a major force in the political and government processes. The phenomenon of television was not new. Milton Berle had been amusing Tuesday night audiences for more than three years. Ed Sullivan was becoming a public figure as the host of "Toast of the Town," and Lucille Ball and Desi Arnaz were beginning to attract large audiences to their Monday night "I Love Lucy."

But the public generally, including politicians and government officials, was unprepared for the shockwaves created by the two national political conventions, which began in June 1952. Television was not a total neophyte in the political process. Governor Thomas Dewey's campaign for re-election in New York State in 1950 was largely a television campaign. Senator William Benton placed heavy emphasis on the medium in his campaign for re-election in Connecticut in that same year, as did Senator Robert Taft in Ohio. President Truman's startling announcement that he would not seek re-election in 1952 was made in a speech delivered on television during the winter of that year.

Both the Taft supporters and the Eisenhower supporters in

their contest for the Republic nomination were aware that television would play a significant role and were making plans for unprecedented use of the medium.

But the public had no forewarning of the excitement that would be generated once the conventions got under way, and even the rank and file in the political community had no inkling that a revolutionary force in politics was gathering strength preparatory to releasing its full force. At a time when the Republican party delegates began to invade Chicago in mid-June, even the broadcast community displayed a curious insensitivity to the potential of their medium. Chairman William S. Paley of the Columbia Broadcasting System was vacationing outside the United States during both the Republican and Democratic conventions. CBS president Frank Stanton came to Chicago for one day between the two party gatherings.

There was some reason for this failure to forecast the full impact of television on the political process. The freeze on the licensing of new stations, which the Federal Communications Commission had imposed in 1949, was not lifted until the spring of 1952 and television's growth had been sharply inhibited for this three-year period. The transcontinental cable had not been opened until September of 1951 and even then only on an experimental basis so that national television was a relatively new phenomenon. News was still a relatively unimportant part of television's program spectrum.

This was the climate that prevailed as television cameras first started probing through the corridors of the Conrad Hilton Hotel in Chicago a week before the Republican convention started. Only a small band of news executives who had been planning for convention coverage for some thirteen or fourteen months had a premonition that they were onto something really big. By the time the Democrats had nominated the team of Adlai Stevenson and John Sparkman, some 55 million American citizens had looked in on some part of one or the other of the two conventions. Congressmen Joseph Martin of Massachusetts and Sam Rayburn of Texas, and Senator Everett Dirksen of Illinois had become either public heroes or villains, depending upon the point of view. Walter Cronkite, unknown prior to the conventions, had achieved a status comparable to that of a Hollywood leading man. Betty Furness became indelibly fixed in the public mind as the country's leading opener of refrigerator doors and ovens. Millions of Americans sat in front of their 10 inch television screens transfixed by the interplay of political forces, the manipulations of the two convention chairmen and the entire nominating process.

If the marriage between television and politics was consummated then, it was to have a relatively tranquil life for almost two decades. Even though the relations were not wholly peaceful during that timespan, generally the majority of the American public was directing a large measure of respect, reliance, and even admiration to television. There were, however, a number of indicators pointing to the fact that the serenity of the relationship would eventually be shattered. Paul Butler, the Democratic national chairman, angrily attacked one network from the Democratic National Convention podium in 1956 for not carrying all of a film produced by the party for showing to the convention delegates and presumably millions of television viewers. Secretary of State John Foster Dulles and President Eisenhower were apparently deeply displeased that CBS carried a "Face the Nation" interview with Chairman Nikita Khrushchev of the Soviet Union in 1957. Printed media critics questioned television's recreation of scenes of disturbances in Little Rock, Arkansas, during the school integration crisis of 1957. Some congressmen were bitter over a "CBS Reports" program broadcast in 1960 under the title "Harvest of Shame," which called attention to the plight of migrant workers. Critics questioned NBC's tactics in subsidizing the construction of a tunnel under the Berlin Wall in 1961. The "Pot Party" staged by CBS' Chicago station, WBBM-TV, in 1969 aroused powerful opposition in Congress, and CBS' support for an abortive Haitian revolt in 1966 first led to conflict between the network and the Investigations Subcommittee of the House Committee on Interstate and Foreign Commerce in 1969. Chairman Harley O. Staggers of West Virginia, who chaired both the subcommittee and the full committee, was not to forget what he considered to be the network's transgressions.

But generally there was a wave of euphoria from 1952 to 1969. The era of good feeling was suddenly shattered on November 13, 1969, in Des Moines, Iowa, when the Vice-President of the United States, Spiro T. Agnew, attacked network news in an intemperate but telling blast against the television news establishment.

The vice-president in a detailed bill of particulars questioned whether power should be concentrated "in the hands of a tiny and closed fraternity of privileged men, elected by no one and enjoying a monopoly sanctioned and licensed by the government."

Repercussions to the Agnew speech were almost instantaneous. Broadcast leaders came to the defense of the embattled newsmen. Persons who had been disturbed by the growing power and influence of television's news and information functions suddenly became vocal. An undercurrent of cynicism and frustration among persons who felt that television had dealt badly with them or their ideas or the persons they supported saw an opportunity to join the throngs in pursuit of a wounded quarry. Vice-President Agnew had sounded the call for the hunt and the pursuit was on.

The vice-president's speech even had its repercussions in the United Kingdom. Some 18 months later in a May Day speech made in Glasgow, former British cabinet member and one of the parliamentary leaders of the Labor Party, Anthony Wedgewood Benn, sounded an almost identical note.[1] Talking about the people and the mass media who "filter the news," the former British Postmaster General said: "Most of these people are accountable to no one, elected by no one and enjoy security of tenure while they continue to please their employers by proving their capacity to hold the attention of mass audiences." The phrase "elected by no one" recalls the exact words used by Vice-President Agnew in his Des Moines speech.

It was in this highly charged atmosphere which still persisted fifteen months later that CBS dropped another bomb: "The Selling of the Pentagon." [2] It was to be expected that the White House, the Pentagon's unfailing supporters in the Congress, and the Pentagon itself would fight back. What apparently happened, however, is that the program served as a catalyst around which all the disparate resentments coalesced, and CBS was vulnerable. Chairman Staggers had been smarting for some time. He had tried to bring CBS to book for its abortive attempt to cover the Haitian revolution which Staggers charged CBS was fomenting. And CBS was clearly vulnerable this time. Its editing had been sloppy at best. In the editing process, sentences spoken by Pentagon representatives had been taken out of context and shifted in position so that they appeared to respond to different questions. One colonel was so edited that statements originally made by the Prime Minister of Laos appeared to be his own.

A careful examination of the printed transcript of their interviews in their entirety compared with the program as broadcast, made by Rufus Crater, New York editor of *Broadcasting* magazine, suggests that the editing did not actually change or even modify the thrust of the interviews.[3] And surely "The Selling of the Pentagon" production staff was not much more guilty of juggling the order of presentation or even the gist of the interview than most other similar documentaries done for television or motion pictures, not to mention newspapers, wire services, and news magazines.

Congressman Staggers demanded the unedited outtakes. CBS president Frank Stanton refused, citing "freedom of the press" as a defence and pointing out that the surrender of outtakes would seriously inhibit news gathering in the future. The Staggers subcommittee voted a contempt citation. The full committee supported the subcommittee, leaving it up to the full House of Representatives to decide whether the contempt citation should be issued and the Attorney General requested to prosecute.

But Frank Stanton was not cited. This was the first time in history that a committee's recommendation for citation for contempt was rejected by the full House.[4] But the vote to recommit to the Staggers Committee, in effect a vote to kill, is not very reassuring to television. *The New York Times* speculated, the day after the vote was recorded, that "if a vote had been taken in secrecy, it would have gone five to one against CBS."

Television had become too powerful, too all pervasive a force in American life. In the process of assuming its lofty position, it has stepped on too many toes and bruised too many chins. Too many congressmen have watched pet-projects go down to defeat because television coverage had been refused when they had requested airtime. They have seen opponents obtain time when they would prefer to have those opponents remain in obscurity. They have been unable to bend television news personnel to their points of view. Some time the underlying resentments will surface again; and when a new eruption does occur, it is conceivable that television's freedom to report will be buried under a massive outpouring of congressional ill will.

The issue between CBS and the House committee, chaired by Congressman Staggers, revolved around the question as to whether the House committee should be given access to the program's outtakes, those portions of the film originally exposed which were dropped out in the editing process. Staggers demanded that he have them, CBS president Frank Stanton said no. Stanton won his victory when the leadership of the House on both sides of the aisle was unwilling to take a stand on an issue which might very probably lead to eventual CBS vindication in the federal courts. A massive CBS campaign to stimulate support from its affiliated stations which were in a position to do big favors for members of congress undoubtedly contributed to the reluctance of the House to penalize the CBS president. But as Julian Goodman, NBC president, who was NBC's deputy news chief before assuming the presidency, stated the day after the vote, the victory may not be long lived.[5]

CBS has taken action to soften any further blows by setting out new policies which will presumably avoid editing errors of the type that made its News division vulnerable. But the editing process will still require cuts, elisions, and some juxta-positions of statements and ideas. As long as this is true, persons whose comments are edited will always complain that their carefully drawn logic has been destroyed and their profound thoughts butchered. The inevitable result is that television as a purveyor of news and as a communication linkage between the governors and the governed will continue to live in a pre-carious state made more so because, unlike the printed media, it is licensed by government and hence subject to regulation and punitive laws. Its sheer size will continue to make it an exceedingly easy target even for shots that would be way off the target, if the target were smaller.

Vice-President Agnew in his Des Moines speech, which shat-tered the era of good feeling, was not wholly critical although this part of his speech was ignored by most news coverage. He cited one aspect of television service that has substantially changed the American public's outlook toward its social and economic problems. Even in his blistering attack on television news, the vice-president paid tribute, somewhat grudgingly, to the contributions to national knowledge made by television news, and to the fact that television's power has been used "constructively and creatively to awaken the public conscience to critical problems." He pointed out that the networks had made hunger and black lung disease national issues overnight, that they had done what no other medium could do to drama-tize the horrors of war, that they have tackled difficult social problems with directness and intimacy, that they have focused the nation's attention on environmental abuses, including pollution of the Great Lakes and the threatened ecology of the Everglades.

The vice-president was notably prescient in calling attention to a curious phenomenon that has developed since television became a major force on the communications scene, the quick rise to the forefront of major issues of public concern and their equally quick demise. There has been a constant parade of issues during the two decades in which the public has become dependent on the picture tube for news and information. Shortly after the historic Supreme Court decision on school integration in 1954, television began to focus its attention on the civil rights issue. Succeeding waves of intensive coverage of various aspects of the issue have been followed by parallel waves of public attention.

Beginning shortly after the Soviet Union launched its first Sputnik in September 1957, there was a major concern of the American public with our apparent shortage of scientists and engineers. For a few months television programs of all kinds were devoted to alleviating the shortage. Pressures were generated to encourage more secondary school students to go into science and engineering in college. Simultaneously, television supported efforts to revise the curricula of the primary and secondary schools in order to place more emphasis on the pure sciences as opposed to social sciences and the humanities. By 1959 the engineer and scientist shortage was all but forgotten and public attention had shifted to Cuba.

During the 1960 election campaign attention turned to the "missile gap." The issue had been raised by the Kennedy forces and hammered home during the remainder of the campaign. Since 1960, these waves of public interest have been coming in more rapid succession as television looked for new problems to focus on. Not too long ago one of the principal items demanding the attention of the American people was the question of hunger in America. After a run of several months, hunger gave way to gun control. The gun control issue was high on the public attention scale after the assassinations of Martin Luther King and Senator Robert Kennedy, until it was replaced by concern over the youth rebellion. The major concern of the public, stimulated by media prodding, then changed to pollution of the earth and foreboding concerning the earth's ecology. Some experts insist that ecology will continue to be a major issue for an indefinite period of time; but following the evolution of issues over a period of the last twelve to fifteen years, it seems likely that ecology will soon be eased out of its position and replaced by another problem that will command equal attention during its short span in the public eye.

All of this poses the question as to what role television plays in the creation of these waves of public concern and their sudden disappearance. It is impossible at this stage to develop any statistical evidence, since there simply is none. But there is circumstantial evidence. Changes have been occurring more rapidly. The public is becoming excited over an issue in a relatively shorter period of time. The fact that television has been devoting considerable time, energy, and money to coverage of some of these major questions and problems suggests that the medium itself has played a significant role in their creation.

If one visualizes the governmental process in the United States as being an equilateral triangle with the White House, or executive, at one apex, the Congress, or the legislative, at another, and the public at a third, the media of communications are the linkages between and among these three elements. The White House uses radio, television, and the newspapers when it wishes to communicate to the Congress and the public. The Congress, when it wishes to communicate with the Executive, uses the communications media to build pressure within the public. The public, in turn, exerts pressure on the White House and the Congress through the electoral process, which is stimulated by communications.

The public, however, does not have the same access to the communications media available to the White House and Congress, and this could be one factor leading to the rise of the action-demonstration technique as a means of attracting attention to a cause or a program. Frustration on the part of many dissident elements inevitably occurs, and those without similar access must use what devices they can to seek out the opportunities to make their wishes known. It didn't take long for dissident elements to find out that television cameras were quickly dispatched to demonstrations, and were in ever greater measure present when the demonstrations turned into violence.

The White House, alert to television's unique capacity to reach the masses quickly and forcefully, has developed highly sophisticated techniques for influencing the public and thus, through the public, the Congress. The White House press conference has been a particularly successful device, as have presidential messages. Both devices have been used more frequently by President Nixon than his predecessors. In the Nixon administration a new director of communications function has been set up in the executive office of the White House to coordinate publicity activities of the president, the cabinet, and the other executive agencies within the national government.

The Congress similarly has been busily at work setting up its own devices. A congressional film and television facility is available to members of the House of Representatives. Senior members of the Congress have become adept at making use of interview time on American networks. They have discovered that it is frequently possible to appear before news teams on the steps of the Capitol or in their own offices, so they can be filmed for presentation on the networks or by groups of independent stations.

Perhaps more than anything else the profound shock within the United States caused by the sudden series of dramatic developments which took place during the early months of 1968 constitute one of the best indicators of the enormous power of television and its effect on the public. While the Tet offensive, for example, surely did not succeed because of television, there is ample circumstantial evidence to indicate that the shockwaves were more pronounced, lasted longer, and had more impact because of television coverage.

It is a matter of record now that statements from U.S. government officials prior to late January 1968 exuded optimism.

The public had been led into a state approaching euphoria concerning the Vietnamese war. And yet Americans were watching every night on their television news programs same-day action from the battlefronts. They were seeing action, guns firing, blood, and death, and injured carried away in helicopters. But the general diagnosis of military leaders and Administration officials was that we were at last approaching some kind of favorable conclusion. The light at the end of the tunnel, as the briefing officers suggested again and again, was becoming clearly visible.

Then came the Tet offensive. In the middle of all this euphoria the viewers saw same-day films from the streets of Saigon showing the Vietcong holding the upper hand. A particularly shocking series of pictures showed Vietcong actually invading the American Embassy in what was supposed to be the best protected section of Saigon.

The impact totally shook the confidence of the American people. That confidence was shaken so badly that the President of the United States decided on March 31 to abandon his plan to run for re-election; in effect, to abdicate. His decision left the country in a state of profound shock. The after-effects undoubtedly contributed to stimulating the demonstrations outside the Hilton Hotel in Chicago during the Democratic Convention in August. The events certainly damaged the Democratic party and contributed to the election of President Nixon. They may very well have caused long-range damage to the entire American system of government. Without doubt they aided in the rapid rise of Senator Eugene McCarthy as a significant candidate for the presidency of the United States.

How much influence did television really have over the surprising events of 1968 and the turmoil which persisted through 1969 and well into 1970? Is there any method of measuring this impact? Has it changed the public response to normal, day-to-day governmental and political activity? Many assumptions have been made concerning the role, significance and impact of television. Many conclusions have been drawn based on circumstantial evidence. Many thoughtful people have given time and attention to trying to determine the precise effect of television. But the answer is still obscure. There are some assumptions, however, which can be supported by circumstantial evidence, and, perhaps, at some time in the future, substantially supported by more concrete data.

Estes Kefauver might have remained an obscure Senator from Tennessee if he had not been the driving force behind the famed Kefauver Hearings which commanded many hours of television viewing in 1951, and the word "Mafia" might never have worked its way into the popular lexicon had not Senator Kefauver been able to summon such fascinating characters as Frank Costello and Virginia Hill before his televised committee hearings during the summer of that year. Civil rights and integration might have remained philosophical and textbook problems had not television cameras recorded the efforts of blacks to exercise their court-supported rights to enter Little Rock Central High School in 1957, and the confrontation between Governor George Wallace of Alabama and envoys from the Attorney General's office at the entrance to the administration building of the University of Alabama in 1962 might have remained a minor footnote in history.

Autherine Lucy and James Meredith became symbols of a black drive for acceptance in Southern state-supported universities because television cameras followed them onto campuses and maintained a pictorial record of their efforts to establish themselves as accepted students on the same plane as the enrolled whites. Martin Luther King owes much of his fame to the fact that television intensively covered the bus strikes in Montgomery, Alabama, and conversely, Bull Connor, the Birmingham chief of police, became a villain along with his police dogs and fire hoses, because he obstructed black progress in full view of the television audience.

Coverage of Southern restaurants and drug stores became a powerful mechanism toward achieving a new state of black equality because television cameras followed the demonstrators from planning meetings into the scenes of their protest. Restaurant owner Lester Maddox became Governor of Georgia but inadvertently contributed mightily to the spread of integration in his state because television cameras were present when he prescribed axe handles properly applied to black skulls as useful preventive measures against a black invasion of his Pickrick Restaurants in Atlanta. The death of three young Northern crusaders in Mississippi, who were aiding registration of voters in the summer of 1964, became a national cause célèbre in large part because television zoomed in on the story and didn't let up until their bodies were discovered deep under a newly built dam.

Television, too, has had a solid impact on the election of public officials and representatives. The public relations factor, however, largely stimulated by television, may not always elect one candidate to office, but it can utterly destroy another.

The late Senator Joseph McCarthy of Wisconsin is a prime example of a victim of television's sharp and perceptive eye. It was almost certainly the image of the cruel, insensitive inquisitor, projected by television, that turned the public against McCarthy, led to his censure by his fellow senators and his ultimate early death. The historic "See It Now" program, produced by Edward R. Murrow and Fred W. Friendly on the CBS Television Network in 1954, exposed the senator's carelessness with fact, his ruthless pursuit of his chosen enemies and his inhumane treatment of those he chose to persecute. Historians generally agree that the program turned the tide against him.

The fascinating and revealing Army-McCarthy hearings which followed only weeks later applied the coup de grâce. McCarthy never recovered from the television image created by his snarling, belligerent, self-righteous performance in the television coverage of those hearings. McCarthy probably would have been brought down eventually, even without television. But in this case the television camera was the penetrating eye that pierced sham and cut through to the inner man. But it may be that the McCarthy case only illustrates that it is easier to destroy than to build, even for the television camera.

Demonstrations and even riots are nothing new on the American public scene. There have been historic confrontations before television, including the Haymarket riots in Chicago and the battle of Dearborn Overpass outside Detroit, but there is evidence that such demonstrations have been more frequent and in many cases more violent since the advent of television. It seems likely, furthermore, that the action-demonstration technique is here to stay. It may not owe all of its popularity to television, but certainly television has been a factor. The tendency to go from peaceful demonstration to forceful demonstration, or even to riot, probably owes some of its popularity as a device for attracting attention to the fact that television cameras are present on the scene. The fact that many old values held by the public seem to be coming unhinged leads to frustration. Frustration, in turn, may in part derive from the speed of television in delivering information from distant parts of the world, and from the dramatic impact of the picture. Print is colder, more remote, and less inclined to emotional color and realism which television furnishes in massive doses.

There are also distortive factors in television which contribute to unrest. Undoubtedly, the heavy concentration of dramatic pictures in television, which leave out the unimportant, unimpressive, undramatic, and colorless, and in contrast deliver a highly concentrated potion of dramatic information in pictorial form can distort actuality. Differences in editing processes have an influence. The fact that the press report is a distillate which goes through a great number of hands and minds before it appears in print extracts some of the dynamism and drama. But the picture itself is not distilled. It appears on the home screen just as it appeared in the camera's lens as the event occurred. And this very realism may exaggerate the impact of a scene far beyond reality of its context.

There is one other series of events which in large part may have stemmed from the influence of television. It is the phenomenon often called the "revolution of rising expectations," particularly as it has affected blacks and ghetto dwellers in the United States. There seems to be little doubt that unrest and dissatisfaction, sometimes leading to riot, have occurred when people in underprivileged areas have been able to see on television screens the manner in which the wealthier elements of society live. Coveting similar wealth and comfort is a natural reaction.

All of this leads to a significant question: Can television's influence on the electorate be described as a safety valve, a factor leading to a more rational social order? Is it a communications channel available to all elements of society? Or is television a clogged channel, an ineffective channel open only to the few, a distortive factor which creates an unrealistic view of American life and of the world outside the United States? Is it an influence for disillusionment, frustration, and despair? Or has it actually brought about a more informed electorate, a more interested people? Has it created a social situation which will be one of turmoil and disillusionment for many years to come, or has it formed the foundation from which a better society can grow— a society based on quick communications, faithful reporting, dramatic presentation of significant and serious information? We know that the individual has the capacity to react and adapt to change but we are not so sure whether institutions have built-in mechanisms which will enable them to respond. Perhaps the resulting lag will lead to more frustration and resultant disorder and turmoil. If so, is television responsible?

The most significant element in relationships between people and their governments, and between people and social forces arises through the interplay of government and politics, conveyed by communications media, of which television is the most realistic, dramatic and colorful. It is vital to know what effect television has had on government, on political mechanisms and processes, on the electorate.

THE BLURRED X-RAY EYE

```
┌─────────────┐
│  ┌───────┐  │
│  │   2   │  │
│  └───────┘  │
└─────────────┘
```

Television's capacity to penetrate sham with an x-ray eye is one of the most widely used cliches of modern politics. The x-ray eye, the theory goes, can expose the warts and blemishes on a man's face; it can penetrate to his inner mind; it can analyze his character; it can lay bare his strengths and weaknesses; and display all of this to the general public on the television screen. Professionals and amateurs alike in the art of political campaigning subscribe to the theory. But does the television camera have this power? Can it actually reveal the individual's inner character on the television screen in a meaningful way?

Behavioral scientists, including Ithiel de Sola Pool of Massachusetts Institute of Technology, Erwin Scheuch of Harvard and the University of Cologne in Germany, and James D. Halloran of the University of Leicester in England, are not so sure. Their evidence suggests that it really is very difficult to assess the impact of television on the individual; that it is almost impossible to develop any meaningful data concerning the effect of continued viewing of the television screen on political campaigns and governmental public relations. There are too many other complex forces, say the behaviorists, playing on the individual to enable the isolation and examination of television as a sole influence. The individual's reaction reflects his own environment, his own past experience and his own emotional and intellectual state as he receives the message.

The Nixon campaign of 1968 was a model of competence, skill, image-making, and candidate management. One of the major reasons for the victory of Richard Nixon in the November 1968 election was the fact that his campaign was so adeptly managed. The candidate at almost all times during the campaign was kept under tight reins; most of his public appearances were in controlled situations; most of the questions that were asked of him in professionally produced programs were asked by persons who had been carefully screened in advance, and whose questions it was possible to anticipate. The candidate himself was thoroughly briefed on all possible questions that might arise, and was in a position to respond in a bland and essentially non-controversial way.

But this leads to some interesting questions: Was the Nixon candidacy so carefully packaged by advertising agencies, public opinion specialists, public opinion pollsters, and expert campaign managers that the average voter was unable to see the real Nixon in action? Was the voter only seeing a candidate who was carefully packaged for him?

If so, where was the x-ray eye? Where was the penetrating lens of the television camera that would cut through the packaging and sham, and reveal the real candidate? Were the wrappings sufficiently impenetrable so the television eye couldn't cut through, so that the packaging alone penetrated to the home screen and was it the package that left its effect on the individual voter? Was Hubert Humphrey the loser in 1968 because he was not so carefully packaged? Because he was much less inclined to take the advice of his managers? Or because the Hubert Humphrey personality was so indelibly imprinted on the voter it couldn't be packaged?

The results of the 1968 presidential election were hardly decisive enough to draw any meaningful conclusions. Richard Nixon, who had been the loser to John F. Kennedy in 1960 by only approximately 120,000 votes out of nearly 70 million cast, won in 1968 by only a scant half million over Hubert H. Humphrey out of a few more than 70 million ballots registered in that year.

Since there is no reliable or acceptable scientific data to indicate the effect on the voter of television campaigning, or even of general television viewing, there is only circumstantial evidence to rely on. And even that is inconclusive. The percentage of voters going to the polls apparently is not the answer. The figure increased through the 1950s, but it leveled off or declined slightly in the 1960s.

It is commonly assumed that the American voter is better informed concerning the issues as a result of television viewing. But there is no conclusive data to back this up; as a matter of fact, there are some students of the impact of television who have come to the conclusion that subjecting the voter to a vastly greater volume of information has served more to confuse than to inform.

Edward W. Barrett, former Dean of the Graduate School of Journalism at Columbia University, would agree. Barrett suggests that one reason for the apparent greater volatility of the voter during the television era is the result of the confusing volume of information to which the voter is subjected. It may be true that the voter reacts more speedily since television to new influences on both the national and international scene, and to new issues and problems because television brings some issues to him more graphically than before, but there is also evidence that he may become bored sooner.

There is no doubt that tremendous interest and a certain amount of measurable reaction has been stimulated by advertising campaigns. During Lyndon Johnson's presidential campaign in 1964 against a hawkish Goldwater, a profound influence on the electorate seems to have been generated by a television commercial showing a little girl licking her ice-cream cone while an atomic bomb exploded in the background. There is little doubt, too, that commercials created by Jack Tinker and Partners for the Nelson Rockefeller campaign for the governorship of New York in 1966 showing accomplishments of the Rockefeller administration prior to 1966 played a positive role in winning re-election for the Governor.

But there is still a lingering doubt. Is there really a rational effect on the voter? Is there greater understanding of issues and current events, better knowledge of the capabilities, intelligence, and administrative competences of the candidate; or is what seems to be sophistication simply an emotional reaction stimulated by sophisticated advertising techniques?

It can be assumed that 60-second spot commercials produced for General Eisenhower had some influence over the 1952 election; but measurement is difficult because it now appears evident that General Eisenhower was going to trounce Governor Stevenson soundly anyway. Furthermore, it is almost totally impossible to isolate the impact of any one single campaign device. Circumstantial evidence indicates that commercials do have a considerable influence, but the evidence can't be supported by statistics. It can only be assembled from the hunches and subjective reactions of campaign workers and advertising agencies.

If an analysis of candidates proves unrevealing, perhaps an examination of the medium might furnish some clues. How faithfully does television report issues; does the x-ray eye cut through sham and packaging; are there safety valves available to viewers to enable them to avoid being duped; does television portray relative realism or might there be built-in distortions in the physical presence of the television camera or in the manner in which television programs are built and presented to the general public?

The potential distortive effect of the electronic camera is one thing. Possible distortive values which arise out of the use of the film camera in creating and editing television news are something else. The former television critic of the *London Times* and now a member of the British Parliament, Julian Critchley, has written of what he regards as the tendency of the film camera to distort in regularly scheduled news broadcasts.[1] Critchley points out that in the editing and production of the television news broadcast, the general commentary and linkages between film elements are the product of careful writing and analysis based on the backgrounds of the writers and editors and a wealth of outside services including wire service dispatches, reports from correspondents, staff research and the general background of the production staff. The film elements which are inserted into the program, however, appear to the viewer on his television screen precisely as they appeared in the lens of the camera at the time they were photographed by the news cameraman. Motion picture film, Critchley points out, can be edited by eliminating portions, trimming, shifting scenes and adding effects, but the raw material, as it comes to the television screen is exactly as it was originally seen. No amount of editing can alter the substance of raw material.

This is in sharp contrast to the newspaper story, which is the product of the eyes and ears and mental observations of one or more reporters, given perspective by the addition of elements from the reporter's own background, including attitudes, memories and experiences. All of these are combined into a distilled report. This distilled product then goes through a process of several more distillations and screenings performed by re-write men and sub-editors before it finally appears on the copy desk. There it is given a final editing before it goes into print.

The printed story thus, says Critchley, has perspective. It has a mixture of background and detail furnished by the whole editing process which stirs, synthesizes, homogenizes and polishes the product.

The film story on television, to the contrary, appears on the home screen exactly as it looks in the camera lens as the event took place. The picture of the Saigon chief of police shooting down a suspected Vietcong in a major square in the Vietnamese capital had a much sharper impact on the viewer because the raw material, the firing of the shot at pointblank range and the collapse on the pavement of the victim, essentially unedited and unfiltered, went from the scene of action directly to the television screen. It was shortened, combined with other events and given an introduction and conclusion, but the shooting itself was undiluted raw material. In print the event lost some of the hardness of impact. It was placed in perspective, related to other similar events, and juxtaposed with other elements in that day's story of the Vietnamese war. Even the still picture of the shooting, which won an international prize for an Associated Press photographer, did not carry the same impact in the viewer's mind because it lacked the shock effect produced by motion and sound.

Memorable film scenes from past political campaigns support the validity of the theory. Many who remember the primary campaign waged by Senator Taft in New Hampshire in 1952 will recall pictures of the Senator, obviously bored with the whole process, pulling one handshaker after another past him with a rather cold and perfunctory, "How do you do . . . glad to meet you." They will also have great difficulty forgetting Senator Kefauver half reclining on a bed in a small hotel room in a middle-sized Wisconsin city with his shoes off, obviously suffering from great fatigue as he talked to a reporter about the exhausting aspects of his sixteen-hour day of campaigning, or Earl Warren, then Governor of California and later Chief Justice of the United States Supreme Court, as he sat at a chicken dinner during that same Wisconsin primary, being harangued by an enthusiastic middle-aged, Wisconsin Republican woman while he was trying to get a bite or two of chicken before going to the rostrum to deliver his next campaign speech.

It is hard to know whether these recollections of Kefauver and Warren had any effect on their ultimate failures to win nomination. But it is almost certain that Senator Taft's obvious distaste for pressing the flesh helped create the atmosphere which led to General Eisenhower's June victory at the Republican Convention in Chicago.

Television news film pictures of the jumpers and screamers as they greeted Senator Kennedy during his campaign for the

Presidency in 1960, and the dissident students as they tried to talk down Vice-President Humphrey in his 1968 campaign, are also unforgettable pictures. The question is, are they distortion or reality? In some measure they are obviously distortion in that they magnify drama and excitement at the expense of the more dispassionate account which appeared in print.

Coverage of the war in Indo-China has been television's classic test. Considering only its agility, flexibility and capacity to perform wondrous feats of electronic legerdemain television has passed with highest honors. This is the first war that has been seen, in some cases live and on the same day, on home screens throughout the world. But from the point of view of the impact of the coverage on world opinion the record is less clear and even subject to doubts.

It is difficult for any American, even at the highest levels of government, to fully understand the Vietnamese war. It is far away. It involves people with a completely different culture. It is an undeclared war. There is a lack of symbols with which the public can identify. Perhaps most importantly, American citizens have not been asked to regard it as a great patriotic crusade and measure of national honor. It was never a situation demanding that we pull out all emotional stops and assure the sacrifices of all-out war.

The big problem in reporting the Vietnamese war involves not only the logistical feat of moving television film great distances, but the fact that there are no valid systems of measurement of gains and losses. There are no battle lines that move backward and forward. There is no taking of key points which clearly represent victory for one side or the other. The best yardstick the military has been able to come up with is the body count; the number of enemy dead measured against the numbers of U.S. and South Vietnamese soldiers killed in any given week. But even the body count is not a very believable system of measurement. It may have been convincing for a week, or a few months, but the public has become inured to it, if not somewhat insulated. The monotony of hearing the enormous numbers of North Vietnamese and Vietcong who have been killed in contrast to the relatively limited numbers from the U.S. and South Vietnamese side, has contributed to suspicion and doubt.

The so-called "five o'clock follies," the daily briefing at U.S. military headquarters, did not do much to increase public interest or confidence because there really wasn't much to be revealed except for the body count. For some months the main measure of victory or defeat as described by U.S. diplomatic and military leaders was the pacification program. More recently it has been Vietnamization. Both pacification and Vietnamization are, if not abstractions, at least hardly measurable indices. And the most favorable statistical data measured by these criteria can hardly compete in the public consciousness with television film of specific battle action, even of patrol or platoon dimension. The film on the television screen appears as reality, even though it may not be as representative of the broad picture as the abstract reports of the briefing officers. This leads to a real dilemma. It suggests questioning whether television coverage may lend an impact to news reporting that may go far beyond the realities of the events it covers.

The utilization of the action-demonstration techniques by students on the American campuses, and the frequent tendency of such actions or demonstrations to get out of hand and result in disruption and violence, also illustrate the tendency of television to exacerbate the more extreme elements of American life. As in the case of political conventions or war, the television picture tube frequently shows only a few bursts of intensive action, and ties these together by skillful and judicious editing.

As a consequence we don't see entended periods of boredom, intervals of peaceful behavior and peaceful marching, and of any restrained speech-making there might be. During the Kent State riot, which led to the deaths of four students and injuries to another ten, television viewers watched National Guardsmen marching towards students, firing tear gas as they approached student ranks. They watched students throwing tear gas canisters back at the Guardsmen. Then they saw shooting, ambulances, students lying on the ground and blood, all in color. They did not see students strolling on the campus before the Guardsmen fired, calmly going from class to class, and other students quietly standing on the sidelines, curious but not participating.

This has been true in the Chicago Loop, in lower Manhattan, outside the United Nations in New York, or on Park Avenue near the Waldorf-Astoria Hotel; on the streets of San Francisco; Cambridge, Massachusetts; Madison, Wisconsin; Athens, Ohio; Berkeley and Santa Barbara, California, and a host of other places. The package that we have seen on the television screen has been a highly concentrated one. It has been intensive, dynamic, dramatic, but there is a real question whether television has furnished any genuine perspective, whether in its intense effort to capture the drama it has not squeezed out the commonplace elements which furnish balance and true realism.

If the Americans, who watched the 1968 Democratic Convention in Chicago, recall the events of that turbulent week, it is not the nominating speeches that they remember, or the balloting, or the acceptance speeches, or the debates over credentials or platform. It is the bloody, riotous scenes on Michigan Avenue, several miles from the International Amphitheater where the convention was held, which left the most vivid impressions. Those riot pictures were made in motion picture film, developed, edited and inserted into the running story of the convention; but they constituted only minutes out of the hours devoted to the convention, something less than one percent of the total time. And it is those scenes of violence that characterize the whole convention and may have destroyed Democratic Party hopes of victory.

It would be useful to know precisely how much influence these events, and their coverage, have had on the American voter. It would be useful to know whether the voter is more or less impelled to frustration, irritation and anger after having lived through twenty years of television coverage of the news, than during the twenty years before television. It would be useful to know whether the turbulence in our political life in the last half of the twentieth century may stem in part from the fact that television is now our most common and useful tool for obtaining the news.

Lest there be any question about television status in the news dissemination spectrum, voter polls conducted regularly since 1959 show that television moved ahead of newspapers as a prime source of news for the general public in 1963 and has continued to increase its lead since. A 1971 poll shows 60 percent of the public replying that they get most of their news of the world from television and only 48 percent rely most heavily on newspapers. 23 percent chose radio, and 5 percent news magazines. In 1968 the margin was 59 percent for television and 49 percent for newspapers. Totals add up to more than 100 percent because of multiple answers.

While science can answer many questions for us, this unfortunately, is one which scientists have not yet been able to devise the formula to measure. Specialists in the behavioral sciences, such as Professor Pool at MIT, point out that the fabric of human experience is far too complicated, and the difficulty of isolating any one stimulus a virtual impossibility. The tracking of a stimulus through the thought and reaction processes of the human individual is a virtual impossibility. Sometimes a device or a system may be found for making such measurements, but until that time the best we can do is make certain assumptions. Applied to the electoral process this probably means a number of things.

Television, it must be concluded, has been a mixed blessing in the political process. It has brought people closer to politics and government, but it may distort the view. It has brought distant events into the family circle and projected them into the living room, but it brings only part of the whole picture— and that part is usually the most dramatic. It has given political managers a new, handy, all-purpose tool for electing candidates to public office. But the all-purpose tool may be just as useful for creating a false image as for projecting the real candidate. It has enormously reduced the physical gap between the citizen and his government, but it has also furnished the manipulators of information about government a handy device for creating events which only barely justify, if that, the effort expanded on them. Perhaps, it has created a new and dynamic interest on the part of the citizen in governmental processes; but it may be just as likely that what passes for interest is simply confusion.

It is conceivable that there now is a greater intensity of interest in political issues, but surely no greater emotion than was engendered by Franklin D. Roosevelt running against President Herbert Hoover in 1932, or by Theodore Roosevelt against Woodrow Wilson and William Howard Taft in 1912, or by the Dewey-Truman race of 1948, or by some of the violent confrontations of the late nineteenth century. The best that can be said is that more people are exposed at greater length and at closer range to both issues and candidates. If we could be sure that the view is clear and undistorted, that the viewer is attentive and interested, that the device itself is a faithful electric mirror, we could conclude that television would help create a more effective government, more responsive to democratic impulses and more reflective of an informed electorate. But evidence to support these conclusions is fuzzy at best. What there is may be more a product of wishful thinking than a sound scientific conclusion.

In fact, the opposite may conceivably be true. The apparent realism of television, the assumption that pictures can't lie, the intimate relationship of viewer to receiver may even distort facts and situations, create false impressions, and provide a handy, ready-made tool for the political charlatan.

Above all, it must be remembered that an overwhelming proportion of television's total program time is given over to pure entertainment. There are some viewers who maintain television receivers in their homes largely for news and information programs. But the vast majority are set-owners because they like Lucy, or the Beverly Hillbillies, or "Bonanza," or "All in the

Family," or the Tuesday night movies. News and information are either an added attraction, a distraction, or an unwanted intrusion. All too often, the latter is true.

In this context, politics and government are dangerously close physically to show business, if not distinctly a part of it. Surely the viewer unconsciously equates an appearance by the president in a conversation with reporters with his favorite dramatic programs—unconsciously, if not consciously. This raises the question: Can a performance by a president, or a senator, or a cabinet member, or even by a network news correspondent or analyst be regarded in the same frame of reference as an editorial page column in a newspaper or an item in a news magazine? And can the producer of the information program divorce himself totally from the requirement that his production appear in a show business environment?

By and large, television executives, producers and correspondents have performed with a high sense of public responsibility and with a remarkable degree of confidence for so new a medium. A high level of esprit de corps has been established and an equally high level of respect has been won from fellow print journalists and political practitioners. But the television journalists, no matter what their competence and their dedication to service may be, still operate in a show business setting, and whether they are affected by it or not many viewers may be, and this is a distorting factor in itself.

None of this in any way belies the fact that television has rightfully assumed a role as the most persuasive medium in political campaigning, the most direct line of contact between government and voter, the most dramatic factor in the political campaign. But how much real influence does it have? The best evidence available suggests that television has probably not affected the number of voters going to the polls, nor has it contributed greatly to the general background, understanding and knowledgeability of voters, or their understandings of issues. It probably hasn't even led to deeper understanding of the political process, even though superficially there may be greater familiarity.

An analysis of the process of campaigning in the mid-twentieth century style doesn't yield much evidence that the voter is better informed, but it does suggest that the campaign managers are not only alert to the presence of television, but have adapted their techniques to its requirements. In doing so they have changed the whole process of political campaigning. Perhaps this is the most significant and most dramatic change that has been accomplished in the era of television, and the one which merits the most intensive study.

In some cases the highly skilled television practitioner has the talent and technical capability to build a cocoon around a candidate who is totally unknown at the beginning of the packaging period. Agency experts and public opinion specialists must have the talent for dressing the unknown candidate as they see fit, giving him a made-to-order personality, image, character and style. But in order to do so, it is essential to keep the candidate out of public view on all occasions when conditions cannot be totally controlled. This obviously was not wholly possible in the case of Richard Nixon in 1968. Mr. Nixon had been a member of the Senate of the United States and prior to that a member of the U.S. House of Representatives. As a congressman, he had been prominent in the Hiss case in the early 1950s. He achieved additional national fame for his aggressive campaign against Helen Gahagan Douglas for a seat in the California senate in 1950. For eight years he had been the Vice-President of the United States and had been given more public exposure than any vice-president in history, and he had run against John F. Kennedy for the presidency in 1960. He had run for governor of California during 1962 in a campaign which was covered nationally. He was hardly an unknown on the American political scene and many voters had fixed attitudes towards him at the beginning of the 1968 campaign.

Additionally, an important safety valve preventing unmitigated image-making was present during the 1968 campaign: the regularly scheduled news program. It would have been impossible in 1968 for Richard Nixon, candidate for President of the United States, to escape the eye of the television news camera. He simply could not avoid appearing in public places and, when he spoke, his image, voice and expressions were there for the camera lens to record. Intensive coverage continued throughout the entire campaign. While it could be controlled to some extent through advance briefings and preplanning of the circumstances in which the candidate would appear, it was almost unavoidable that the television news camera would catch a glimpse of the real Richard Nixon, no matter how effectively his managers tried to conceal him.

It is true that until late in the campaign, candidate Nixon succeeded in avoiding appearances on discussion or interview programs. He didn't make his "Meet the Press" and "Face the Nation" appearances until the last ten days before the election. These appearances could not be as tightly controlled by the Nixon campaign staff as his arena programs, but he could be thoroughly prepared and a skilled fencer like Richard Nixon is able to steer a panel interview show in almost any direction he wants it to go. As it developed, the candidate demonstrated considerable skill at avoiding dangerous pitfalls. But if the Nixon campaign may be generally regarded as the ultimate in image-making and the use of sophisticated techniques to protect the candidate from undue exposure, the Humphrey campaign can be regarded as a dismal failure. The Humphrey character was well known to the public as he had just completed a term as vice-president. But Humphrey had a number of overwhelming disadvantages. His campaign was much less adequately and expertly planned. Perhaps, more importantly, there is nothing bland about the bouncy, ebullient, gregarious and garrulous Hubert Humphrey. Confining the Humphrey image within an air-tight package was the ultimate test of a political public relations man's packaging ability.

The John F. Kennedy campaign of 1960 was an expertly planned venture managed by the most competent political advisors of the time, including Mr. Kennedy himself. It was backed up by the most sophisticated use of polling techniques ever employed for political purposes, including Ithiel de Sola Pool's "people machine." The "people machine" utilized public opinion polling and computerized analyses to create a model of the American electorate. By use of the computer-developed data the impact of campaign efforts could be instantly analyzed and potential effects of new themes predicted with uncanny accuracy.[2] The devices used were designed more to present the candidate as he was and to project his real personality than to hide problems in his personality, or to create a non-existent image. The Nixon-Kennedy debate series also presented both candidates face-to-face in a confrontation in an environment which they could not control. For the first time they were placed in a situation where television could live up to the claims of its partisans that it could penetrate the artificial wrappings of packaging.

The television commercial leads to even a more profound quandary. Can use of the most sophisticated techniques of television advertising create attitudes, images, and even personal responses which are not genuine? Is the commercial an elaborate, diabolical device for deceiving the voter and selling him a bill of goods he would not otherwise buy? It seems to be the good fortune of the United States electorate that so far good judgment and concern for the public welfare has generally prevailed over excessive and unethical salesmanship. But that is a conclusion that deserves much more intensive examination, particularly in the light of the hard-sell emotional excesses which characterized the congressional campaign of 1970.

One matter of major concern to public and social scientists alike is the question as to how far the television camera may go toward actually distorting reality. Television has been condemned for having played a significant role in stimulating

rebellion and riot; in encouraging the use of the action-demonstration technique; in creating a distorted or unreal picture.
Charges have been leveled and not just by Vice-President
Agnew that the picture the viewer sees is sometimes shaped by
the television camera or even a creation of the camera.

In 1952 Kurt and Gladys Lang, highly respected sociologists
who have observed television both from staff positions at the
Canadian Broadcasting Corporation and from faculty assignments at American universities, conducted an intensive analysis
of the visit to Chicago in that year of General Douglas Mac-
Arthur. The General was returning from his service in the Far
East. He had just been removed from his job by President
Truman and was coming back to the United States as a triumphant hero. Chicago officials scheduled what they hoped
would be a massive demonstration on behalf of the returning
war hero and American patriot. The Langs, prior to Mac-
Arthur's arrival, did a careful analysis of all television, radio
and newspaper reports concerning the general's impending
arrival, preparations made for the demonstration on his behalf,
and the expectations which were being raised by advance
publicity.[3]

On the day of the demonstration itself, they assigned experts
to monitor programs of the four television stations in Chicago
and stationed researchers at each of the points along the route
of march which would be covered by cameras and at some
other points at which the general was to make appearances. The
Lang findings suggest that the demonstrations as seen by the
researchers in the street were vastly different from what was
seen by the viewers on the television screen. The curious on
the streets saw relatively little excitement. They saw even less
of the MacArthurs as they drove by in an open car. When the
general and his entourage stopped to make a short speech to
the public, the speech was made only to a very few persons
who were close enough to see the general and his family in
person and was unintelligible to those who were several tiers
deep into the audience.

All in all, very little excitement seemed to be generated. The crowds in the street were smaller than anticipated, and the Chicago transit system indicated that only a fraction of the persons expected came to the Loop for the demonstration. On the other hand, television viewers got quite a different impression. MacArthur Day, as seen by the television viewer, was one of enthusiastic crowds, dramatic excitement, the triumphant general passing through jam-packed streets, and of adulation paid by cheering throngs along the route of the parade.

The difference in the two points of view, according to the Langs, was caused by a number of circumstances. In the first place, television and press alike, during the days preceding MacArthur Day, had built up the event by predicting that vast numbers of people would swarm into Chicago for the day. They described the anticipated excitement to be generated by the impending visit of the hero of the Pacific, and of the valiant efforts being planned by Chicago police to maintain order. When the day itself arrived, the television commentators were imbued with some of the excitement which had been generated by their own pre-MacArthur Day buildup. But more importantly, the television cameras, rather than roaming through the streets where the public gathered in somewhat less volume than was anticipated, concentrated on those areas, in range of the limited view of the camera lens, where there was excitement. They caught the general and his entourage in the heart of the Loop area, stopping from time to time before clusters of cheering Chicagoans. But they didn't show the stage waits, the faces of the mildly curious by-standers or the thin line of viewers between pre-set stops. The Langs concluded that television showed the television viewing public in the Chicago area an entirely different MacArthur Day than actually took place—or, at least, than was seen by the persons who were in the Loop.

A somewhat similar picture was drawn by the Langs of the 1952 political conventions, which they studied in comparable detail.[4] Television cameras were constantly at the points of greatest excitement. When the events taking place inside the

convention hall were relatively dull, they were in the committee
meetings at the Blackstone or Congress hotels, or at the Conrad
Hilton. Rather than show the sometimes bored delegates, they
were focused on the speaker's platform which, during both
conventions in 1952, was crammed with people and teemed
with controversy and excitement.

The Langs made another interesting point concerning convention coverage. They pointed out that the conventions as
seen from the three television networks furnishing the coverage were vastly different events. One of the television networks
expressed bafflement with its lack of understanding of the events
taking place and spoke constantly of confusion. It left the
audience with the impression that the conventions were care-
lessly planned, that the convention chairmen had very little
control over the proceedings, and that the whole political
process was one of chaos and disorder. The second network
was more concerned with showmanship. It focused on personalities and dominant party members. It regarded the convention
as a pageant. The third network concentrated on the convention as a news story. It related everything happening within
range of the camera to the development of the main news
theme, the interplay of political forces leading toward the
nomination of candidates for the presidency and the vice-presidency. The Langs, while not identifying networks one and two,
concede that network three was CBS.

As a result of differences in approach, the picture drawn
by the viewer of the two conventions in that summer of 1952
was strongly conditioned by the outlook and approach of the
network which he happened to be watching at any given
time. It is clear that the convention has been shaped and even
distorted to cater to the requirements of the television camera.
Seconding speeches and demonstrations have been reduced so
that these rather non-essential aspects of the convention are
given only minimum time. Political party management has
endeavored where possible to expose to the television-viewing
public only what it considers to be its most attractive personnel

and to downplay or hide wherever possible those members of the party who are considered less attractive. This still leaves the decision as to what is attractive and what might be repulsive to amateur decision-making processes, usually influenced by political considerations.

A potentially distorting feature of the television camera, however, may be considerably more influential than convention management, or even of delegate reaction. Cameras inevitably focus only on those scenes which have high audience interest value. By actual percentage of time, cameras are directed toward proceedings on the floor no more than half the total time the convention is in progress. At other times they zero in on individual delegates, switch to demonstrations outside the hall, observe comings and goings of party leaders and candidates, leave the hall completely to interview party leaders in hotel rooms in the city centers, pick up meetings of committees outside the convention hall, and cover developments which are far removed from the immediate business of the convention as it is being conducted in the convention hall.

The net result is comparable to what the Langs found on MacArthur Day in Chicago. The view which the average television viewer gets from his home television screen is one of a highly concentrated, condensed series of events which create an aura of excitement, and of constant motion and action. But the picture fails to reflect the long stage waits and the periods of utter boredom which are experienced by the delegates and onlookers in the auditorium. The very immediacy of the television camera may also contribute to distortion. The fact that the television camera brings the event directly to the viewer without any filtering, screening or analytical process, may distort the event rather than show it faithfully to the public.

The Democratic national convention of 1968 will be discussed, debated and analyzed for years to come by political scientists, politicians, and behaviorists. Every conceivable weakness of the convention system manifested itself in Chicago while delegates were trying, not always enthusiastically, to carry on their political party business. Hubert Humphrey ascribes much of the reason for his loss of the presidential election of 1968 to distortive factors that arose during the convention. The Democratic party feels that it may take years to recover from the blows suffered in Chicago.

It is difficult for the average television viewer to know precisely what did take place in Chicago, because of the mélange of views of the convention and its environment which were obtained from television. They saw the normal, dull convention routine; the sometimes bitter jockeying for position in regular convention business including accrediting of delegations, approving a platform, and nominating and electing candidates. But they also saw physical combat on the floor and flaring tempers. Juxtaposed with this was the rioting in Lincoln Park, on Michigan Avenue, and outside the convention hall. A communications workers' strike prevented live coverage of Loop events and forced reliance on sharply edited film which was projected long after events occurred. The television viewer was consequently disoriented and unable to keep events in proper time perspective.

Former Vice-President Humphrey and members of his staff feel that the presence of the television cameras on the convention floor was a major contributing factor toward creating the impression that there was not only excessive wrangling among the delegates, but evidence of a virulent form of bossism. They believe that television contributed in considerable measure to disturbances which took place on the floor. Humphrey feels very strongly that the presence of the television camera on the floor contributed to excesses by delegates who saw their opportunities to perform for the television public and made maximum use of those opportunities.

The imperturbable Walter Cronkite lost his cool for one of the first times in the memory of many of his millions of viewers when CBS correspondent Dan Rather was apparently punched by unidentified security personnel while trying to obtain an interview. No one who saw Rather as he picked himself up off the floor, out of wind, and barely able to describe the events that had taken place, will soon forget that incident.

Likewise, few will forget an angry Mayor Richard Daley sitting front and center directly under the speaker's rostrum as he was chastised by Senator Abraham Ribicoff of Connecticut. Television's descriptions of the ring of hard-eyed guards who surrounded the Illinois delegation did not lessen the impact of the confrontation between the senator and the mayor, and the feeling that events were under tight boss control.

The Humphrey entourage was particularly irritated by the reporting efforts of NBC correpsondent Sander Vanocur during a good part of one session. Vanocur reported in detail and knowledgeably on the theoretical candidacy of Senator Edward Kennedy of Massachusetts. The Humphrey people argue that this was an obvious example of a television correspondent creating a false story about a candidacy which was not to occur.

In the midst of the chaos on the convention floor came pictures of bloody rioting on Michigan Avenue outside the Hilton and Blackstone hotels. Surveys made by the three television networks indicate conclusively that the actual minutes of rioting shown were only an infinitesimal fraction of the total time given to the Democratic national convention; but the impact of those pictures was felt around the world and left an unforgettable impression. Memories of the convention cannot be separated from pictures of policemen beating demonstrators and hauling them off to paddy-wagons parked on side streets.

Was the picture as seen on television faithful to the facts, or a distortion? Were the events as violent as they appeared to be? Was the attitude inside the hall as consistently explosive? Were the Democrats in such irreparable disarray? Were the breaches between elements of the party as irreparable? Was anger among the disputing groups as intense as the television pictures indicated?

Again, we have no precise way of measuring. We can only assume that the camera skipped from highlight to highlight, that film and tape editors deleted many of the duller portions of the convention, that television camera directors concentrated on items of intense emotional interest at times when there was nothing but boredom on the floor. The picture as seen on the home screen was a concentrated potion of tension, antagonism, bitterness and anger. It was almost certainly an exaggeration, but the impression left was indelible, partly because it appeared real. It is likely that the television view was distorted. But any one of the fragments of the story which contributed to the whole chaotic scene may have been wholly accurate. It was their juxtaposition, if anything, which made them false. Distortion arises not through the ability of the camera to portray faithfully and accurately, but rather through the editing process which combines events of high emotional intensity piled one on top of another to create an overall impression which cannot be sustained by a more dispassionate and rational view of the whole pattern.

A single event occurring in the San Francisco Opera House in September of 1951, during the Japanese Peace Conference, illustrates how an innocent event, magnified by television, can almost cause an international incident. In 1951, at the height of the Korean War, delegates of the Soviet Union participating in international conferences were in the habit of rising to their feet and striding out of the hall whenever statements to which they took exception were made by other delegates.

The television crew representing the combined American networks was well aware of this idiosyncrasy of Russian official behavior and took steps to cover such a walk-out the minute it started. The several cameramen assigned to the pool had each been drilled during practice sessions as to precisely what to do at the moment any person in authority was to give a code signal "the Russians are walking." One camera was to stay tight on the delegation, another to pick them up in the aisle and follow them to the rear of the hall, a third was to wheel up through the lobby and catch them coming out the door, a fourth camera outside was to go to the driveway at the side of the building and focus on the limousine which would presumably drive up to take the delegation back to their quarters.

Halfway through the third session of the Peace Conference when everything seemed to be going smoothly, Andrei Gromyko, chief of the Soviet delegation, suddenly arose from his seat and proceeded toward the aisle. The signal went out and cameras immediately snapped into position. Mr. Gromyko worked his way to the center aisle and started toward the back exit. Members of his delegation followed him. The carefully rehearsed television cameras proceeded as they had rehearsed for the event.

By the time the Soviet delegates got to the rear lobby, a crowd had gathered around and the lobby camera followed delegates and curious onlookers. As expected the traditional black limousines wheeled into the driveway and it was evident to everybody that the Russians were "taking a walk." The outside camera followed the three limousines into position and waited for the delegation to use the side exit and board their cars. After a few minutes of milling around in the lobby the Russians peacefully reentered the Opera House, marched down the aisle, returned to their seats, and sat down calmly as if nothing had happened.

Actually, nothing did happen. But certainly the television viewer who had been alerted to the possibility of a Russian walk and had been told by commentators that a walk probably would mean a serious hitch in efforts to bring the peace conference to a successful fruition were convinced that an event of dramatic significance was taking place. Did the television cameras distort the event? Did they create excitement when there should have been none? Did they read into the peace conference an element of international tension—a tension which actually never existed? Or were they simply faithfully covering the events of the peace conference as the camera saw them?

No one has ever successfully explained why Gromyko and

his assistants rose to leave the hall; whether it was only for a smoke in the lobby or some other purpose nobody really knows. The crowd gathered around the delegation was so large that the camera lost them. It is conceivable that they might have felt they could create diplomatically useful tension by walking out, but the fact that on their return everything went smoothly, and the signing of the peace treaty took place on the fourth day without any further dispute, would indicate that the event had no significance in international affairs. On the other hand, when it is considered that the Russians had been using opportunities of this sort to register their displeasure with international diplomacy, it appears that the television crew was fully justified. Considering the Russian record for walking out of conferences, the television director on nine occasions out of ten would have been right. In this case, however, television can logically be charged with distorting the convention.

The German election of September 1969, which in many ways was a classic example of the most sophisticated use of television by two political parties, the Christian Democratic Union and the Social Democratic Party, saw another example of television's power to create a situation which might otherwise never have developed. Willy Brandt, the leader of the Social Democrats, in the view of many experts in Germany, won the prime ministership by his imaginative and skillful exploitation of the medium *after* the polls had closed on election night.

As ballots were being counted, the Social Democrats were running in second position to the Christian Democratic Union —not quite as well as had been anticipated. The Free Democrats were a poor third with slightly less than the five percent of the total national vote. A minimum of five percent was required to enable them to have parliamentary representation. Brandt knew that if the FDP were to achieve the five-percent level, a coalition of SPD and FDP would give the coalition a parliamentary majority and enable him to form the government and become chancellor. Brandt foresaw this possibility and had earlier in the day discussed with Walter Scheel, the leader of the Free Democrats, plans for such a possible coalition. Under the terms of the agreement Scheel would become foreign minister.

As the night wore on, Brandt was reasonably certain, certain enough to gamble, that the Free Democrats would achieve the five-percent level. On that still shaky assumption he played his hole card. He informed television executives that he was ready to go on the air with a definitive statement. Once on the air he announced with complete assurance that he was setting out immediately to form the new government and in this move he had the full support of the Free Democrats. As soon as Brandt had finished his highly optimistic statement, the camera cut to Christian Democratic Headquarters and focused on the incumbent chancellor, Mr. Kurt Kiesinger. Kiesinger was so shocked by this turn of events that he couldn't fail to register his dismay in front of the cameras. He was caught totally unprepared for Brandt's audacious ploy and his face fully registered his concern and despair.

Millions of Germans at their television receivers followed the drama, and it is the opinion of many experts in German politics that this apparently innocuous episode was a major contributing factor toward Brandt's ability to move ahead with confidence the next day to form the government. It is believed that a confident Christian Democratic Party, with a confident leader at its head, could have responded vigorously to Brandt's exaggerated claim, thus forcing the Free Democrats to reassess their position. The result could have been a CDU-FDP Coalition with Kiesinger remaining in the chancellorship. The CDU succeeded in winning more votes than the SPD and in running somewhat more strongly than expected.

As it was, there was no doubt in anyone's mind after Brandt had spoken that the Social Democrats had won; Kiesinger's shocked and dejected reaction on camera sealed it. Willy Brandt would be the next chancellor. The Free Democrats would join with him to give Germany its new government, at least in part because Brandt gambled with the television camera and created an atmosphere of victory for himself and defeat for Kiesinger. While this cannot technically be described as distortion of an event, it is an illustration of the power of the television camera to record what apparently is a minor event and give it a significance totally out of reasonable proportion. Brandt guessed he could catch Kiesinger off guard. The plot worked and a minority party won control of the government over a party with a slightly higher percentage of parliamentary membership. The television camera became the key so skillfully manipulated by the SPD.

This, in effect, was a staged event on a small scale, but with a large impact. With the arrival of television on the reporting scene, staged events of all sizes have become commonplace. Some are designed for sharp and immediate impact, such as the Brandt ploy in the German election; some for longer term, more generalized results; some to provoke instant and occasionally violent reaction as in the case of the SDS Weathermen's demonstration in Chicago in 1969, or the peace march to London's Grosvenor Square in October 1969. There have even been cases in which television crews themselves have staged events.

The charge that television news film crews recreated scenes to obtain better coverage of presumably spontaneous events was brought forcefully to my attention in September 1957, following the Little Rock school integration disturbances. Both *The New York Times* and the *New Yorker* carried stories charging that CBS News crews had asked demonstrators to repeat actions which had been missed or inadequately covered. Investigations confirm that the critics' accounts were accurate. No physical clashes had followed, but they could have. This was really nothing new; it had been standard newsreel operating procedure for years. But the realization that such recreation was commonplace, however, was deflating.

The old "March of Time" not only recreated scenes but

frequently used actors to play key roles. No one gave a second thought to the ethics involved. "See It Now" could never have gone on the air without arranging to have events occur in front of its bulky 35 mm sound on film cameras. "Person to Person," Edward R. Murrow's highly rated personality program in which guests were interviewed in their own homes, appeared wholly spontaneous, but, in fact, had to be carefully rehearsed in view of the volume of bulky equipment required to display guests in their homes to Mr. Murrow sitting in a studio many miles or a whole continent away and to the millions in the viewing audience. The complexities of moving cameras and tripods around the narrow confines of the interviewee's dwelling quarters made careful logistical planning and rehearsing an absolute necessity.

One of the classic "staged" events in American political history was the so-called "cabinet meeting," broadcast from the cabinet room in the White House just prior to the 1958 election. All the cabinet members were present, and President Eisenhower was in the chair. The president called on each of his departmental chiefs to report, starting with Secretary of State Dulles and moving around the table one by one. Reports were so terse, the timing so carefully planned and ad libs so carefully discouraged that the whole meeting fitted very neatly within one hour of television time.

The Democrats obviously screamed in outrage, since the event took place only eight days before the congressional elections, and since it was unmistakably designed to have an influence on the electorate.

The story behind the manner in which the event was scheduled on the CBS Television Network clearly substantiates the Democrats' strong suspicion that this was in fact a "staged event," designed for no other purpose than to create favorable climate for Republican Party candidates, and ironically I was largely responsible for its execution. The story of the scheduling of these events for television began on a late Sunday afternoon when I received a telephone call from CBS's president

Frank Stanton. I was president of CBS News at the time and Stanton asked whether I might have any interest in covering a meeting of the full cabinet, presided over by the President in the cabinet room in the White House.

Since in a sense this would be an historic event, a television first, and a first opportunity for the public to see inside the cabinet room, watch the Secretaries at work and observe the interplay between cabinet members and President, it all sounded like a good idea. Stanton would say no more, except, "If you would like to pick up the affair, call Jim Hagerty at the White House. He is available right now."

I called and Hagerty was indeed instantly available. He somewhat laconically agreed that the meeting could be covered but he had to know immediately, because it would be necessary to start at once to set the complicated machinery in motion. CBS also needed all the time available to assign crews, survey the cabinet room for camera placements and lighting, notify affiliates, and be sure that all technical facilities were in order. The decision was made at CBS to go ahead. I first called CBS's Director of News & Public Affairs in Washington, Theodore F. Koop, to begin the job of marshalling up crews and facilities, then the network's Operation Department in New York to make arrangements to cancel commercial commitments and substitute the cabinet meeting.

Accordingly, the only "cabinet meeting" to be shown to the American television viewer was conceived and planned. Hagerty now says that he has difficulty remembering just whose idea it was or how the original suggestion was made to CBS. But it is obvious enough to me that it somehow was suggested to William S. Paley, the chairman of the board of CBS, and then was passed down from Paley to Stanton, and from Stanton to me. And then I served as the eager and not sufficiently alert dupe for the plan.

Every presidential press conference is, in effect, a staged event, every presidential message, every meeting or conversation of the president with correspondents, every White House news conference, every White House trip where public appearances are made. Senators, congressmen, governors, movie stars, business executives, leaders of pressure groups, and almost anyone with a public ax to grind, knows in some measure the value of the staged event, which is conceived largely to obtain television coverage.

The tactic was not an invention of the age of television. It has been used for years to obtain newspaper coverage. After the development of radio it was used to attract microphones. Television, because of its more dramatic impact, has simply accelerated the development of the technique and has given it new prominence and presumably new impact. The measure of the medium, however, should not be based solely on its idiosyncrasies. It can influence events and people, it can distort reality, it can create illusions which are at variance with fact, it can compress events in time and space in such a way as to exaggerate their importance, and it can furnish a platform for charlatans.

But it can also create new interest in significant events, provide a dramatic platform for responsible officials to exercise leadership, unmask the disingenuous and, perhaps most importantly, form a new communications linkage, enabling governors to govern more effectively, and citizens to respond to their leadership more quickly and forcefully. The power to do either good or evil is enormous. How the medium is used for the public good is obviously a matter of gravest concern to every level of society.

A NEW MEDIUM FOR POLITICS

3

The era of the 1950s and 1960s was a period of quick, sometimes revolutionary change in political methods. This change has been reflected most dramatically in the cost of political campaigning. The total cost of the 1952 election campaign, primaries and final elections, at the precinct, ward, congressional districts, state and national level, ran to about $150,000,000.[1] By 1964, a relatively uninteresting national election, dominated by the big victory won by Lyndon B. Johnson, cost about $200,000,000. By 1968 the figure had exploded to $300,000,000, twice the 1952 figure.

In 1952 about one-fourth of the budgets of the two national candidates was spent on television.[2] In 1968 about two-thirds of all such expenditures went into television advertising and promotion. Total expenditures for television thus rose from one fourth of $150 million or $37.5 million in 1952 to two-thirds of $300 million or $200 million in 1968—a six-fold increase in 16 years. Of the approximately $200 million spent on television, approximately three-fourths went into production and placement of spot announcements.[3] The ballooning increase in cost, and the enormous rise in the percentage of budgets going to television sufficiently suggests the degree of preoccupation with television as the predominant medium for political campaigning.

45

The obvious result has been a revolutionary change in the form of the campaign. The set speech has given way to the question and answer or arena type program. There has been a proliferation of ten, twenty, thirty, and sixty-second commercial spots. The telethon, the man in the street program, and various other types of question and answer shows have become commonplace. Candidates have been increasingly responsive to invitations to appear on network discussion shows, straight face-to-face interviews and in regular television news programs, both network and local. While debates have not been scheduled since the 1960 campaign on a national level, they are a common device in state and local races.

This is a vast change from the era of Franklin D. Roosevelt, when the set political speech, normally on a national network, was the predominant form of campaigning. The set speech and the rear platform appearance persisted through 1948, the last year before television became a major factor, but by 1952 they were settling back into history.

As campaign mechanics and media changed, techniques had to change too. The old-time political managers either had to adapt or give way to new experts, particularly those specializing in the broadcast media. The two national committees in 1952 employed broadcast personnel on their staffs, but in secondary positions. The directors of publicity for both parties were former newspaper men who were concerned almost entirely with the press. An assistant with little prestige and less power worked on radio and television programs. This had been the standard practice through the 1930s and 40s.

But starting with 1952, a new cadre of specialists began to appear who knew how to relate television and politics. They understood the requirements of politics, and how they could be met by the most sophisticated use of the capabilities of television. Among the pioneers were Carroll Newton and John Elliot of BBD&O, both working on behalf of General Eisenhower; Ted Rogers of Senator Nixon's personal staff; and Leonard Reinsch of the Cox stations in Dayton and Atlanta, who had been broadcast advisor to Franklin D. Roosevelt and Harry Truman, and filled a similar role for candidate Adlai Stevenson. Also in the Stevenson camp were Louis G. Cowan, a highly successful radio and television package producer, and Victor Sholis, general manager of the WHAS stations in Louisville, Kentucky.

A few advertising agencies had had some experience with television, but most of them had specialized in radio. Then in 1952 agencies began to be interested in both television and politics. BBD&O, Young and Rubicam, and Kudner for the Republicans, and Milton Biouw Inc. and the Joseph Katz agency for the Democrats started the movement. Since that time, counting both local and national elections, more than a score of agencies, including most of the nation's largest, have operated actively in the television political field. In the process they trained a corps of experts to form a specially qualified breed of political practitioners in television. Finally, what has been happening in the United States has similarly been happening in virtually every section of the free world where there is a meaningful election process. This includes Western Europe, Japan, and, to some extent, South America.

The new emphasis on television has changed the whole profile of the political campaign. The vastly increased costs and the complexity of campaigns which utilize new technological devices available to political campaigners have made it necessary to tighten up the whole process. The increased costs are not due entirely to television. The rising curve affecting the whole cost structure influences everything for which political managers spend. There is more travel, more communication, larger staffs, more requirement for office space and hotel rooms all at higher prices, more office equipment to be rented or bought, and greater allocations for travel, subsistence and entertainment. But the real problem is television, and the charges for time on the air, high as they may be, constitute only a fraction of the whole.

Television advisors, producers, directors and writers load a new and heavy factor onto the normal staff and talent budgets. The whole production process, involving camera crews, film editors, studio rentals, equipment leasing or purchases, and laboratory processing and printing, is a wholly new and heavily burdensome addition to the political budget. The whole range of television production, from ten, twenty, and thirty-second spots through straight speeches and interviews and question and answer programs, up to one-hour film documentaries, soaks up budgets at a rate far exceeding anything previously known. Television time charges are the target of most of those critics who lament the amounts of money being spent for television purposes. But it is rarely noted that production costs will frequently match and sometimes exceed time costs, particularly when staff costs for television personnel are included in the production and talent columns.

Some campaigns in the era of television stand out as models of intelligent use of the medium, of careful planning, efficient development of staff, knowledgeable usage of media and sensitive analysis of voter attitudes, interests and possible reactions. The first classic, as has been suggested, is clearly the 1950 Dewey campaign for the governorship of New York. In this primitive age of television, the Dewey staff pioneered in developing strategies and techniques which were to set the pattern for the two decades which have followed.

The younger members of the campaign specialists club of the 1970s look on John F. Kennedy's campaign of 1960 as the model for all future campaigns. The Kennedy managers were shrewd observers of campaign tactics and strategies during the 1950s. When the time came to make their run for the nation's top political prize, they had amassed a wide array of talents and a bulging bag full of new techniques, not the least important of which aimed at television. Planning the John F. Kennedy campaign for the presidency in 1960 actually began in earnest in August of 1959 at the Kennedy compound in Hyannisport, Massachusetts. There's little doubt, though, that John Kennedy had been running for the presidency since the conclusion of the

Democratic national convention in Chicago in late August, 1956. The experts who participated were largely new on the national scene, but they included persons who were later to become famous as political technicians. Lawrence O'Brien, Kenneth O'Donnell, Theodore Sorenson, Richard Goodwin, Pierre Salinger and, perhaps most importantly, Robert Kennedy.

The Kennedy team fully understood television, its strengths and weaknesses and how best to utilize it in the support of the presidential campaign. They further understood all the ramifications of political techniques, not all of them gentle. They knew how to win delegate support. They knew how to apply pressures at the right time and place to hold delegate support through the convention. And they knew when, how and through whom to apply pressure. Furthermore, the members of the Kennedy entourage knew that it was essential that the time of the candidate himself be booked almost to the very minute throughout the entire period of the intensive campaign, and that the most sophisticated communications had to be used to tie the various national headquarters to the candidate's personal staff and to the advance men out ahead of the presidential party.

Perhaps most importantly they realized that public opinion polling techniques were essential to shape the original campaign themes and that they were further essential to be able to modify those themes as time went on. They further realized that the indices of public opinion had to be available instantly to speech writers and simultaneously to the presidential candidate's personal traveling group. Individual members of the leadership group, plus the candidate and his brother, had to be in a position to make quick and sometimes tricky decisions in order to keep up with unexpected developments and remain supreme opportunists.

From all points of view, not the least of which was the fact that their candidate won, the Kennedy campaign was an enormous success. It was a success due to the care, skill and thoroughness of the advance planning, to the creative and imaginative use of new techniques and to the decisiveness of the leaders who apparently made their decisions quickly and firmly, stuck with those decisions and enforced them cooly and confidently.

The Richard M. Nixon campaign for the presidency in 1968 is another model of efficiency, careful direction, intelligent use of media and a tightly controlled organization. Some critics describe it as a ruthless steamroller, using television to create an attractively packaged candidate kept in a thoroughly sterilized container. Nixon supporters, anticipating the probability that their candidate would win the Republican nomination in the summer of 1968, started preparations at least a year prior to the nominating convention. Memos such as those outlined in Joe McGinniss' revealing book. *The Selling of the President 1968,* were written during this pre-convention period. They outlined the direction that the campaign should take, the controls that should be exercised, the media that should be used, the themes that should be employed and the weaknesses of the candidate that should be concealed from public view.[4] The plans were carried out almost to the letter. The infinite care and attention to detail gave rise to widespread complaints among Mr. Nixon's opponents. They argued that this was the first case in which a candidate had been packaged for the presidency by advertising agency methods. Image, they argued, had become more important than substance in the campaign for the presidency.

"Packaging" and "image-making" are representative television era terms, used to connote excesses deriving out of show business origins. Whether they fully measure up to the negative connotations they evoke is another matter, and one worth deeper consideration.

The fact is that the Nixon campaign, for all its care in isolating the candidate, restricting him from the political rough and tumble experience, and limiting public appearances to those carefully screened and controlled, did not succeed in creating a new Nixon. The best the Nixon campaign staff could hope for was to emphasize the strong points in the Nixon personality, stress his experience and his areas of competence, and restrict or downplay those elements which might have caused an adverse reaction on the voting population. The campaign plan was carried out with precision and calculated efficiency. Television was used exactly as it had been projected. The voters saw only what the Nixon managers wanted them to see. History records that the candidate won. Even though the margin was slight, and even though no votes may have been won away from those leaning to the opposition, at least few of those leaning his way were lost. The Nixon campaign of 1968 must, therefore, be regarded as an immense success.

There are campaigns which have been equally noteworthy as failures. The Nixon organization in 1968 did not have to look very far to find one. The Nixon campaign of 1960 is a classic example. Supporters of Vice-President Nixon in that year, including some of the most competent, skilled and experienced holdovers from the Eisenhower campaign staffs of 1952 and 1956, laid out a campaign which in substance is really not too different from that which was planned for candidate Nixon in 1968. There was one essential difference. The candidate failed to listen to his campaign managers and failed to carry out their recommendations. Their skillfully conceived plans were lost between conception and execution. Through this almost total failure of communications between campaign managers and candidate, the themes so carefully plotted during pre-convention months evaporated. The devices which had been so skillfully plotted on the drawing boards were abandoned as the presidential candidate went his own way in his own style.

It had been agreed that the candidate would not engage in debate with his opponent, but—he did, in four such debates, the first of which may have cost him the election. It had been agreed that there would be regular consultation with campaign manager Leonard Hall, advertising manager Carroll Newton, and the remainder of the campaign staff. There was substantially no contact. It had been agreed that changes in travel and public appearance plans would be plotted out in consultation between the candidate and his personal staff on the one hand, and the headquarters group on the other. Instead the candidate operated almost wholly on his own, consulting only with his personal aides, Robert Finch and Herbert Klein. Campaign plans so carefully considered in late spring and early summer lay in desk drawers and filing cabinets at campaign headquarters. They were never implemented.

How significant the failure to campaign according to plan and the abandonment of a carefully drawn strategy may have been provides an enigmatic footnote. The total popular vote for Richard Nixon was essentially the same in 1960 as it was in 1968. His margin of loss to John F. Kennedy in 1960 was approximately the same in total votes as his margin of victory over Hubert Humphrey in 1968. Perhaps the only difference is that in 1968 he followed his campaign plan and won. Does this demonstrate that chaos and disarray will serve as well as machine-like precision and that haphazard use of television serves as well as infinite care in the planning and execution? Or was Nixon simply lucky that his 1968 opponent was even more disorganized and haphazard in planning and execution than the Nixon of 1960?

Evidence indicates the latter was true. This time Nixon was the beneficiary of an opposition that was unready, impoverished and failed to achieve an organizational efficiency before mid-campaign. The evidence strongly indicates that Hubert Humphrey lacked either the arrogance or the will to believe until the fact was accomplished that he could be nominated as the Democratic candidate for the presidency of the United States.

The nomination for which he had aspired so long, dating back at least as far as the convention of 1952, seemed to have come to him after the traumatic experiences of the spring and summer of 1968 as a distinct surprise, even though it seemed inevitable that he would win the nomination—a fact of which he must have been very well aware. When he finally strode forward to the rostrum on the tongue of the speaker's platform in Chicago's International Amphitheater at the end of August of 1968, he had no written campaign plan, no formal staff organization, no television advertising plans. In fact, he was represented by an advertising agency he was going to drop in just two weeks time. Perhaps most damaging of all, he had no money. The Democratic treasury was bare.[5] To add to his miseries, the Democratic party had been ripped apart by the disastrous sequence of events in Chicago immediately preceding and during the convention. It was suffering from shock, disillusionment and apathy.

The campaign started slowly. By the time the first active steps could be taken, it was already well into September. Campaign manager Lawrence O'Brien wasn't appointed until after the nomination during the last week in August. He only then started writing a campaign plan. Doyle, Dane & Bernbach, the advertising agency which had represented the Democratic Party under the presidential administration of Lyndon B. Johnson, was dropped as the agency of record for the party in the second week in September. All its planning disappeared with its dismissal. The Lennen & Newell agency was not appointed to succeed Doyle Dane until September 13, less than seven weeks before election day. Television advisor Allan Gardner wasn't even invited to join the campaign staff until that same date, September 13. He was in Detroit attending a bar mitzvah for a nephew when he got a call inviting him to take the next plane to Washington to discuss terms and conditions for accepting the assignment. The wonder is that the campaign machine ever started to move at all.

Yet the fact is that during the month of October the steady, decisive hands of Lawrence O'Brien, Joseph Napolitan, and Ira Kapenstein, backed by a dedicated staff and a revitalized candidate, began to get the inadequately prepared Democratic campaign in motion. The surprising result was that they almost succeeded in winning the election. Some political experts have speculated that if the campaign had only run 48 hours more, Richard Nixon would have been denied the electoral vote sufficient to win him the presidency without going through the House of Representatives. A clear Humphrey victory, had the campaign been longer, is regarded as having been a realistic possibility.

The records of candidates who have had tight, efficient organizations, time to prepare their campaigns, and resources to effectively employ television, furnish ample evidence that the techniques of political campaigning have become both a science and an art. The new element on the political scene which has rendered obsolete the haphazard and carefree campaign organizations of the past is television. It is television that places new stresses on organization and planning. The logistics of television are too complex, the variety and numbers of required talents too varied and too numerous, the media selection requirements too demanding, the necessity for new techniques and new uses of technology too pervasive to leave campaigning to the amateurs and campaign control to old-line politicians. At the same time, the overall cost figures have grown so burdensome that television has made finance and administration essential elements to the successful political campaign.

The most overworked word in recent political campaigns is "image." There is talk of image-makers, image-candidates, image-campaigns, image-programs, party image, candidate image and just plain image. As a result the word has taken on a curious mystique. Image has for many become a sine qua non for political success and lack of image a major element in political failure.

Concurrently with a rise of concern with image-making has been concern with the whole question of candidate packaging. As early as 1956, a book entitled *The Golden Kazoo* was written by a former advertising man named John G. Schneider. Schneider's fictional treatment traced a presidential candidate through a campaign to his election, branding him as a piece of putty in the hands of an advertising agency which shaped him and packaged him to conform to the agency's analysis of what the majority of the voters would like. The candidate was a nonentity. He was a tool in the hands of the advertising agency president, who created him, molded him, breathed life into him, put words in his mouth and ideas into his head.[6]

While *The Golden Kazoo* obviously exaggerated the case, concerned people have been worried about the twin questions of packaging and image-making. They wonder whether it is possible to so reshape a candidate so that his character is altered and he becomes a tool of the manager rather than a leader of the public. The publication of Joe McGinniss' book, *The Selling of a President 1968,* has stimulated a new wave of concern over image-making and candidate packaging. The mechnical efficiency of the Nixon campaign for the presidency in 1968 with its tight controls, efficient administration and effective media use, has heightened interest in the question.

The question is more than a matter of what might be ethical and what not. It really goes to the basic substance of politics. Is it possible that the use of new, refined skills and techniques can package an inferior candidate in such a way that he can be elected to the highest office in the United States government?

Can a small group of self-interested, self-willed men find the most likely candidate for conversion to a vote winner by image-making and packaging processes in order to win control of the United States government for themselves? Or, even more disturbingly, can they discover an attractive and pliable tool, short of talent but long enough on show business talent, and mold him to win elections? The basic question is: How much can you shape the image? As a corollary, is it possible to create attributes in a man which were not previously there? Can you make something out of him which he is not?

The fact is that you probably cannot. Skilled political advertising men of the new breed, like Allan Gardner and Barry Nova who represented the Lennen and Newell Agency in the Humphrey campaign, suggest that there are built-in checks and balances in the system which would prevent the image-makers from maintaining complete control over a candidate. Older specialists, such as Carroll Newton, Robert Mullen and James

Hagerty, concede that it is possible to make a candidate more effective, but not to make him a different candidate.

It is inconceivable that any American citizen as well known in public life as Hubert Humphrey, who has been a prominent figure on the national political scene since 1948, could like a leopard suddenly change his spots. And it was also evident from the career of Lyndon B. Johnson, that very little could be done to change or modify the Johnson image. Some of his detractors charged that he tried to make himself a Walter Mitty which simply did not fit the strong-minded, strong-willed, dynamic president. This effort to create a Walter Mitty image for himself was probably a major factor in building an adverse public reaction during the last couple of years of his administration. The mild, gentle, thoughtful Johnson was simply not believable.

There have been major image-making attempts of various degrees of effectiveness. It could be said, for example, that Nelson Rockefeller's sudden affinity for walking through Jewish communities in lower east side Manhattan and Brooklyn all the while chewing on blintzes could be a factor in an effort to build an image. His "Hi ya fella" greeting could likewise be a part of the effort to build an image of informal affability. Many of these campaigning expeditions were covered by television news film cameras. The exposure on news programs was undoubtedly more important to the governor than the personal contacts or the flavor of the blintzes.

Mayor John Lindsay of New York made it a point in his 1969 campaign to visit synagogues. Out of deference to the large Jewish electorate in New York City he appeared in the traditional yarmulke. Television cameras followed the Protestant mayor as they followed the governor and film appeared on the nightly news broadcasts.

Senator Barry Goldwater tried to get away from an image of recklessness and incaution but was unable to shake the stereotype, partly because of his own proclivity to the rash statement or at least diction which was vulnerable to interpretation by the opposition as being rash, and partly because the Democratic party and its advertising agency, Doyle, Dane, Bernbach kept constantly on the attack, searching out the inevitable vulnerable statement and giving it wide exposure.

Since the question of image is so tightly intertwined with the efforts of the advertising agency, it seems appropriate to analyze the two together. Advertising agencies have long played a signficant part in political campaigns. Previous reference has been made to the fact that the George Batten Company represented Charles Evans Hughes in 1916. From that year on, advertising agencies frequently played some part in developing newspaper advertising programs, direct mail campaigns, billboards, carcards, transportation displays and the like. It can be reasonably said, however, that the advertising agency really came into its own as a major force in political campaign techniques and strategy after General Eisenhower was nominated and before the campaign began to gather momentum in the fall of 1952.

Not every technique, however, came out of intensive planning sessions. An innovation that was to gain significance in later campaigns was born almost by accident. One of the more innovative, creative minds in the advertising business is Rosser Reeves, an executive at the Ted Bates Company. Reeves decided that there were many advantages to be gained by adopting a new form of political advertising—the short, spot commercial. He had a hunch that the 60-second advertising spot could be used in the way the soap, food and cigarette companies were using them with spectacular success.

Reeves approached a key figure in the Eisenhower group, J. H. Whitney, later Ambassador to the United Kingdom, who expressed an interest in hearing more of his plan. Arrangements were made for Reeves to come to a dinner meeting at the 21 Club in New York with story boards and a full description of his technique. As Robert Mullen describes the event, Jock Whitney had talked to Reeves at length prior to the dinner at 21. Whitney's associate Walter Thayer, Washington state political leader Walter Williams, chief executive of the Citizens for

Eisenhower, and Sidney Weinberg, the Wall Street head of the financial end of the Eisenhower campaign, were already at 21 when Jock Whitney came in, as Mullen says, with stars in his eyes.

Shortly after Whitney's arrival, Reeves appeared with story boards and made what Mullen describes as a "magnificent presentation." As Mullen puts it, "he hit the jackpot." Before dessert was finished, a special television committee was formed to raise money for a spot advertising campaign. Whitney was appointed chairman of the committee, but he assigned the job of raising the funds to Ogden White of the White Weld Company in Wall Street.

In order to develop a theme for the spot advertising campaign, Albert Cole from the Reader's Digest Corporation was brought into the group. *Reader's Digest* was of key importance because it possessed one of the largest mailing lists in the United States and had had substantial experience in the use of direct mail selling. It was decided to break out small carefully selected segments of the *Reader's Digest* mailing list in an effort to test themes which might be useful in the announcement campaign which Rosser Reeves was to prepare. Three separate mailing lists of 10,000 names each were chosen. Letters were prepared to send to these lists of 10,000, each one to stress one potential theme for the Eisenhower spot advertising campaign. The results would determine which of the three potential themes would be selected for the final campaign.

The first of the three themes to be tested described General Eisenhower as "the man to bring fiscal responsibility to Washington"; the second, that the Republican Party and General Eisenhower "would clean up the mess in Washington"; the third acclaimed General Eisenhower as a "man of peace." The results overwhelmingly supported "Eisenhower, the Man of Peace," as the theme which would attract the most national attention and would gain the Republican Party and General Eisenhower the most votes.

This was hardly a surprising result. The unpopular Korean

War, a conflict which was incomprehensible to millions of citizens, had been in virtual stalemate for many months. Like the Vietnamese conflict, which was to follow a little more than a decade later, objectives were difficult to understand and measurements of success or failure obscure. After nearly two years of this baffling conflict, the public would probably have voted overwhelmingly to get out.

It was this mood which led to the enthusiastic response to the peace theme and to the committee's decision to campaign on the slogan "Eisenhower, The Man Who Will Bring Us Peace." This slogan was then taken to General Eisenhower for his approval prior to the preparation of scripts for the advertising spots. The general took a quick look and surprised his advisors by reacting negatively. He told them that he could not guarantee to bring peace; therefore, he would prefer not to be falsely described as "The Man Who Will Bring Us Peace." It didn't take the committee long to make an adjustment that satisfied the general's complaint. A few words were knocked out, a preposition added and the slogan which was to dominate campaign efforts right down to election day was born: "Eisenhower, Man of Peace."

Raising the required half million dollars didn't take much more time than deciding on the theme. Reeves himself then set about to write the commercials. The scripts were largely taken from speeches and statements which had been made by the candidate. The general was brought to a film studio. Reeves arrived with his portable typewriter. With a stack of Eisenhower speeches beside him, he pounded out the text for the 60-second commercials. As he completed them, he brought them to the general for approval. The required modifications were made to conform to the general's desires and Reeves went on to the next one. In the course of one long day, the commercials were written, edited, and finally narrated by General Eisenhower himself. And the first spot commercial campaign in history was officially launched.

There is no method for measuring the influence of this

precedent-shattering commercial campaign from the election vote, but the influence on future campaigns is self-evident. The fact that three-fourths of all television expenditures in 1968 were devoted to spot commercials seems ample proof that the advertising spot has won a dominant role in the campaign spectrum. But there were sharp-eyed critics even in that early era. Shortly after the conclusion of the 1952 campaign, a rather acid bit of verse written by Marya Mannes, read:

> Hail to BBD & O
> That told the Nation how to go
> It managed by advertisement
> To sell us a new President
> Eisenhower hits the spot
> One full General, that's a lot
> Feeling sluggish, feeling sick
> Take a dose of Ike and Dick
> Philip Morris, Lucky Strike.
> Alka-Seltzer, I like Ike

Irrespective of Marya Mannes' cynicism, there were subtantial reasons for placing emphasis on the spot commercial. Reeves explained two of them when he pointed out that the 60-second spot would attain a satisfyingly low cost per thousand, the prime measurement of the efficiency of any type of advertising; and that it would attain higher ratings than a half-hour set speech or a special program, because it would inherit the rating from the program in which it was inserted or from the one it followed.

The reasons are easy to understand. With the 60-second spot the viewer could have the commercial and his favorite program too. He didn't have to miss Milton Berle and "I Love Lucy" or Gene Autry because the regular program was pre-empted to be replaced by a dull political speech. Since the 60-second commercial was only a minor intrusion, ratings held up and the cost per thousand-viewers-reached was low.

Lower cost per thousand and higher ratings are important considerations, but the "spot" brought other bonuses. It offered a chance to reach individuals already committed to the candidate but also those who were non-committed or even supporting the opposition. The regular set political speech is normally made only to those persons who are already deeply committed to the cause. Rarely do non-supporters watch, except occasionally to scoff. The short political program is somewhat more effective; it may catch the deeply committed, some of the partially committed and a few neutrals. But the 60-second commercial spot, because it is not long enough to interfere with entertainment programs, is likely to reach all the persons who are watching those entertainment programs and thus reaches a wide spectrum of degrees of interest or disinterest in the candidacy of any particular individual.

There are also structural advantages in the use of the 60-second announcement. There's a single theme; a single copy approach; an opportunity for colorful and terse writing, and for attention-compelling graphic arts. The theme can be projected in an uncomplicated way that makes it understandable to virtually all watchers of a given channel at a given time. To the campaign manager its greatest charm is its complete flexibility. One of the axioms in political advertising, or for that matter any form of political campaigning, specifies that the candidate and his managers keep a close watch on those areas which are either safely committed so no additional efforts are required; still in contention so they demand additional campaigning; or definitely lost, so they can be written off, with no wasted time, effort or money.

The use of the 60-second commercial or, more recently, of the 30, 20 or even 10-second spot, gives campaign managers the opportunity to use public opinion polling techniques or less sophisticated gut reactions to spot trouble areas which demand immediate attention to shore up a weakening position or direct a barrage of pressure against a wavering voter. A spot campaign can be mounted in a matter of days or shifted in a matter of hours. And it can be pinpointed at limited target areas.

It is the ability of the spot to hold the audience, though, that makes it most attractive to advertising strategists. Carroll Newton once pointed out that the thirty-minute set political speeches achieved average ratings 34 percent below the programs they replaced. Fifteen-minute political programs, he added, lost an average of 24 percent, and five-minute political programs between 5-10 percent. In contrast, the 60-second commercial spot showed no loss. In view of the fact that the political campaigner must constantly try to win over the uncommitted, or supporters of the other side, the advantages of the spot are clear.

Justifications for using the advertising agency in the political campaign were obvious long before the advent of the spot announcement. The complexities involved in placing advertising in such diverse media as newspapers, magazines, radio and television, and contracting for billboards, transportation displays, carcards, lapel buttons and bumper stickers, are sufficiently obvious to indicate that they would be very difficult operations for a rank amateur to perform. Add to these the printing of posters, brochures, leaflets and assorted mailers, and the job becomes very complex indeed.

An orderly approach to an advertising campaign involves a number of complicated steps, demanding a high degree of expertise. The constituency is analyzed to determine what appeals will be likely to command attention and win support. Geographical areas and population strata are surveyed to determine where appeals would be most effective and where a campaign would be wasted. Media must be selected, favorable positions in media obtained and contracts signed; the advertising message designed, written, polished and produced in print, sound or motion picture to achieve maximum effectiveness and results analyzed to measure their effect before a new or modified campaign is launched.

Whether we like it or not the advertising agency is the only respository available possessing this entire range of talents and experience. Agencies are acquainted with media buying processes and pricing policies. An agency through its normal business channels has acquired experience in contracting for time on radio or television, in buying space in magazine and newspapers, and in purchasing the additional paraphernalia of campaigning including lapel buttons, posters, carcards, transportation displays, billboards and the host of other devices which may be of use in supporting the political campaign. Modern technology, and specifically the use of the sophisticated techniques of television, has only increased the role of the advertising agency and the necessity for the employment of a particularly competent agency to support the political campaign.

The Kennedy campaign of 1960 provides some excellent examples of skilled agency use of television. No Roman Catholic had ever been elected to the presidency, and it was generally assumed that an adherent to the Catholic faith would run with so many obstacles in his path that election would be a remote possibility, if possible at all. Fundamentalist Protestants had long trumpeted that a Catholic candidate for the presidency, once he succeeded to the office, would be under an obligation to the Vatican—at least spiritually, if not politically as well. This obviously was a political weakness which could be exploited to the ultimate degree if the opposition saw fit to do so. The dependence of the candidate on the Vatican could be used as an example of the possible subservience of the United States to a foreign power. The Kennedy staff was very well aware of the dynamite in this issue. The question was how to combat it.

There is some dispute as to the precise reasoning behind Kennedy's final approach to the issue. The Louis Harris organization, including Harris himself, insisted that it was Harris polls which showed that the best way to combat the Catholic issue was to meet it head on. A second behavioral research group organized under the name of Simulmatics and led by Professor Ithiel de Sola Pool of the Massachusetts Institute of Technology also concluded that the best way to approach the Catholic religion issue was the frontal attack.[7] Both organizations, Harris and Simulmatics, concluded that any votes which were to be lost, had already been lost, and could hardly be won back. On the other hand, solidifying the Catholic vote, which had previously been heavily Democratic, behind the Democratic candidate would probably more than offset any minor losses which would occur as a result of the blunt and open approach to the religious issue. The Kennedy staff and the candidate himself were won over. They decided to run the risk and not attempt to conceal the issue. An opportunity presented itself in Houston, Texas, in early September. The Houston Protestant Ministerial Council had scheduled an appearance by Kennedy before the full membership.

It was a daytime meeting. This seemed the ideal opportunity to test the head-on attack theory on local television when audiences were substantially smaller than during prime time hours. The Kennedy advertising agency, Guild, Bascom & Bonfigli, made arrangements with Channel 13 in Houston, managed by Willard Walbridge who later played a prominent role in giving the performance national exposure, to carry the program. The Kennedy strategy called for making a short statement and then answering as frankly and bluntly as possible the questions raised by the Protestant ministers.

The results are now history. Walbridge was so enthusiastic about the program that immediately after its conclusion he called the offices of Guild, Bascom & Bonfigli in New York to express his enthusiasm to Reggie Schuebel, the media buyer for the agency. Walbridge urged Miss Schuebel to set about immediately buying national network time to give this program full national exposure. Miss Schuebel responded at once. She got in touch with Robert Kennedy to relay Walbridge's recommendation and urge quick implementation. Robert Kennedy, while expressing interest in the idea, suggested that his brother, the candidate, should make the final decision. It was ultimately John F. Kennedy himself who gave the orders to go.

There was one major deviation from the Walbridge proposal. It was decided not to buy national network time for an edited version of the Houston speech, but rather to use the taped program in areas where the Kennedy schedule called for personal appearances. Television in such areas was to be saturated during the seven days prior to his arrival. The technique thus served as effective advance promotion and as additional evidence of Kennedy's full willingness to bring the issue out into the open.

The Kennedy campaign had been planned so as not to waste any time in states which were firmly committed to the Democratic party or those in which Nixon had an insurmountable lead. There were 10 states which without question remained in the undecided column. These ten states were the battleground. It was these which would furnish the electoral votes necessary to elect one man or other to the presidency. The Kennedy staff was determined that the candidate campaign in these states and not dissipate his efforts where activity would be futile.

The Houston appearance thus became an integral element in the campaign ammunition stockpile in these ten states. The entire question and answer session was edited down into a compact half hour. It obviously was essential that the editing be done in such a way that there could be no charges of deletion of elements potentially damaging to the candidate. The edited version had to be so representative of the entire meeting and so fair in every respect that not even the most cynical critic could discover slanting. The delicate editing process was apparently performed without exposing any targets. Republican strategists carefully avoided exploiting the religious issue and Kennedy managers used it as they had planned.

The results of the 1960 election are history. But it was almost noon on the day after the election before it was finally decided that John F. Kennedy had won the presidency. California, Illinois and Texas, where the Kennedys had campaigned hard, were crucial states. The religious issue could have been damaging to the Kennedy cause in any or in all of the three. That he won is testimony to the courage of the Kennedy strategists in nullifying the religious issue and using television to expose it to public attention.

The campaign may have been less important, however, for the introduction of imaginative, creative, new uses of media than for solid, tough political organization and campaign management. The political professionals who made up the Kennedy campaign staff had an instinctive feel for the use of media and whether their employment of television was innovative is besides the point. They used it effectively.

The national campaign is so widespread geographically and so complex in terms of personnel, appeals, media buys, and sub-groups that it is difficult to investigate in detail. A state-wide campaign, however, furnishes an opportunity to draw a sufficiently detailed profile to permit an exhaustive examination. One such campaign was Congressman Robert P. Griffin's run for the Senate from the state of Michigan in November 1966. The campaign was managed by Robert Smalley, an executive of Whitaker & Baxter, a San Francisco political public relations firm which had been retained by Griffin supporters.

The Griffin campaign was built around three essential issues. The issues were selected after exhaustive analysis of Michigan politics, the Griffin record and attitudes of Michigan voters. Strategists were mindful particularly of the candidate's identification with the Landrum-Griffin Act, which had dealt with problems of both education and labor and was credited in some circles as being "the working man's bill of rights," although labor leadership was hardly unanimous in agreeing with the designation.

With this background, it was decided to drive home three themes during the course of the campaign. The first was Griffin's experience with education; the second, his experience with labor; and the third, his interest in and knowledge of how to deal with the disparate problems of inflation. In order to cater to the large labor vote, which is crucial in Michigan, it was decided to refer to him as a spokesman for the working man.

Once the theme was set, the campaign went forward. The first step was to determine how much money could reasonably be raised and how a budget could be based on this reasonable expectation. Sources of funding were the GOP State Central Committee, which would allocate funds both to the campaign of George Romney for the governorship, and Griffin for the Senate; local Griffin clubs which were to be set up throughout the state; and efforts at special fund-raising by Whitaker & Baxter. The campaign plan called for combining travel, largely by private auto, with heavy use of broadcast media and some newspaper advertising.

Television was to be concentrated largely in the Detroit area, with the McCann-Erickson advertising agency handling the media buys. A Washington television and film production firm sent representatives to Detroit and under Smalley's supervision prepared two five-minute programs, three sixty-second spot commercials, two twenty-second spots, and two ten-second spots. While this advertising, once it was scheduled for air, was exposed largely in the Detroit area, it was later seen on television stations throughout the state through the efforts of the Griffin clubs. The Griffin clubs raised their own funds, placed their own advertising and promoted interest in the advertising in order to increase viewing. Between $50,000 and $75,000 of added financing, all spent on television, was raised in this way.

As one feature of the television production effort, a rock-and-roll song with the Griffin theme was composed, recorded and included as background in television advertising. The song was introduced on television, after which approximately 20,000 plastic discs were distributed widely throughout the state. Some old-line Republican regulars tried at various times during the campaign to have this modern music removed from the Griffin effort, but by the time the protests grew loud the theme song apparently had caught hold among college student and black groups who constitute a large percentage of the population of the city of Detroit.

While utilizing the pre-prepared spot commercials, the

Griffin party was well aware of the advantage of appearing on news broadcasts, interview and question-and-answer programs on the many radio and television stations in the state. Griffin headquarters made up a file of television program schedules for all stations in the state and identified those which would be most likely to serve as outlets for personal appearances. An advance man traveling ahead of the Griffin entourage arranged for news coverage of the candidate for special interview programs where such programs were available, and scheduled interviews on women's programs for Mrs. Griffin.

Considerable stress was placed on this feature of the campaign since it was the feeling of the campaign managers that the most effective device for promoting the candidacy was appearance on regularly scheduled television news programs. The second most useful outlet would be the informal interviews with local personalities. Both, it was felt, were infinitely superior to spot announcements, newspaper advertisements, billboards, carcards, and the other devices normally used in political campaigns.

During the last three weeks of the campaign, the two statewide candidates, Romney for Governor and Griffin for Senator, joined forces to participate in five separate telethons. Each of the telethons ran for one hour. There were twenty minutes of Griffin answering questions alone, twenty minutes of Romney, and twenty minutes of the two working together. Normally, two or three-station networks were hooked up for the performances. The last of the telethons was broadcast from the Detroit area. All five were scheduled within a two-week period beginning from a point three weeks before the actual election. The response according to Smalley was "terrific."

Since one of the potentially troublesome problems for the Griffin campaign was the question of what labor would do, special efforts were made to increase Griffin's appeal to the laboring man. Fortunately for the Griffin forces, the state AFL-CIO had scheduled a convention at Detroit's Cobo Hall, to take place only a short time before the election. Griffin had written a letter to the convention managers asking for an opportunity to speak, but the AFL-CIO had refused. Griffin didn't reveal that his request had been rejected until the morning the convention opened. On that morning he held a press conference a few blocks from Cobo Hall during which he showed reporters the letter from the AFL-CIO officials, informing him there was no spot on the program for him.

A reporter asked whether Griffin would go to Cobo Hall and ask for a chance to be heard. He immediately responded in the affirmative and the whole entourage started for the convention site—the candidate himself, his managers, pencil and pad reporters, radio reporters with their microphones, and the television film crews with their cameras and audio equipment. As they arrived at the auditorium, the United Auto Workers' chief Walter Reuther was blasting Griffin on the platform. The Griffin party was, of course, stopped at the door. As doorkeepers made explanations as to why Griffin could go no farther, microphones were open and film cameras were grinding away.[8] The scene made for a highly dramatic episode on television news broadcasts later that day, and was not overlooked on front pages of the daily press. From that date on Griffin had an audience wherever he went.

As to whether the episode might have been set up in advance, Smalley, with a half smile, says, "Well, let's just say that it was not entirely unexpected that a reporter would ask whether the candidate would go over to Cobo Hall and ask directly for the opportunity to make his speech."

Governor Nelson Rockefeller's campaign for a third term as governor of New York in 1966 is regarded as a model of ingenuity, creativity, craftsmanship and as a superb example of campaign planning. Rockefeller's own experienced campaign staff combined with the efforts of Jack Tinker and Partners to build a two-stage campaign. But the governor's problems were baffling. Most of the national Republican apparatus regarded him as a renegade. They would never forgive him for the pressure he applied on Richard Nixon during the

1960 GOP National Convention. He was also the nominee of a party which held only minority status in New York State. This posed a baffling problem. The Rockefeller group had to defend a somewhat unpopular record and at the same time find a position where it could stand off the most violent attacks that the Democrats could make.

The campaign, which was planned during the spring, was broken into two parts for one principal reason: the identity of the Democratic candidate would not be known until after the Democratic state convention on September 12th. It was consequently decided to schedule phase one to run from early July until the Democratic state convention, and phase two from the Democratic state convention to the election. During phase one all the stress in a highly sophisticated television campaign was put on the record of the Rockefeller administration. During this phase the governor himself never appeared on the screen. Commercials dealt with the state's new narcotics law, its Medicaid bill, the governor's highway program, his efforts to combat air pollution, and his program for aid to higher education.

By the time Frank O'Connor was nominated by the Democrats at the September 12 convention following a bitter internal fight, the Rockefeller group was ready to shift gears. It was possible to leave the governor's face off the screen prior to the Democratic convention because, completely contrary to the Griffin experience in Michigan, the governor was widely known throughout the state and instantly recognizable. He had already been governor for two terms of four years each, had traveled widely throughout the state and had campaigned intensively and aggressively in both of the previous election campaigns. As an added bonus, he was a national figure as a result of his early service in the administration in Washington and his two campaigns for the Republican presidential nomination.

With a candidate who needed no personal build-up campaign managers concluded that it was the Rockefeller program which was the key to re-election. The decision was supported both by the governor's own advisors and by agency personnel assigned to the account. The advisors were also convinced that the long political speech would not be an effective method for selling the governor's program. So concentration was placed almost entirely on sixty-second commercials prepared by Jack Tinker and Partners.

After the Democratic convention, the advertising campaign swung into a new phase—an effort to give the Rockefeller program a forward look. The intention was to convince the public that the governor's plans were not static, that they were not finished and that only by the re-election of Governor Rockefeller could the program be carried to its ultimate end and successful conclusion. The final phase, scheduled for the last two weeks before the election, was designed to give extensive exposure to the candidate himself. This was done through a new set of commercials and through personal appearances on interview programs and debates and constant availability for coverage on regularly scheduled daily news broadcasts, including blintz-eating forays into Brooklyn, which were not entirely by coincidence in the most populated borough or city in the state.

The Democrats remained in a state of disarray throughout the entire campaign. Franklin D. Roosevelt Jr., who had wanted the Democratic nomination, was thwarted by the Democratic party and as a substitute accepted the Liberal nomination. This resulted in an erosion of O'Connor's voter base and diluted Democratic financial support. O'Connor's nomination came at a date so close to election day that it was difficult to mount an effective advertising and promotional campaign. Competent personnel were selected but they were never adequately coordinated.

In the meantime, the governor's campaign went forward, spending huge sums of money and creating an atmosphere that ultimately led to the election. Candidate O'Connor frequently charged the Rockefeller group with buying the election. It is a matter of record that, according to such data as are available, the Rockefeller campaign outspent O'Connor by nearly ten to one. Rockefeller expenditures apparently ran in the vicinity of $2,000,000 from the July 5th beginning through election day. The O'Connor campaign cost about $200,000. Rockefeller received 2,700,000 votes; O'Connor 2,300,000. If votes can be calculated on a price per vote, each ballot cast for Nelson Rockefeller cost approximately 74¢ whereas the X's in the O'Connor column cost about 9¢ each, a ratio of more than eight to one. Of the total two million dollars spent by the Rockefeller group, some $450,000 was spent on television programming between July 5th, the starting date of the campaign, and September 12th, when Frank O'Connor was nominated by the Democratic party.

Violent attacks were subsequently launched against the Rockefeller campaign by Democratic State Chairman John Burns and by candidate O'Connor. Rockefeller was charged with having bought the election, with having used advertising to distort the accomplishments of his administration and with having destroyed the integrity of political campaigning by reducing it to a matter of Madison Avenue advertising techniques. The complaints fed fuel to the simmering controversy about the role of the advertising agency in the political campaign. They stimulated new critical speculation about the so-called image making processes and about many aspects of the new campaign methodology.

The election of Richard Nixon to the presidency in 1968 is frequently referred to as an outstanding example of the use of image-making. And the witty and very successful book written by Joe McGinniss, *The Selling of the President 1968*, has contributed greatly in the public mind to the impression that the image makers were working overtime on behalf of Mr. Nixon. It seems more likely, however, that the Nixon campaign managers, with a good deal of skill and understanding of their man, combined with a sensitive approach to the voting public, did much more to highlight Mr. Nixon's strong points than to create a new image out of the man who had been in public life for more than twenty years before the 1968 campaign. They admitted that they could not create a new Nixon even if they tried. They were only trying to lend emphasis to his experience, acquaintance with an enormous range of problems, his thoughtfulness and capacity to maintain an efficient and orderly government. Admittedly they tried to erase his reputation for belligerency and for political machination, but not by remaking the man. They rather presented him in situations where he could appear thoughtful, confident, decisive and compassionate.

It's even questionable how far this expert job of political managment succeeded. Allan Gardner and Barry Nova, who directed Hubert Humphrey's 1968 television efforts, insist that the Nixon campaign won no new converts to the Republican party or to the cause of Richard Nixon, but only succeeded in holding on to those votes which would have accrued to a Republican party candidate under almost any circumstances. They further insist that the public was getting thoroughly bored with the bland Nixon toward the end of the campaign, and that had the campaign run for another week or two, this boredom would inevitably have led to defeat. This question raised by Democratic campaigners reopens the conundrum: How important was image-making with respect to the 1968 campaign for Mr. Nixon?

Television has been the major factor creating this new interest in image-making. It is television which widened the range of campaign technology, placed new emphasis on personal communication and bred a new corps of specialists in presentation for the television camera. The function performed, however, is one of adapting to new mechancial devices, not of creating new personalities. Preparing oneself to appear before a public audience, whether it be on the lecture platform, the old style Chautauqua circuit or before a television camera, has always demanded experience, training, audience analysis, and the ability to communicate to the audience. William Jennings Bryan was a good deal more of an actor than candidate of the television era. It is a reasonable question whether the dramatic Bryan, who electrified his partisan audience from the convention podium when he delivered the Cross of Gold speech, was less a performer than Richard Nixon appearing in an arena style program answering the questions of five or six carefully selected citizens before a similarly carefully selected audience of between fifty and one hundred people. If dramatic skill alone is the criterion, Bryan must be acknowledged the winner, hands down. If impact on the electorate in the latter half of the twentieth century is the measure of success, it may be that Richard Nixon is the new champion.

Franklin Roosevelt did not have the opportunity to use the television medium, but is generally regarded as having employed the most consummate skill in his radio fireside chats. Is this skill in the use of the most effective medium for reaching his constituency unethical because it is image-building, or is it simply a matter of making use of the tools at one's command to operate most effectively in the political or governmental milieu?

There probably isn't much point in becoming concerned that the Golden Kazoo will destroy honest democratic government. The average voter may not be a wholly rational being, but he has certainly seen enough television of all types to be able to apply some cynical standards to the actor who represents form rather than substance. On the contrary, the electorate may be better off if the candidates on whom he must decide come before him with well-planned campaigns, highlighting strengths, pinpointing significant issues and suggesting reasonable solutions. Then modern technology, mainly television, can serve the voters' interests by using its powers to clarify issues, candidates' strengths and weaknesses, and to stress differences between opposing aspirants to the same job.

It seems to make sense that to govern successfully, the candidate use every aid he can get. Theoretically it should make him a better leader if he learns how to use his most important assets to exercise leadership more effectively. If his managers equip him with background briefings, analyses, projections, and public opinion polls, he should logically be better informed concerning the issues of the election and those which concern the public.

The television camera may possess some of the attributes of the x-ray eye, but it is not an x-ray eye that will inevitably penetrate to show warts and blemishes in the candidate. It is the candidate himself who will give himself away over the period of any extended campaign.

This doesn't mean that a healthy cynicism is not in order and that a little skepticism concerning excessive amounts of superficial showmanship wouldn't be useful. The voter can afford to be skeptical and cynical but, most importantly, he should apply his own method of evaluation and judgment to the candidate and to the issue. Television should help him do so if he will give it a chance.

There is one significant trend in recent American political party methods that undoubtedly has been influenced by the new importance of television and its resultant emphasis on new campaign methods. The old-time political boss is becoming increasingly impotent. The combination of the role of the advertising agency and the television campaign are giving another shove to the power broker. The voter in the modern era is demonstrably less susceptible to the blandishments of the precinct worker, much less dependent upon him for favors. He can now get his information from radio and television whereas in an earlier age, unless he happened to be an avid newspaper reader, he depended largely upon word of mouth.

Television alone could not have destroyed the power base of the political boss. Greater affluence, a weakening of the hold of ethnic loyalties over the individual, a greater mobility of the whole population have all contributed. The Thanksgiving turkey basket, the precinct chairman's promise of an introduction which could lead to a city job, or even the social life at ward headquarters, no longer have the charmed effect on metropolitan areas they once had. The new immigrant is no longer very new; he is acquiring new confidence in his own capacity to serve himself. His horizons are extending beyond the homogeneous precinct or ward, and even beyond the city.

While this natural evolutionary decay of the roots of political bossism was proceeding, television was furnishing an entirely new information source, a source that was colorful, easy to understand and created a new set of heroes—the television news broadcasters. Chicago is still dominated by the remnants of an old-time political machine, guided by a master at blending old-time loyalties with new and modern approaches. But other American cities have shaken off the dominance of the machine and are demonstrating a new television age volatility.

Television with its strong grip on the time and attention of millions of householders has not been the sole factor in the demise of the once all-powerful urban political leader either. Labor union efforts, volunteer organizations, and a much more broadly-based political organization, have all contributed toward establishing an independent contact with the individual voter. But the information he gets from television and the impressions he forms on the basis of his viewing have made him more receptive to new political structures unconnected with the old political machine. Some of the campaign advisory role, formerly played by the political leader, is passing on to the advertising and public relations agency.

One of the interesting matters for speculation is the role the advertising agency will play in future campaigns. At the beginning of the television era relatively few agencies had any experience or even any interest in political campaigning. Numbers swiftly grew through the fifties and sixties and toward the end of the decade there were at least a score in the New York City area alone that had had significant experience on the firing line.

But the political campaign, while a fascinating challenge, is a major disruptive element to an advertising agency. The agency makes its bread and butter out of continuing accounts day after day, year after year. The political campaign, to the contrary, puts an inordinate amount of pressure on agency personnel for a few months every second or fourth year. Many agencies are less than enthusiastic about accepting the strain on their personnel and facilities. Regular accounts must almost inevitably suffer in some measure through the diversion of creative talents and production facilities to the cause of the campaign. While agencies are becoming more skeptical of participation in political campaigns, expertise in the art of political advertising, including planning, writing, producing, and media buying, is being acquired by individuals who are tending toward full-time careers in politics and issue-oriented campaigns. Others in agency life are becoming so fascinated by politics that some are leaving to enter politics as a career.

It is conceivable that a new form of advertising organization may develop in the near future to represent national parties and local campaigns. Such an organization would depend upon a director of communication at the top of the structure—an executive who is skilled in media with emphasis on television and in public relations, publicity, news reporting and editing methods, and skill in producing film and tape programs in the broad range of problems posed by creating and placing political advertising. It is even conceivable that the national parties will soon build miniature advertising agencies attached to national headquarters under the supervision of a director of communications.

A permanent organization need not be large. Many services could be purchased from the outside, including media buying, film and television production, graphic arts and public opinion analysis. The prime need of the permanent political party house agency would be for a skeleton staff of discriminating department heads, experienced experts who would be able to apply standards of quality to the selection of sub-contractors to carry out the operating function. Only the skeleton staff need be on a permanent payroll; all others could be employed either on short-term contracts or on a retainer basis.

The proposal is not a radical one. Production facilities are now usually obtained on contract by advertising agencies from established production houses. There is no reason why the political party organization couldn't follow the same procedure. Media services have traditionally been furnished by departments within the agency, but there has been a significant trend in the last few years for media personnel to break away from advertising agencies and establish media buying houses, as middle men between advertising agencies and clients on the one hand and television and radio stations on the other. There is no reason why a director of communications for a national political party wouldn't be able to engage the services of such a media-buying group for the duration of his campaign, and thus not have to rely on the frequently reluctant advertising agency to perform these services. Graphic arts are likewise frequently purchased by agencies from independent contractors. There is no reason why the party couldn't do likewise. Public opinion analysis, polling and copy-testing are logically services to be performed by outside contractors.

The major exception to outside contracting would most likely fall in the news and information programming areas. Guidance and special consultation will certainly continue to be obtained from the political public relations specialists, including the David Garths, Charles Guggenheims, Joseph Napolitans, Stephen Ailes, Spencer-Roberts, and Whitaker & Baxters. But the party machinery will still need an internal staff to maintain contact with party leaders and candidates, coordinate information policies, establish and preserve news service contacts, arrange television and radio appearances and newspaper and magazine interviews, and perform the multitude of functions of the publicity, public relations, and information experts.

The assignment is a particularly sensitive one in that most political experts are now convinced that the best possible exposure for the candidate is on regularly scheduled news broadcasts and interview shows, both news and entertainment-oriented. It would be difficult for an outsider to maintain the close contacts required for the party organization and candidates with media personnel. The small staff, aided by expert service organizations for the duration of the campaign, should be adequate to perform the function.

An organization of this sort probably would not work in the case of campaigns for lesser offices or in less populated areas simply because the cost of maintaining the staff would be excessive; but for the large, well-financed national organizations it is possible that major savings will accrue.

Whatever the future may bring, there is no doubt that the requirements of television for political campaigning make it mandatory that the skills and talents which are now found to a very considerable extent in the advertising agencies will continue to be required, and will continue to develop as the new methodology progresses. Increasing costs, growing sophistication in the use of communications technology, the introduction of new technology and the accelerating development of new techniques to propagate ideas and campaign themes point toward the necessity of establishing a corps of permanent campaign media experts. The growing disillusionment of advertising agencies with the distractions inherent in gearing up for a short term political campaign may hasten the change. The enthusiasm of recent converts to using media to support campaigns whether within the agency or outside, could provide the final push to the national parties.

Whenever the change occurs, television will certainly be the prime area of concern. It is television that shook up the old order and forced the new assessment, and television in one form or another, for better or for worse, will continue into the indefinite future to dominate the political campaign.

POLLS, PROJECTIONS,
AND ELECTIONS

$$\boxed{4}$$

Public opinion polling can be said to have been a part of the electoral process since the disastrous *Literary Digest* poll dug its own grave and that of its parent magazine by badly misgauging the temper of the country in the presidential election in 1936. Since that time scientific sampling has largely replaced the wholly unscientific approach used by the *Literary Digest*.

It would be an error to say that the use of the scientific sampling method of political campaigns is directly related to the use of television as a campaign tool, but the two have worked hand in hand and there has been a distinct relationship between them.

The Eisenhower "Man of Peace" campaign theme was developed in 1952 out of a sampling of names on the *Reader's Digest* mailing list. Later that year, the BBD&O agency in support of the Eisenhower candidacy devised a simple and inexpensive telephone polling system to keep the agency abreast of public attitudes and interests and to identify any shifts in public opinion which should be noted by the campaign directors in planning speeches and media campaigns, with special reference to television.

The first use of statistical projection on a broad scale by a network in covering a political campaign also occurred during the 1952 election. Prior to 1952 the networks, then largely radio, had relied more or less exclusively on the wire services, principally the Associated Press and to a lesser extent United Press, to furnish election returns. Network reporters traveled on campaign trains and made some ineffective efforts to gauge public opinion, but most political reporting seemed to have been a product of reporters talking to reporters rather than to a sample of the voting population.

CBS Television was planning to use a simplified projection system in a few sample areas to speed voter projection on election night of 1952, but had little hope for more than a sketchy and limited success until a CBS executive learned that Remington-Rand might be willing to make its Univac computer available for performing on a vastly larger scale. Negotiations were hastily completed, and in late August Dr. Max Woodbury, a mathematician then teaching at the University of Pennsylvania, began constructing a model which would anticipate the pattern of returns on election night and presumably furnish early indications of voter preference.

There was no time to build sophisticated models relating to specific geographical or population areas. The only available data which would serve the purposes in the short time available were the records of election returns half-hour by half-hour as reported on the CBS radio network in the 1948 and 1944 national elections. These statistics were supplemented by some Associated Press and United Press returns, also on a half-hour by half-our basis for the same election years.

There were some serious built-in hazards. Population shifts had drastically altered suburban patterns in a number of states and voting laws had changed poll closing time in some others. Notwithstanding the possible errors these changes might cause, Dr. Woodbury went to work to develop his model. He had barely finished programming Univac when the first returns started sifting in from the early reporting precincts in New Hampshire, South Carolina and Kansas.

Contact between CBS Television election headquarters and the Univac center had to be maintained by telephone between the election studio in Grand Central Terminal at 42nd Street and Park Avenue in Manhattan and the Remington-Rand headquarters building at 23rd Street and Fourth Avenue. Returns had to be channeled from election headquarters to the Remington-Rand building, processed for feeding into the computer, and results called back to the CBS Television studio. The remarkable fact is that even in the face of the awkward communications structure, the Univac projected returns almost precisely as they would eventually come out, and this only a few minutes after 8:30 P.M. on election night. That first Univac projection showed odds of 100 to 1 that General Eisenhower would defeat Governor Stevenson by an overwhelming popular and electoral vote.

CBS television viewers didn't see or hear these early results, however. Dr. Woodbury was concerned with some small aberrations in his results and decided to do one more run with some new correction factors before releasing the figures to the impatient CBS news executives who were not aware at that time that one run had been made.

The new projections released a few minutes after 9:00 P.M. showed that General Eisenhower would win with odds at 8 to 7 over Governor Stevenson and a very close race in prospect. By that time CBS correspondents had already concluded that an Eisenhower sweep was in progress. As one of them commented: "Univac must be a Democrat." It was not until the next day that the first almost perfectly accurate projection was released, and a new style in projecting election returns was launched.

By 1956, NBC News had concluded an arrangement with the International Business Machines company to perform a similar service. CBS Television again used Remington-Rand's Univac in the congressional election of 1954 with mixed results and in the 1956 national election with another bull's eye.

The 1954 projections were complicated by the fact that state-wide elections are much more complex than national elections. Within the relatively simpler senatorial races in which emphasis could be concentrated on key races, projections were reasonably accurate. But the House of Representatives posed problems that were too complicated for the state of the art in 1954.

By 1960, CBS had switched to IBM replacing Remington-Rand, which by then had become Sperry-Rand. NBC utilized the RCA computer built by its parent company. The 1960 election marked the first genuinely sophisticated use of computer-processed projections. IBM ran its first projection for CBS at 8:12 P.M. Eastern Standard Time. At that time only 4 percent of the precincts had reported. IBM quoted the odds at 11 to 5 on the election of John F. Kennedy as President and forecast that Kennedy would win 297 electoral votes to 240 for Mr. Nixon, with the further forecast that Kennedy would win 51 percent of the total popular vote and Nixon 49 percent. It is now a matter of record that Senator Kennedy reecived 303 electoral votes, 6 more than IBM had projected, and Vice President Nixon 219, or 21 fewer. The popular vote was almost a dead heat, with less than 120,000 votes out of nearly 65,000,000 separating the two candidates.

Since 1960 all three networks have devoted substantial resources to constructing faithful models in representative election precincts throughout the United States. As a result of this careful attention to detail and intensive checking of previous results, the technique of projecting election returns has developed to a fine art—light years ahead of the primitive efforts by Dr. Woodbury, Remington-Rand and CBS Television long ago in 1952.

CBS News in 1960 pointed the way toward the more sophisticated use of early election returns during the Wisconsin primary in April of that year. An intensive analysis was made in Wisconsin voter districts prior to the election through the combined efforts of Bernard R. Berelson and William N. McFee of Columbia University, Elmo Roper, IBM statisticians and CBS News.

The objective was to see whether there were any patterns developing in the Wisconsin primary election returns which would suggest the directions the parties would follow in the pre-convention period and the issues which might predominate in the national campaign which would follow during the summer and fall. In view of Senator Kennedy's vigorous campaign, voter reaction to the religious issue was carefully studied. Wisconsin voters were broken down into urban and rural classifications, Catholic and Protestant, farmer and labor, tenant farmers and farm owners, relatively wealthy farmers on large plots of property which they owned themselves and less affluent farmers, either scratching out a living on inferior acreage or renting from large landowners. Ethnic groups were also isolated out and classified by income, occupation, religion, political preference and area of residence.

A number of quick conclusions were drawn on election night, more detailed findings a few days later. Senator Kennedy's Roman Catholic religion was obviously a factor in the campaign, but evidence indicated that Catholicism helped him rather than hurt. Senator Humphrey ran strongly in the less affluent farm areas in the lake and scrub forest country of northwestern Wisconsin but was unable to achieve any substantial margin in the labor dominated areas in the industrial southeastern part of the state. Senator Kennedy's support seemed to be broadly based through both urban and rural areas, labor and agriculture, and he had an overwhelming margin among Roman Catholics, whereas Humphrey's margin was substantially less among Protestants. Relatively weathly German Catholic farmers in the Fox River Valley supported Kennedy overwhelmingly. Impoverished Scandinavian Lutheran farmers in the barely productive farms carved out of the forests of northwestern Wisconsin were for Humphrey, but there were fewer of them.

Careful attention to these returns might have foreshadowed Kennedy's later smashing victory in West Virginia which took Senator Humphrey out of the race.

There are many thoughtful persons who question the use of scientific sampling and public opinion polls. They argue that the candidate and his party are simply building a program to cater to interests which they know are there, rather than to exercising any effective leadership. Superficially, this makes a good argument. But as Ithiel de Sola Pool argued when under attack for devising his "People Machine," the public may be better served by a leader who is armed with a fund of information than one who insulates himself from opinion.

The case for televison's use of public opinion polling is much more clear cut. The employment of sophisticated techniques for sampling public attitudes makes it possible to identify issues which might otherwise remain hidden, to anticipate trends relating to both candidates and issues, to isolate specific population groups for microscopic examination of reaction to campaign appeals and to anticipate factors which will influence voter preference on election day.

A function of television in the political process is to report; to report as thoroughly, honestly, objectively, and meaningfully as its resources permit. Effective use of scientific sampling techniques furnishes a new and useful tool to the medium, a tool which supplements the efforts of its reporters, checks the validity of their findings and introduces a new objective element into what is essentially a subjective process.

The public is the beneficiary. When scientific surveys of public opinion are knowledgeably and effectively used, the voter has at his disposal a mirror which faithfully reflects public attitudes and a barometer which suggests future trends. He had these tools before television entered the political scene, but television has given them new dimensions. Television has brought new methods of using results, speed in reporting them, and an audience far surpassing that delivered by radio and the press and magazines in the 1930s and 1940s. In the process, television has enormously accelerated the process of tabulating, analyzing and reporting election returns, even to the extent that it has dramatically altered the process of reporting those returns.

Prior to 1964 the two wire services, Associated Press and United Press International, assumed the responsibility for gathering results from precincts, wards and counties, tabulating them in regional tabulating offices, and feeding them into central election bureaus. Beginning in the 1964 November election a new national election bureau was formed, a bureau in which the three television networks, all of them armed with their carefully programmed computers and armies of gatherers of returns at the precinct level, began to play a dominant role. Whereas in previous years computation was done almost entirely manually in newspaper or wire service offices, by 1964 the task had been assigned to computers. Delays involved in hand tabulating in city or state bureaus were avoided as details poured directly into central headquarters in New York.

Anxious partisans of Richard Nixon and Hubert Humphrey still had to wait for hours before they were certain of the outcome of the 1968 election, but that was a result of the closeness of the race not the slowness of the counting process. It could conceivably have taken hours longer to determine the winner had not television and the computer become integral factors in the election tabulating scene.

Some political observers have been concerned since as long ago (in television terms) as 1960 that early projection of election results based almost entirely on scattered and fragmentary returns in the eastern and some midwestern states could exercise a profound influence on voter behavior in the Rocky Mountain and Pacific Time Zones. They speculate that a projection made at 8:30 P.M. Eastern Standard Time, which would reach the Pacific Coast at 5:30 P.M. or from two-and-one-half to three-and-one-half hours before polls close, could generate a bandwagon effect on behalf of the leading candidate. They theorize that such an early projection would either cause discouraged voters to stay away from the polls or undecided ones to swing to the candidate designated by the projections as the probable ultimate winner.

There is little reliable evidence either to support or to deny the theory. Network specialists argued that western voters have behaved essentially as they were projected to, thus suggesting that any effect of the broadcasting of early predictions on their behavior patterns is limited to such an extent that there is no meaningful evidence of a shift in the final returns. ABC News undertook a study in 1964 which indicated that the impact was negligible.[1]

Nothwithstanding this inconclusive evidence, president Frank Stanton of CBS has called for uniform poll opening and closing times throughout the country so that there could be no suggestion of improper influence. His suggestion has stimulated little support, however; and the concern of the critics seems to be abating as the use of the projection technique becomes more commonplace.

The combined influence of television and scientific sampling techniques has, though, been subject to some abuses and some errors on the part of network news personnel. Some mistakes have been made in projecting final election returns on the basis of inadequate results or faulty programming. Television reporters have from time to time misused data, either because it has not been properly interpreted for them or because they have jumped to unwarranted conclusions. Generally, however, the process has been used responsibly, but unscrupulous use of polling techniques, coupled with the impact of the television image, could do irreparable damage to the political process. By and large, however, the marriage of television, scientific sampling and computers has been a happy one and one for which a long relationship can be predicted.

THE CHANGING CAMPAIGN: FROM WHISTLE STOP TO TV SCREEN

The 1968 presidential election campaign reached a new high level in the use of television as a campaign device. The lessons learned in previous campaigns, both regional and national, were put to work with a sophistication born of years of experimentation and observation by a mixture of hardened experts from previous elections and fresh young newcomers who had been keen observers of the electoral process.

More money was spent than ever before. Herbert Alexander, a director of the Citizens Research Foundation, estimates that some $300 million dollars were invested in supporting all candidates at all levels.[1] This represents a fifty percent increase over 1960; and a higher expenditure than ever before went into television. Advertising agencies played an increasingly significant role, as did the so-called "campaign planners," a new breed of specialists in advising and counseling candidates, suggesting campaign themes, commissioning and interpreting public opinion polls, producing campaign films, coaching the candidate in television performances and staging rallies for maximum effect. Spot announcements were used more frequently than ever before; and the Nixon staff picked up Governor Dewey's device of the street corner interview, used so effectively in 1950, and developed it to a new degree of perfection in his so-called "arena-type" programs.

Hubert Humphrey made a valiant effort and by reason of a last ditch, stretch-run campaign, directed by a group of political pros, led by national chairman Lawrence O'Brien, who gained his national experience in the Kennedy campaign of 1960, and his political public relations partner, Joseph Napolitan, nearly nosed out the frontrunner and favorite.

But it was the Nixon campaign that reached new heights of efficiency and succeeded in creating a blend of techniques from previous campaigns with new tactics developed to cater to the strengths and weaknesses of the candidate.

The campaign was directed and executed by a battery of experts, including representatives from advertising agencies, a former editorial writer of the *New York Herald Tribune,* a number of holdovers from previous Nixon campaigns, and a senior executive of the Columbia Broadcasting System. The effort was supported by the Fuller & Smith & Ross advertising agency, which was beefed up by the "anchor and loan" system in order to give it the expertise to function at maximum efficiency over the short period of time consumed by a campaign. Under this system, expert volunteers were recruited from other agencies for the campaign's duration, after which they returned to their more prosaic careers advertising soaps, cereals and automobiles.[2]

Nixon advisors, more than in any previous presidential contest, concentrated on that mysterious characteristic called "image." A decision was made many months before the campaign actually got under way to give Mr. Nixon an "image" which would be attractive to the American electorate. It was determined that he should not appear pugnacious or belligerent, but that he should reflect reasonableness, thoughtfulness, intelligence, knowledgeability about a wide range of domestic and foreign affairs, and ease in conversing with the public on the most reasonable and down-to-earth basis.

In order to maintain this image, it was decided to restrict his appearances to tightly controlled situations. There would be no chances taken: no debates, a minimum of formal speeches; and a heavy degree of concentration on what was called the "arena" style of political performance. The arena performance required a controlled situation in which an audience was carefully screened in advance. Five or six carefully selected interviewers were to ask what would appear to be blunt questions of the candidate. While the candidate did not know in advance the precise wording of the questions, it could be relatively certain that none of them would be embarrassing. Each would be designed to give him an opportunity to launch into a statement regarding an area in which he was knowledgeable and in which he had had ample opportunity to prepare himself. These appearances would be scheduled for locations around the country where the subject to be discussed would have strong regional appeal and were frequently broadcast on regional networks. Of course, the regional television network was nothing new. It had been used as early as 1952 by Dwight Eisenhower. The Eisenhower managers had purchased limited network time in his very first campaign swing through the south in August 1952. John F. Kennedy had made extensive use of the regional network in his presentation of his side of the religious issue in 1960. An edited version of his appearance before the ministerial association of Houston, Texas, was prepared for extensive use in a number of regions. But the regional network was developed to its fullest extent in the scheduling of Mr. Nixon's arena performances in 1968. National networks were avoided. Nixon advisors arranged for the programs to be carried by a number of stations in the immediate vicinity of the origination point. If an arena performance were to be made in Kansas City, Missouri, time on stations within a limited radius of Kansas City would be bought for the performance. If the performance originated in Atlanta, Georgia, stations in Alabama, north Florida, South Carolina and Georgia carried the program.

The national television network news broadcasts became another major target of opportunity in 1968. Nixon personnel made it a point to have a release available for television news recording purposes every day at 3:00 P.M. Eastern time. They reasoned that a three o'clock release in any portion of the country could be transmitted to New York in time for inclusion in the evening news programs of that day. The candidate himself, however, was rarely made available for these statements. He was kept under tight wraps and the statements were normally made by persons other than the candidate himself. Humphrey supporters were also conscious of the requirements of television news. While their plan was not developed to the careful precision of the Nixon system, some attempt was made to reach network television news programs every day.

Political experts were present in great numbers on both sides: Lawrence O'Brien, Joseph Napolitan, Ira Kapenstein, William Connell, Ted Van Dyk, Agriculture Secretary Orville Freeman, and two newer men, Allan Gardner and Barry Nova on the Humphrey team; Harry Trealevan, E. R. Haldeman, John Ehrlichman, Patrick Buchanan, Leonard Garment, Frank Shakespeare and Ray Price, in addition to old regulars Robert Finch and Herbert Klein on the Republican side. Most of these men had had previous campaign experience and were regarded as masters of the political art.

The Democrats had an enormous disadvantage in that their team really was not put together until the conclusion of the Democratic national convention in late August. The advertising agency, Lennen & Newell, which brought both Allan Gardner and Barry Nova into the campaign, was not actually employed to support Humphery until September 13, or approximately seven weeks before the election. But while the year 1968 saw political campaigning on television reach new heights of concentration, intensity and sophistication, the real beginning occurred some eighteen years earlier with Governor

Thomas E. Dewey's 1950 campaign for the governorship of New York.

Some television had been used in the 1948 Dewey presidential campaign, but the medium then had penetrated only a few major cities along the East coast. Chicago and Los Angeles had active television stations, but they were not interconnected with Eastern origination points. The number of receivers in American homes totaled only 400,000. While many bars had become, in effect, community viewing centers, the audience was hardly large enough to be of any significance. The important fact during the 1948 campaign was that there was some opportunity for experimentation with techniques.

In 1950, very early in the campaign, months before the June nominating conventions, Governor Dewey had selected the advertising agency of Batten, Barton, Durstine & Osborn to plan his campaign. An important factor in the selection was the agency's politically oriented president, Bernard (Ben) Duffy. Duffy was a skilled craftsman, a superb salesman, and a hard-hitting executive who had been born on New York's West Side. He was a born politician with an instinct and a flare for the game of politics. It was a very simple matter for Duffy to blend the capabilities and technical skills of his advertising agency, which was one of the world's most successful, with the requirements of a political campaign. He also had on his staff men who were curious about politics and interested in it, enthusiastic about plunging into the great game. They included Carroll Newton, who was to continue working on Republican Party campaigns through 1960, John Elliott, who worked extensively in the 1950 and '52 campaigns, and later became president of Ogilvy & Mather and Al Cantwell, one of the agency's best producer-directors.

Dewey himself had an alert and innovative staff, interested in steeping themselves in techniques of the new medium. They included his political expert, Herbert Brownell; and his media specialist, James C. Hagerty, who, unlike some of his former newspaper colleagues, was adaptable and flexible enough to learn the requirements of the television business.

Months before the nominating conventions (actually, in January and February of 1950) BBD&O began to buy prime time slots for the 1950 campaign. Agency personnel discovered it was possible to put together state-wide networks so that New York City, Albany, Utica, Schenectady, Syracuse, Rochester, and Buffalo, could all be reached simultaneously. They also reasoned that by buying time early they could select time periods which would have the most impact during the final days of the campaign. They were not particularly concerned that the time would be bought in vain, because, as Hagerty put it, "it was no mystery that Governor Dewey was going to be renominated."

The assumption was made, and quite logically as it turned out, that the formal political speech was well on the way to oblivion. They concluded that the campaigner would have to be flexible and informal, and that he would appear at much greater advantage on television in a question-and-answer situation than he would in a formal speech. As a consequence, plans were made for what later developed into the arena concept employed so successfully in 1968 by the Nixon campaign, and the telethon, which at that time was in vogue for money raising purposes.

The highlight of the Dewey campaign was an eighteen-hour marathon telethon, which was conducted on the weekend before the November election. The governor appeared for 15 minutes out of each hour. Questions were asked largely by persons on the street, with Happy Felton, a broadcaster with the Brooklyn Dodgers, recruiting the personnel and working as a relay man between interrogator and governor.

The fact that Dewey was an easy winner is now a matter of record. More significant from the point of view of the impact of television on U.S. politics, however, is the fact that the campaign team trained during the Dewey run for the New York governorship had tested techniques, tried new formulas, experimented with new devices, and had formulated a set of standards and policies which were to be put to use two years later in the nomination and election of Dwight D. Eisenhower as President of the United States.

Batten, Barton, Durstine & Osborn was not involved in the early stages of the Eisenhower campaign, but Ben Duffy was an advisor. The principal role was played at this stage by another prominent New York advertising executive, Sig Larmon, president of Young & Rubicam. Larmon, a friend of President Eisenhower's, had offered the services of the Y & R agency during the period required to achieve the nomination for President Eisenhower. Except for the fact, however, that the advertising agency was different, the personnel supporting Eisenhower included many of the faces that were involved in the Dewey campaign of 1950, including Dewey himself.

Young & Rubicam, like Batten, Barton, Durstine & Osborn, had had extensive experience with television prior to the 1952 campaign. The agency, during the later '40s, had been a predominant producer of radio programs which were then placed on the networks, and in the early 1950 period it was in the process of converting some of its radio program facilities to television program production, this before the period when the networks took over the principal burden of production of programs themselves. Y & R was largely responsible for preparing the advertising, planning much of the public relations, and some of the campaign strategy leading up to the 1952 Republican convention which began in late June. Y & R personnel worked closely with the principal supporters of General Eisenhower: Henry Cabot Lodge, Paul Hoffman, General Lucius Clay, J. H. Whitney, and some of the Dewey people who had been deeply concerned with the gubernatorial election in 1950 in New York State.

The man selected to head the publicity and public relations activties was Robert Mullen, who had been with Paul Hoffman in the Marshall Plan program and had had considerable experience as a government public relations man. The whole group was aware of the success of Governor Dewey in using television in 1950 and apparently was convinced at an early stage that television would play a significant role in the pre-convention maneuvering.

The first major television effort was General Eisenhower's Abilene, Kansas speech and press conference in early June. Eisenhower strategists decided that the kick-off to the campaign should take place in the general's old home town. There was one major problem involved. Bringing television to Abilene was a costly affair. The closest mobile facilities were in Kansas City and Omaha, some 200 miles away, and the nearest microwave relay connection was an equal distance. Y & R executives in conjunction with representatives of the general's campaign succeeded in convincing CBS and NBC that the $80,000 expenditure necessary to put in temporary microwave relays would be a well worthwhile venture.

While Mullen was generally in charge of the program and the press conference which was to follow, it never occurred to him that the television audience could be more important than the crowd gathered in the historic Kansas town. And since the performance was booked to take place in the town's baseball park, it was scheduled for daylight hours. Mullen now concedes that if it it were to be done again, the sponsors never would take the risk of having this kick-off speech done in the open air. It would have been scheduled in an auditorium so that weather and climate conditions could have been controlled. The principal thrust of the speech would have been directed at the television audience rather than at the audience present in the arena.

The serious consequences of the error were soon clearly evident. A downpour struck Abilene just as the festivities were beginning. The general was already soaked when he reached the lectern set on an open platform in the park's infield. As he started to speak one of the local committee members tried to hold an umbrella over his head and his manuscript; but the water poured down off the umbrella onto the manuscript, soaking the pages. As Mullen describes it, "you could see the gen-

eral grow more and more irritated." At least at one time during the course of the presentation the umbrella bearer moved
aside and some of the rain began to pelt the general's bald
head, which irritated him even more.

Added to the problem was the fact that the general was not
terribly enthusiastic about the speech which had been written
for him by Bryce Harlow. Harlow incidentally later became
one of his favorite speech writers. It was a highly philosophical
speech and it was the first time that Harlow had written for
him. Rain and an unfamiliar manuscript took their toll. Boredom was so pronounced, the general couldn't conceal it. Mullen felt the affair was a total disaster. James Hagerty, who
didn't go to Abilene for political reasons (Governor Dewey
was holding him in reserve for later), agreed.

But much of this lost ground was recovered the next morning during a press conference held in an Abilene theater. The
theater was not the ideal location for a press conference. It was
long and narrow, in the country town movie theater tradition.
CBS and NBC had been asking since the Abilene press conference was first announced, for the privilege of bringing their
electronic cameras in for a live pick-up. Since they brought their
electronic gear out from Omaha and Kansas City, they felt
that this was an important part of the Eisenhower meeting, and
it was time for television to assert its own independence.

As Mullen describes the story, the press threatened to boy-
cott the meeting completely if television were permitted in.
At one time when Mullen suggested to representatives of the
wire services that he was considering the request of television,
he was told by their representatives that if Mullen allowed
television coverage, they would bring patrols of Boy Scouts
into the hall as messengers. As the candidate answered a question his answer would be written on a scrap of paper and given
to a Boy Scout to take to the nearest communications center.
The turmoil and inconvenience this would have caused, the
clutter that would have inevitably developed in the aisles and
the noise and commotion stemming from the constant move-

ment of the messengers would obviously have disrupted any of Mullen's efforts to conduct an effective conference. Mullen could only tell the television representatives on the scene (Paul Levitan and Fritz Littlejohn for CBS and Joseph McConnell and Ad Schneider for NBC) that there would be no live television. They could attend as pen-and-pencil reporters, but the electronic cameras were barred.

On the morning of the press conference itself, William S. Paley, chairman of the board at CBS, called his chief news executive even before commuter trains started for the city and asked whether it might not be a good idea to cover this conference. Paley was told that CBS News had been trying hard for weeks but that every request had been bluntly rejected. Paley suggested then that perhaps the alternative was to muscle in. This, of course, was exactly what the CBS personnel had been waiting for; a call went out immediately to Paul Levitan in Abilene, the director of special events, instructing him to move his gear in and to inform Eisenhower officials that he and the equipment could be ousted only by physical force.

Levitan had taken the trouble to move his cameras and switching gear to a position in the lobby of the theater the night before. His technicians were on call ready to move it in, assuming something of this sort might happen. So, seconds after Levitan took the call from Paley, the machinery was in motion. NBC, in the meantime, being understandably pessimistic about the opportunity of covering the conference, had packed its machinery onto a truck and sent it on its way to Kansas City. So NBC was effectively out of business.

Mullen learned shortly before the press conference while en route to the General's quarters to escort him to the conference site that CBS cameras were in the theater and that Levitan was refusing to be ousted. As he walked over with General Eisenhower, he described to the general what had happened as tactfully as possible and suggested that there would be quite a commotion if the cameras were to be removed from the hall.

Conversely, there was the threat of a reaction from the press if they were not.

General Eisenhower asked Mullen whether he didn't think it was a good idea to leave the cameras in the hall. Mullen replied in the affirmative. The cameras stayed. NBC, its cameras en route to Kansas City, called CBS for a feed. CBS replied that NBC could have a feed if NBC engineers could arrange with AT&T to obtain the signal from New York, which they did seven or eight minutes late—and General Eisenhower's press conference went out to the country live, at first on one network, then on two.

General Eisenhower handled himself in the conference with what was regarded as warmth, professional skill and a firm hand. He was far more relaxed and interested than he was in the rainstorm the night before. Boredom had disappeared. The performance was considered a huge success by those in the hall and by many of those who watched on television. Political experts who observed the performance felt that it did much to rectify the damage that had been done the night before. However, it did much more than that. It created the first crack in the then existing impenetrable barrier between the printed press and representatives of television. It would be several years before television would have fully demonstrated sufficient strength to insist on equal treatment; but a long step forward was taken in the Abilene theater. The conference also pointed the way toward later live television coverage of presidential press conferences. This was not to come to fruition until the winter of 1961—almost nine years later; but a precedent had been established. The successful television campaign for equal participation led to one more significant result which has had a profound effect on political campaigning in the United States and later throughout most of the free world. It brought television into the campaign process in a big way; it established the electronic camera as a major factor to be reckoned with by political campaigners; and it forced campaign organizers to start planning techniques to harness the device for maximum impact in the political process.

The Eisenhower strategists who were television-oriented from the beginning were quick to take advantage of the medium's capacity to aid in upsetting the Republican party's old order. Combining the talents of Young & Rubicam with the inner corps of Eisenhower campaigners—Henry Cabot Lodge, Paul Hoffman, Senators Duffy of Pennsylvania and Carlson of Kansas, Walter Williams of Washington state, and the Dewey group from New York City and Albany—a strategy was developed which was to place a primary stress on the use of television.

Eisenhower supporters knew that the bulk of Republican party machinery was in the hands of the Taft wing of the party, and that the Taft hold could be dislodged only by maximum effort aimed at rank and file Republican party members throughout the country. It was felt that an image had to be created for the campaign effort which would dislodge the hold of the regular party supporters and permit the strength of the masses of Republicans to make itself felt. The ultimate aim was to wrest control of the party machinery from the Taft wing and open up the convention to an Eisenhower blitz.

It was foreseen that the major battleground was to be the credentials committee of the Republican national committee, which would meet prior to the convention. The Eisenhower effort was designed to make it appear that the only Republicans who were capable of winning the election, after a long twenty-year GOP drought, were on the Eisenhower side. It was felt that television would reveal the difference between what was regarded as the tired, old-line party regulars who were supporting Taft, and the young, fresh, new broadly based Republicans who were for Eisenhower.

The credentials committee was chosen as the site for the major effort, because only by dislodging Taft delegations from Southern states and replacing them with younger, more aggressive Eisenhower supporters could the Eisenhower forces break the Taft stranglehold on the convention. But there was a basic weakness in the Taft position which Ike supporters had carefully evaluated. The traditional Southern Republican party official was a staunch conservative, who held party office only to dispense patronage in such years as the Republicans might win national office. Holding on to this position year after year was relatively simple, because there were so few Republicans in a one-party region. But in 1952 a mass switch began to take place and the new Republicans, mostly Eisenhower sympathizers, were frustrated because the party machinery was in the firm grip of the old-timers who selected the convention delegates.

Eisenhower tacticians made every effort to get their candidate and his supporters on television. They were quick to recognize the value of news programs, and enthusiastically accepted invitations for interview and discussion programs. At the convention itself they set up machinery to make it possible to cooperate fully with television personnel, and, while they lost the battle for live television coverage of the credentials committee meeting, Eisenhower supporters never passed up opportunities to appear before television cameras conveniently set up just outside the credentials committee meeting room.

Following the convention the Republican National Committee engaged the Kudner advertising agency, which had represented Taft in the pre-convention period, to plan the Eisenhower campaign for the national party. Young & Rubicam, which had been the principal Eisenhower agency, was given the responsibility for supporting the Citizens Committee for Eisenhower, a broadly-based group with representation from Democratic regulars as well as Republicans. The Citizens Committee was to make a special effort to enlist the support of younger voters and disillusioned Democrats.

It wasn't long before the Eisenhower supporters became disillusioned with the support the Kudner agency was giving them, and a call was put in for Ben Duffy, the old political warhorse from BBD&O. Duffy came to Denver and was asked whether he would work with the Kudner agency in developing the Eisenhower campaign. His answer was that he would work on the campaign only if BBD&O had the primary responsibility. The Eisenhower leadership agreed to Duffy's terms and Kudner was thereby relegated to a secondary position. This brought into the campaign the expert services of the BBD&O group, including Duffy, Carroll Newton, John Elliott, Al Cantwell and the production and direction personnel who had been working on live network television programs for BBD&O clients.

Two startling changes in campaign tactics were accomplished relatively early in the campaign. The first involved a breakaway from the old methods of scheduling campaign trips and media coverage; the second, the birth of the spot announcement as a political force.

A two-day Eisenhower trip to six southern cities taken during late August marked a dramatic change from old campaign procedures in three principal respects. In the first place, it pointed the way to the quick demise of the traditional campaign train. Use of air transportation made it possible for the general to cover six cities in three states in two days' time. Secondly, rather than depend upon major rallies in large auditoriums, which could be scheduled only at night, day time appearances were arranged so that the meetings could be held at airports or public squares. This enabled the general to leave his plane, move to a platform with microphones and cameras, or travel by motor coach to the city center. There he appeared before reporters and television cameras in addition to the party faithful and curious onlookers of either party. This technique meant that a lesser number of faithful Republicans might be able to see and hear the general in action; but television exposure and the opportunity to reach the uncommitted were regarded as more than adequate compensation. The third tactical change saw television given an equal break with the printed press.

The most dramatic development, however, was the virtual

extinction of one of the most colorful and traditional political techniques, the whistle stop campaign. Candidates had been whistle stopping for almost a hundred years. A private car for the candidate and a few personal aides, additional Pullman and lounge cars for members of the campaign staff, and sufficient sleeping cars to accommodate representatives of the press were tied together in the yards and started off on extended trips that sometimes lasted for two or three weeks. Advance men, keeping a day or two ahead, drummed up curious crowds along tracksides. Frequently they succeeded in getting school officials to declare holidays so that cheering school children could liven up the audience. As the train ground to the stop, a band played, a local party official—frequently the mayor—appeared on the rear platform and in his best campaign oratory introduced "the next President of the United States." While the candidate delivered his set speech, revised only to fit in the name of the town where he was appearing and a few names of local party faithful, a selected few key party supporters were permitted to board the lounge car for the journey to the next town, where they would be replaced by a new contingent. If they were very lucky, they might have a short chat with the presidential candidate, or at least a handshake.

The press meanwhile, or those who were sufficiently curious to do so, ran down trackside from their cars stationed toward the train's head end to see for themselves how the candidate might vary his set pattern and to pick up any political tidbits they might from the trackside onlookers. On signal, they dashed back to their own cars to jump aboard before the train pulled away, leaving them to find their own transportation to the next scheduled stop. At trainstops, while the candidate met privately with the most influential visitors or conferred with his personal staff, reporters gathered in the bar with the lesser party supporters or talked with them in the smokers. As deadline time neared, they went to typewriters and workcars to prepare copy for filing through the nearest Western Union office.

As night fell, the train usually chugged its way into a larger city where an auditorium rally was scheduled. Reporters normally went with the candidate's caravan to hear the speech, seize up the crowd, and try to spot a few knowledgeable local experts to round out their stories. But some, bathless for days, headed for hotels to try to clean up a bit while there were a few spare moments. Then it was back to the train, perhaps sleeping aboard their own Pullmans in the yards at night, or making a long run to a distant section, where the routine was repeated over and over again in almost identical pattern.

Before the advent of television the whistle stop was a device of critical importance. A successful whistle stopper who achieved rapport with his trackside followers had the same kind of advantage that the effective television performer now has—he just couldn't reach as many people. President Truman was effective at the art, but Governor Dewey was seriously hurt by a sharp comment which he was overheard to make when his engineer started the train before the governor had finished his performance.

Eisenhower's whirlwind tour in August virtually marked the end of the whistle-stop campaign. There has been some whistle-stopping since. In 1968 President Nixon spent a day traveling by train in Ohio. Senator Robert Kennedy did a day of rear platform campaigning in California prior to that state's presidential primary in 1968; but the technique of using the train as both a conveyance and platform for speaking to political rallies effectively died on the day that General Eisenhower went south. It was a death that was mourned by few reporters or candidate staff members. As James Hagerty puts it, "with the availability of television, you don't have to take this traditional backbreaking ride around the country for 23 or 24 days."

The other major breakthrough in the 1952 campaign related to the first use of the spot announcement. No real consideration had ever been given to the use of the short, hard-sell message prior to the arrival at Eisenhower headquarters of Rosser

Reeves, a brilliantly creative executive at the Ted Bates Agency. Reeves suggested that General Eisenhower be asked to appear in a number of these spots. The spots would then be placed on local television stations in those areas where additional support seemed most necessary. After some discussion, Reeves was given the commission in September to prepare the scripts, and General Eisenhower agreed to record the announcements once they were written and approved.

Once the commercials were finished Reeves tried to place them through the Bates Agency, but had great difficulty in doing so largely because the presidents of the two major broadcasting networks—CBS and NBC—were opposed to the use of spot announcements to deliver political messages. They were regarded as undignified, excessively abbreviated and only a caricature of the candidate's views. BBD&O then undertook the responsibility for placing the messages. The first step was for Carroll Newton to see Frank Stanton of CBS and Joseph McConnell of NBC. After considerable persuasion the two agreed to permit the spots to be used on the stations owned by these two networks; whereupon BBD&O set up the schedule. But there was still some controversy. Many felt that political campaigning was being reduced to a hard-sell, package-goods type of performance, and that the dignity of the presidential office and the presidential campaign would suffer as a result of the huckster aspect of the standard commercial.

It has become evident, however, that political campaign managers and candidates in subsequent elections were not unduly concerned about these doubts. The twenty-second, thirty-second, and sixty-second spots have since become a standard part of the political campaign process. One of the main reasons that more than half of television campaign expenditures in 1968 were devoted to spots derives from the high costs in time, effort, and money devoted to planning spot campaigns and placing advertising messages in those areas where they are most likely to win votes or hold votes inclined to defect to the opposition.

While the Eisenhower managers were making maximum use of television for the first time in American national campaign history, the Stevenson staff was busy too. The Joseph Katz Agency in Baltimore, beefed up with the addition of a great number of Stevenson advisors who had had considerable experience in the youthful television business, set out to establish a pattern for the Stevenson campaign. Among the advisors were Louis G. Cowan, who later became president of the CBS television network; Victor A. Sholis, the president and general manager of the WHAS stations owned by the *Louisville Courier Journal* and *Times;* Leonard Reinsch, president of the Cox stations in Atlanta and Dayton, who had been a Democratic advisor on the use of broadcast media since 1944; and a young Chicago lawyer named Newton Minow, who was later to work with the Kennedy campaign of 1960, and to become chairman of the Federal Communications Commission in the Kennedy administration.

Governor Stevenson unfortunately had a weakness in his television performances that was to destroy much of the careful planning of his media supporters. He didn't seem to be able to time out his speeches to complete them within the thirty-minute periods which were normally bought for the purpose. Often after his time had run out, the Governor was cut off the air before he came to the punch lines and vote-seeking conclusions. Reporters grew all too accustomed to seeing Governor Stevenson still talking as the screen went black.

The result is history now. President Eisenhower appeared at a triumphal session in the Grand Ballroom of the Commodore Hotel before midnight election night, backed by the saccharine music of Fred Waring and his band, to claim his victory and to congratulate Stevenson for putting up a hard fight. Ultimate victory by a wide margin had been predicted several hours earlier by another device new to elections and campaigns. CBS News had programed a Univac computer with results of the 1944 and 1948 elections in such a way that the Univac was able to call the election results almost as they

ultimately came out, by approximately 8:30 P.M., Eastern
Standard Time. At 8:30 Univac called the odds at 100 to 1 that
Eisenhower would win more than 400 electoral votes out of
531. He actually won 442.

Following the election came the post-mortems regarding
television's contribution to the campaign. Broadcasters who
had been involved speculated that the country was entering
an entirely new era in political campaigning. They predicted
that candidates thereafter would be younger; that persons
relatively unknown on the national scene could be propelled
quickly into stardom; that campaign travel would be drastically
reduced; that campaigns would be shortened; and that voters
would be better informed and more enthusiastic about going
to the polls.

William S. Paley, the chairman of the board of the Columbia
Broadcasting System, appearing before the Poor Richard Club
in Philadelphia in January of 1953, made a strong plea for
shortening campaigns to no more than six weeks. He coupled
his recommendation with a frank prediction that extensive
travel on the part of presidential candidates was a thing of the
antique past; that television would enable the candidate to
remain, except for a few major extravaganzas, in one central
spot and do his campaigning from that one location. And that
there might well be a return to the front porch campaign of
the past. Mr. Paley, of course, turned out to be dead wrong.
Candidates are traveling more than they ever did before.
Richard Nixon and John F. Kennedy set travel records in 1960,
and Humphrey and Nixon almost duplicated those records in
1968. Campaign time, contrary to Mr. Paley's prediction, has,
when all aspects are taken into consideration, lengthened rather
than shortened. While it might be said that the Kennedy
campaign for the presidency in 1960 began at the conclusion
of the Democratic national convention in Chicago in August
1956, Kennedy campaign machinery was actually in full motion
by early January 1960. Intensive efforts at campaign planning
began on Cape Cod at an August 14, 1959 meeting of Kennedy's

campaign staff, more than fourteen months before the 1960 election.

The Nixon 1968 campaign was similarly planned in great detail in 1967, a year before the election. In fact Vice-President Humphrey suffered severly from lack of preparation time. For some unaccountable reason nothing was done to create an overall campaign plan until his nomination was assured by the Democratic convention in late August. The vice-president might have made a stronger run had he not waited until after the convention to make his final plans. The Humphrey organization even changed advertising agencies after the convention. Doyle Dane and Bernbach, representing the Democratic National Committee during the Johnson administration, was discharged and Lennen & Newell not employed until September 13, only seven weeks before the election. Humphrey thus began the final two months with no basic campaign plan, no advertising agency and an almost total lack of financial resources. As a consequence, the Humphrey campaign remained in a high state of chaos and disorganization until the last four or five weeks prior to the November election. This lack of planning and organization, coupled with a paucity of resources, undoubtedly was a major factor in preventing the vice-president from catching up with his well-organized, well-financed, and well-planned Republican opposition.

The contrast between Richard Nixon's careful preparations and Hubert Humphrey's state of disarray, however, only makes it all the more puzzling in considering television's influence on the final results, for despite Humphrey's obvious handicaps, Nixon won by only the thinnest of margins, about a half million votes out of some 73 million ballots cast. It is evident that changes forecast by Mr. Paley in Philadelphia in 1953, and by scores of other people, following the election of 1952, proved not to be valid. But what effect did television really have? What changes in campaign methodology have resulted from television's central role? And what changes can we anticipate for the future?

The effect on the process of the campaign itself has been profound. In the age of the electric mirror, campaign costs have been rising in a geometric progression. It is now estimated that the entire campaign of 1968, primary and final, local, regional, state, and national, cost more than $300,000,000, compared to the $150,000,000 costs of 1952.[3]

We know that much greater sophistication has been added to the process of image making. Public opinion polls, which were a relative novelty in the early days of television, have become a regular facet of preparing campaign plans and maintaining flexibility throughout the course of the campaign. Specialists in the art of image creation and symbol manipulation have become required elements in the campaign organization. A thoroughly and tightly drawn campaign plan prepared weeks or months before a campaign actually gets under way has become an absolute must; and constant testing of public opinion state-by-state, and region-by-region enables a campaign to maintain ultimate flexibility up until the very last moment.

It is clearly evident that the role of the advertising agency has been expanded and enlarged and has become an essential adjunct to the campaign. The advertising agency in politics is not an innovation of the age of television. The George H. Batten Company represented the Charles Evans Hughes campaign in 1916, and agencies were commonly used through the 1930s for the placement of newspaper and radio advertising and for booking of radio time for national campaign speeches. But, since 1952 and the advent of television, the role of the agency has become vastly more complex. Now, in addition to media services, agencies work on the production of commercial spot announcements, influence candidate performance, set standards for decorating and lighting halls where meetings are to be conducted, and direct television performances. The agencies' creative staffs are busily engaged in assessing the candidate's strengths and weaknesses and recommending styles of performances calculated to influence voter attitudes. Simultaneously with the growing power of the advertising agency we have witnessed a mushrooming of political public relations firms: companies like Spencer Roberts in Los Angeles; Whitaker and Baxter in San Francisco; Charles Guggenheim in St. Louis and Washington; David Garth in New York; and Joseph Napolitan and Lawrence O'Brien in Springfield, Massachusetts, and Washington, D.C. Scores of other lesser known specialists in political public relations techniques have proliferated since 1952.

Perhaps most interestingly, since 1952 there has been a distinct shift in the selection of candidates for vice-president and president from persons who have achieved their principal fame as governors to those who have achieved fame on the national scene. During the six national elections from 1952 to 1968, six major party candidates for president came from the ranks of senators, and only two from the ranks of governors. Since 1960, all six major party candidates have been senators. Contrast that with the five elections from 1932 through 1948, when only one presidential candidate had been a senator prior to his nomination. That was Harry Truman, who succeeded to the office as the result of the death of Franklin D. Roosevelt. Eight had been governors, and one, Herbert Hoover, had been a member of the cabinet. Only two men who had previously been senators were elected to the presidency in the first half of the twentieth century, Warren G. Harding and Harry Truman.

It is possible to debate at length as to whether television has had any pronounced influence on this distinct change in the preference by the two parties for their candidates. But there is circumstantial evidence that television may have played a significant part. Senators who are selected for six-year terms have much more opportunity to achieve national television exposure than members of Congress and governors. Thus, when a campaign begins, they have a substantial edge on governors and members of Congress whose invitations to television programs are much more limited. The case of General Eisenhower is quite different in that he had achieved both national and worldwide fame as the commander of the Allied forces in the European theater during World War II.

The greater preoccupation of the United States with foreign affairs since the Second World War has also provided a distinct advantage to senators who have an opportunity to gain a greater reputation as experts in foreign relations. This recognized expertise may furnish a substantial advantage over those whose principal experience has been gained as governors of states in which foreign affairs do not play a very significant role. Conversely, it may also be true that television has directed more attention than in the past to foreign affairs, thus creating a favorable environment in which a senator starts with a built-in advantage. The leading prospects for candidacies in both major parties in 1972 support this assumption. Those most prominently mentioned on the Democratic side are all senators: Hubert Humphrey, Edmund Muskie, Henry Jackson, Edward Kennedy, and George McGovern, Birch Bayh and Fred Harris. A full year before the election *no* governor had been prominently mentioned for the office. On the Republican side, former Senator Richard Nixon, unless a cataclysm occurs, will be the Republican nominee.

Since the advent of television, styles of campaigning, scheduling travel, and setting up party rallies have undergone revolutionary changes. The whistle-stop tour, the rear platform speech and the civic auditorium rally have almost become museum pieces. The airplane has virtually become the presidential candidate's office and bedroom, in addition to being his swiftest and most convenient conveyance. The airport, the super market parking lot and the public square have succeeded the public auditorium as the locale for public speeches and meeting the electorate. Local and regional television dutifully cover the events as news before the candidate goes on to repeat the same act step by step at the next stop. Changes occur only when dictated by geography or special political considerations. There are relatively few occasions when national television is called for as often as national radio used to be used in the period prior to 1952. Primary emphasis is devoted now to informal appearances on television in question-and-answer sessions, rather than in set formal speeches. This leaves more time to be devoted to clandestine meetings with party functionaries and potential financial supporters.

Pierre Salinger, shortly after the completion of the 1960 campaign, said that he foresaw no reduction of travel in future election contests, because there would always be a necessity for energizing the local party organization. Salinger could foresee very few occasions for big, national rallies, except on election eve and on other special occasions. The historical record has proven him an accurate seer.

Candidates in the second decade of television have been much more willing to subject themselves to appearances on such question and answer programs as "Meet the Press," "Face the Nation," and "Issues and Answers," and on the nighttime interview programs conducted by such television personalities as Johnny Carson, Merv Griffin, and Dick Cavett.

Being responsive to invitations to talk and interview programs provides greater flexibility, greater opportunity to keep surveillance over the areas which need additional intensive campaigning and the opportunity easily to switch concentration on issues as seems to be required by polling and subjective analysis of voter reactions.

A greater reliance on news broadcasts was much longer in coming. In the early 1950s, most of the public relations men, representing the national parties of the candidates, were selected from newspaper ranks. Their orientation was largely toward newspaper publicity. The value of the clipping and the clipping book was unassailable. The interest of newspaper publishers in politics and editorials endorsing candidates in many newspapers enhanced the prestige of the printed media for political propaganda purposes.

It took time before the regularly scheduled television news program was able to assert its own influence. The change, while slow in coming, brought about a revolutionary change in campaign publicity. The regularly scheduled early evening network news broadcast eventually became a prime target taking its place alongside the wire services and the big, high-prestige dailies. This led, in turn, to the widespread acceptance of what has become known in some circles as "Guthman's Law." This refers to Edwin Guthman, a member of the Kennedy campaign force both in 1960 and 1964, and now an editor on the *Los Angeles Times*. Guthman's Law was relatively simple. It suggested that three minutes on the early evening news program was worth any amount of exposure on any other medium at any time of the day.

Very few experienced political campaigners will question the validity of Guthman's Law. The principal early evening television news broadcasts, the CBS Evening News with Walter Cronkite and the early evening News on NBC reach audiences of as many as 40 to 50 million persons during the height of the winter season and will easily reach 30 to 35 million during the normal political campaign period of late September and October. The audience obviously is made up of partisans of both political parties. There is a high degree of loyalty of viewership and an intensity of viewing through the course of the entire half hour. Through the regularly scheduled news broadcast, the candidate has the opportunity of reaching those committed to him, the uncommitted, as well as supporters of his opponent. This means that in addition to reinforcing the attitudes of his loyal followers, he has some opportunity to win over additional support.

What is true of the regularly scheduled national network news program is true in even greater measure of the regularly scheduled local news program, except for the fact that the geographical area and, therefore, the total population covered is smaller. If anything, the degree of loyalty to local news broadcaster is greater than to the network reporter and ratings are higher. Additionally the candidate can couch his approach on the local news broadcast in more intimate local terms and thus appeal more directly to his immediate audience.

The ascendancy of news in the political campaign occurred despite an unusual legal constraint which broadcasters ignored. Section 315 of the Federal Communications Act of 1934 was written so that it could be interpreted to require granting of equal time on news broadcasts to all candidates for a given office if mention were made of one. The absurdity of application of this rule to a presidential campaign is obvious. With sixteen to eighteen candidates in the field, the news broadcast would either have had no news of the campaign or, in its efforts to achieve balance, would have had time for nothing else. The bookkeeping problem alone would have been horrendous. Fortunately, Congress somewhat clarified the diction in the Section prior to the 1960 election, specifically exempting regularly scheduled news, news discussion or interviews and documentaries from complying with the provision.

During the 1968 campaign, the Nixon campaign managers hit upon a simple device which proved to be highly effective. They offered the availability of candidate Nixon himself for extended interviews with either the chief news executive of a local station or a principal news broadcaster with a wide following. The stations were inclined to be flattered at the offer and the candidate had the opportunity to expound his views to a local audience under the auspices of a person with strong local indentification, and at no cost to the campaign. If the station which had been so favored by the Nixon entourage were a member of a group under common ownership, it was frequently suggested helpfully that other stations in the same group might be interested in running the same broadcast. This added to the exposure and at the same time, theoretically added to the prestige of the originating station.

In addition to regular news boardcasts, campaign managers have not failed to overlook the regularly scheduled news interview shows: both the afternoon programs which are especially adapted for women's audiences, and the more masculine-oriented, politically dominated programs. In 1968, Mrs. Hubert Humphrey, who campaigned separately from her husband, was available and seen on many such programs. Mrs. Robert Griffin, who traveled with her husband in the Michigan Senatorial Campaign of 1966, appeared on the women's interviews programs, while her husband was campaigning in men's circles.

There are several other major changes which have occurred during the era of television. One is a revision in the methods of using motion picture film. It has become standard procedure for a biographical film built around the candidate to be commissioned as part of the basic campaign plan. One of the first steps taken by Joseph Napolitan, after the 1968 Democratic convention and the appointment of Lawrence O'Brien as campaign manager, was to commission Shelby Storck of Kansas City to prepare a biographical film on Senator Humphrey.[4] This was done before there was a single penny in the Democratic treasury and before Napolitan had the slightest idea how Storck was to be paid. The money was eventually obtained, and the Storck biographical documentary of Humphrey was presented during the course of the Humphrey telethon on election eve.

A principal innovation in political campaigns, however, is the use of film to illustrate campaign themes by showing the candidate out in the field observing institutions, studying problems, interviewing persons on the scene and reacting to his discoveries. If, for example, it is felt important to make a statement on Medicare, the candidate might visit a hospital, call on a doctor in his office, and appear at a medical convention. Film cameras would accompany the candidate's entourage and literally thousands of feet of negative would be exposed, capturing the candidate in all possible situations and talking to all types of people. Candidates similarly inspect construction sites, ride subways, admire cattle and, if running for office in New York, swim at Coney Island and eat blintzes. Enthusiastic news coverage is a bonus.

A careful editing job, discarding all but a few kernels of color and wisdom out of all of the thousands of feet exposed fuses the residue into one solid, hard-hitting statement, em-

Senator Estes Kefauver (center), shown here on a television news program, held Senate Crime Investigation Committee hearings which dramatically revealed the power of organized crime. Extensive television coverage of the hearings led to a Kefauver Presidential campaign at the Democratic Convention which netted him a Vice Presidential nomination.

LEFT: *Senator Joseph McCarthy, here seen with members of his Senate Investigations Subcommittee, was to make extensive use of television to become a powerful national political figure. And yet the television coverage he sought so eagerly eventually contributed to his downfall by widely exposing his tactics in the Army-McCarthy hearings.*
BELOW LEFT: *Shown here shortly before his censure by the Senate, McCarthy was still trying unsuccessfully to use television to regain his former prominence.*

Television coverage gave added impetus to the emergence of civil rights as a major national issue, covering major events such as the desegregation of Little Rock Central High School in 1957 (seen here), sit-ins, and freedom marches.

As the civil rights issue grew in national interest, Martin Luther King, Jr. and other leaders became increasingly effective in making use of television news coverage.

OPPOSITE: *The series of Presidential debates during the 1960 Kennedy-Nixon campaign was a major breakthrough in the use of television in the political campaign. The aftermath of the first debate, hosted by CBS, brought protests from the Nixon staff at their candidate's unflattering appearance on television.*

By the final debate, a split screen appearance by the candidates from Los Angeles and New York, Nixon's appearance seemed to improve. Nevertheless consideration of the risks of television debating has caused most candidates to avoid its use.

While television news was contributing to the exposure of discrimination and poverty in America, its coverage of the Vietnam War brought the visual impact of what had once been only a headline, such as the bombing of the American Embassy in Saigon in 1965, into the homes of millions of citizens.

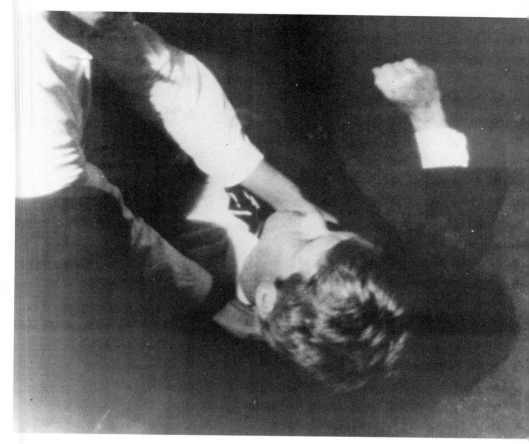

But the violence of the '60s at home was brought alive just as vividly. Here Senator Robert F. Kennedy lies wounded moments after being shot in Los Angeles.

Perhaps the most heavily criticized TV news coverage in recent years was at the 1968 Democratic National Convention in Chicago. Democratic leaders later charged the TV press with contributing to their defeat by over emphasizing the violence at the convention.

Antipathy towards television newsmen rose so high at the Democratic Convention that there were several incidents between convention personnel and TV reporters. Here CBS correspondent Mike Wallace is ejected from the convention floor.

bellished with human interest pictures, brief interviews and comments from persons who were on the scene while the cameras were grinding. The resultant material can be used in sixty-second commercials or in five-minute presentations or as even adjuncts to formal speech or arena type programs. The process is a costly one, in view of the enormous amount of footage exposed and unused and the many hours of expensive editing time required to eliminate the nonessentials and cut the film down to its final presentation length.

This type of presentation has been particulary effective in the five-minute program, a development of the 1956 campaign which has since been widely accepted. Reggie Schuebel, the veteran time buyer who represented the Democratic party on behalf of Norman, Craig & Kummel advertising agency in the 1956 campaign, is given credit by Democrats for the five-minute program. Robert Kinter, who was then president of NBC, is credited by Republicans for having first suggested the idea.

Wherever the credit should be given, there is no question concerning its advantage over longer programs in holding its audience. A viewer will apparently tolerate five minutes of well produced political programming while he is repelled by thirty minutes.

There are also substantial cost savings. During negotiations conducted while the 1956 campaign was in progress, both Batten, Barton, Durstine & Osborn representing President Eisenhower and Norman, Craig & Kummel for Governor Stevenson succeeded in winning over the networks to accepting five-minute programs at one sixth of the normal half-hour program rate. Rate cards usually required something closer to one third. Since they did not displace a complete program, but only required editing to eliminate five minutes, there were no pre-emption costs to pay. Previously, a political advertiser would be charged not only for time but also for the production cost of the program replaced, a figure as costly as the time charges if not more so.

Thus, through the use of the five-minute trimming or "barbering" practice, as Carroll Newton refers to it, the price was reduced to only a fraction of what it would have been for the full half hour. Additional advantages included the fact that the audience ratings remained higher. Persons who had been interested in the twenty-five minutes of the half-hour program which was being trimmed to accommodate the 5-minute political, would generally stay to watch the political program itself, awaiting the next regularly scheduled entertainment show. Half hour political programs normally repel entertainment-seeking viewers in droves.

There is also a reasonable possibility that some supporters of the opposition candidate wouldn't take the trouble to turn away for so short a time. Thus, the candidate or his supporters would have an opportunity to recruit support which they otherwise would not be able to reach. As a result, the five-minute program has become a standard feature of political campaigning.

As political campaigning grows in complexity and as utilization of media becomes more varied and costly there will be inevitably a proliferation of specialists in the field of campaigning for both ideas and candidates. Television unquestionably has contributed and will contribute substantially to this growth. The capabilities of television are so much more varied and the technical knowledge required so much more complicated that the need for specialists is vastly greater than it is in the relatively uncomplicated matter of newspaper advertising. Writing the newspaper ad, achieving the most effective layout and planning the most effective media buys, require a high degree of technical competence, imagination and creative skills. But television demands much more. It demands expertise in personal performance, scripting, staging, costuming, lighting, make-up, direction, and film or tape editing. Media placement is more complicated. Ordering of physical facilities requires specialized experience, and crowd handling at a rally can't be overlooked.

Critics such as Joe McGinniss have frequently speculated: Has the agency become too important a factor in political campaigning? Has it led to placing too much emphasis on technique and too little on substance? Can the agency like the image-maker hide the warts and the blemishes and create a silk purse out of a sow's ear?

Probably not. The agency, like the make-up man, must start with a human being, or with an idea. It can highlight the pluses. It can downplay the minuses, but it's doubtful if it can create a candidate or a policy out of a vacuum. Additionally, the complexities of production and media placement are so great that it would be only the rare candidate and the rarest candidate managers who would be able to perform the role without the assistance of experts, whether it be within an advertising agency or within a unit of the campaign organization. There are just too many skills required to leave it to the amateurs.

When campaign managers became interested in television and began to assess its potential influence, it was originally assumed that they could relax in their efforts to get out the vote. It was thought that a new interest in voting generated by television would bring voters out in greater numbers than ever before. It is doubtful, now that the evidence is in, that the assumption is accurate. The percentage of persons going to the polls in national elections was high in 1952, when Republicans saw a chance of driving the Democrats out of the White House after a twenty-year reign. It held up very well through 1956 when President Eisenhower was an easy victor, rose to an all-time record level in 1960 during the neck and neck Kennedy-Nixon race; but fell off somewhat in 1964 when President Lyndon Johnson won a smashing victory over Senator Barry Goldwater. More significantly, it did not rise again to the 1960 level in the bitter campaign between President Nixon and Vice-President Hubert Humphrey in 1968.

The evidence seems to be piling up that "get out the vote" campaigns conducted by party functionaries themselves have been more influential than television coverage. They seem to have brought more voters to the polls than intensive television reporting. It may be that an intensive "get out the vote" campaign launched by the AFL-CIO's forces in the fall of 1968 was much more responsible for Humphrey's last minute surge than the candidate's appearances on television. This theory assumes that many voters who made a last minute decision to support Humphrey had previously planned to sit out the election. It seems evident that the parties will have to continue their own "get out the vote" efforts, perhaps supported in many cases by television. Television's role in building broader voter interest has yet to be proved.

Notwithstanding its doubtful effect on numbers of voters casting ballots, it is impossible to minimize its overall influence on the political process. It is only necessary to enumerate the profound changes in campaign methodology which evolved since 1950: shorter speeches, more interviews, spot commercials, airport and supermarket rallies, arena-type performances, stress on television specialists in the campaign organization, more reliance on the advertising agency and political public relations firm and a staggering increase in budgets.

It is unlikely that the campaign specialist of 1948, or even of 1952, would be able to adapt himself easily to the requirements of the campaigns of 1972 or 1976. For there is today a rapidly evolving set of competences and techniques required for successful management of the campaign and image building.

THE TELEVISION CAMPAIGN
GOES ABROAD

The heavy concentration on television as a device for political campaigning in the United States has been reflected through all those parts of the world where there is widespread distribution of television facilities and freedom to campaign for public office. Candidates and the parties they represent have been quick to realize the advantages offered by television as a medium for reaching the people.

Television as a campaign device was later in developing outside the United States. But television itself grew somewhat more slowly. By the beginning of the campaign year of 1952 some 30 to 35 percent of all of the homes in the United States, were equipped with television receivers. Similar set density figures were not achieved in most Western European countries and in Japan until late 1950s or early 1960s.

While many countries followed patterns set in the United States, each had to make the necessary modifications to conform to its own political system. The American system stresses the election of a president who functions as the head of state, in addition to being head of government. In the parliamentary system, the Prime Minister is both a representative of one parliamentary constituency and the leader of his party. But he appears on the ballot only in his own parliamentary district. He becomes the head of the government by virtue of his role as leader of the party in power. This fixes the election focus in a parliamentary system on the party rather than the individual. The leader is a significant representative of the party but so are other potential members of his government. Each runs only in his own parliamentary district and any campaigning done outside his constituency is done for the party rather than for himself. Television thus becomes a device more important for the support of the party than for the individual. The whole national campaign thus assumes a different form and coloration.

Relationships between television stations and government also vary widely from country to country. In the United States, privately-owned, commercially-supported stations dominate both in financial strength and audience support. Public broadcasting, while gaining strength, still lags far behind commercial competition. In contrast, European broadcasting is for the most part conducted by government corporations supported to a large extent by license revenues and subject generally to a greater degree of government regulation. The freedom of choice of the viewer to select a television signal is restricted. In England, there are only three signals available, two operated by the British Broadcasting Corporation and one by the Independent Television Authority. In Germany, two are operated by the government-licensed Arbeitsgemeinschaft der oeffentlich-rechtlichen Rundfunkanstalten der Bundesrepublik Deutschland (ARD) group of stations and one by the second German network, Zweites Deutches Fernsehen, also a government corporation. In France, Italy, Holland, Sweden and Spain the viewer, unless he lives near an international border, has access to only two signals. There are wide differences among the five countries with respect to the precise manner in which the broadcasting companies are chartered, operated and financed; but in each case the government plays a significant role, a substantially greater one than in the United States. Elsewhere in Europe, the viewer has no choice. It is either the government-sponsored channel or no television at all. Japan is a bit more complicated in that a considerable degree of latitude is permitted for privately-owned, commercially-supported stations, but the only full national network as such is the government-sponsored Nippon Hoso Kyokai (NHK). As in the case of the European networks NHK is supported by license revenues and derives its power from the government. Its principal officers are elected by the government.

Variations in methods of governmental regulation have a profound effect on the manner in which television conducts itself during a political campaign. The degree of government interference or control varies widely among European countries from the tight news control imposed in France to the relative freedom accorded to broadcasters in the United Kingdom. Generally, however, restrictions are tighter and regulations more detailed than in the United States. National traditions also have a significant impact on the manner in which television functions in the political campaign.

The United Kingdom has a long history of freedom and a great respect for traditions which permeate its political life as well as its business and social customs. The present governments of Japan and Germany are both of post-1945 creation and have little governmental tradition. Japan, however, has particularly strong ties to its social, cultural and religious past. These factors of tradition, custom, culture and religion play a role in creating differing environments in which politics and television can live together. They create differences in methods of campaigning on television and in the types of regulations which are imposed. But even though the differences are great, the similarities are striking.

There is striking emphasis on the same election techniques and strategies that prevail in this country. Party managers outside the United States emphasize charisma, image, on-camera appeal and the talent for communicating on the screen as do their American counterparts. They devote the same degree of attention to campaign plans, analyses of voter preference and the basic appeals which are likely to attract the votes. Party leaders are almost universally concerned with bending party strategy to the most effective television presentation, whether it be by straight speech, interview, film presentation or any other of the devices available to the television producer.

The entire campaign structure has frequently been modified in such a way as to allow it to adapt itself to the most effective use of television as a campaign tool. Communication specialists with television background are achieving positions of increasing importance within party structures. Substantial portions of party budgets are being allocated to television purposes. Party strategists, conversant with the capacity of television to develop favorable party and candidate images, are achieving positions of increasing stature within the party structure. The widely reported Kennedy-Nixon debates in the United States in 1960 have been imitated in some way in nearly every country in which television figures prominently in political campaigns. Contrary to the American pattern which has not yet seen a repeat of the 1960 confrontations in presidential campaigns, debates have become a standard feature of political campaigning in a significant number of countries.

In the United Kingdom the liaison between government, politics and television began almost concurrently with its development in the United States. Political leaders and cabinet ministers appeared on television in accordance with formuli which had been originated by BBC Radio in the 1930s, and gradually evolved through the years. But the BBC, through the application of a self-denying ordinance, had refrained from permitting its high prestige news department to cover a political campaign prior to the 1959 general election. The reasoning of the BBC leadership was that an appearance by a candidate on a news program equated with his appearance on a specifically designated campaign program. Therefore, the BBC had no right to make the time available.

The BBC abstinence resulted in a number of absurd situations. During the election in the winter of 1951, Prime Minister Winston Churchill in a speech delivered during the campaign had urged that there be a meeting at the Summit, involving the leaders of the United Kingdom, the United States, France and Russia. Because this speech was delivered during a political campaign, the BBC refused to report on it within its regular news broadcasts. BBC news personnel, recognizing that they could not black out so crucial a story, were forced to refer to dispatches from Washington in order to mention even in the most casual way the Churchill recommendation.

A significant event in British broadcasting development occurred in September of 1955 when a competitive, commercially supported system, under the supervision of the Independent Television Authority, took to the air. The independent television program contractors, each licensed to serve specific geographic areas, were instructed under the terms of their charters from the Independent Television Authority, to create a third national service entity known as Independent Television News. ITN was to be jointly owned by ITV program contractors. Its purpose was to furnish a news service to ITV stations, but only a news service. ITV program contractors would produce their own documentaries and educational and cultural programs. The program contractors by pooling their output and using country-wide ITA micro-wave links and transmitters constituted a full national network.

Geoffrey Cox, now Sir Geoffrey, who became editor of ITN in early 1956, and one of its principal correspondent broadcasters, Robin Day, found themselves increasingly restive under the BBC's self-imposed ordinance against covering news of elections. They determined to make an effort to cover a by-election as a test case. If the test failed to create a storm of opposition and a governmental crack-down, they believed they could give full coverage to a general election whenever one should be called. In an effort to prepare themselves, they experimented with some dry run coverage of by-election campaigning in 1957 which they later decided to broadcast. An hour and forty-five minutes after the official closing of the polls, they felt that the experiment was successful and that forcing the issue would be eminently worth while.

The BBC decision to refrain from coverage was based upon its interpretation of the Representation of the People Act passed by Parliament to govern the conduct of elections. This act, passed in 1949, included a Clause 63 which specifically exempted newspapers from responsibility for violating the corrupt practices portion of the act, if they were to furnish any coverage of a campaign. BBC executives interpreted the absence of any mention of television to mean that if television were to cover a campaign, it might be charged with having made a financial contribution to the cause of the campaign and thus could be sued for malfeasance. BBC executives also felt that the victorious candidate who had been covered in the process of his campaigning could be unseated as a result of the violation by television of the election code. ITN leadership, on the other hand, felt that this was an erroneous interpretation and one which would never be enforced. All that was needed, they concluded, was someone to take the intitiative.

In February 1958, a conference on political broadcasting was called to take place at Nuffield College at Oxford. Attending were representatives of the political parties and of BBC, ITA, the ITV contractors, and ITN. In the course of the conference, Cox tried to get a ruling on by-election coverage, but was told by the Director General of the ITA, Sir Robert Fraser, that this was not the occasion for such a decision. Upon return to London, however, Cox did raise the issue and insisted on the right to cover the by-election which was to take place in Rochdale, during the spring of 1958. Unfortunately for the ITN personnel and their efforts to break the BBC tradition, one of the candidates in that election turned out to be an ITN reporter-correspondent named Ludovic Kennedy. Cox was told he must not interview the candidates or cover their speeches because if it did so, ITN might be charged with favoring one of its own staff members. But he was permitted to put out a filmed report on the campaign which described the constituency, showed the candidates, and summarized their election policies. This was shown on the night of January 31st and was the first broadcast of an election campaign in Britain.

At this juncture, one of the ITV program contractors took a decisive step toward breaking the tradition. It presented a program in which not only was the constituency and its problems surveyed but the three candidates for office were interviewed by a reporter. By doing so the BBC's self-denying ordinance had been violated by Granada Television and for the first time in British history, a campaign had been covered by broadcasting as a news event, even though that coverage consisted of only one program. Since there were no unfortunate repercussions to Granada's election program, ITN personnel under Cox's leadership went ahead to make plans for intensive coverage of the next general election which was expected during the fall of 1959 and actually took place during the first week in October that year.

In the meantime, BBC had appointed a new Director General. General Sir Ian Jacob, who had held the post during most of the 1950s, surrendered his position to Sir Hugh Carlton Greene. Among a considerable variety of positions Carlton Greene had held within the BBC was the directorship of the corporation's very excellent news department. He too had been restive under the self-imposed regulation and, since he was much more inclined to risk-taking than the former army general who preceded him, one of his first decisions was to mobilize his forces to give intensive news coverage to the campaign as soon as it was officially declared.

Consequently, when Parliament was dissolved in September of 1959 and the beginning of the three weeks campaign was officially declared, both the British Broadcasting Corporation and Independent Television News had their plans made, their crews assigned, their strategy determined and they were fully ready for action. As in the case of the by-election in 1958, there was no adverse reaction from persons in authority. It can be conjectured that restrictions would have been difficult to impose in view of the intense interest on the part of the general public in the television coverage. It may also be true that the enormous power of the two news organizations intimidated any potential critics bent on a crack-down. At any rate, BBC and ITN proceeded to do their best to relate to their viewers the story of the election.

In subsequent campaigns, ITN has restricted itself largely to straight news coverage. It has the disadvantage that it has no outlet for documentary production, discussion or question-and-answer programs; documentaries are the self-assumed prerogative of the program companies, a prerogative that has never been challenged by the ITA. The BBC on the other hand has gone far beyond straight news coverage. It has, on occasion, sought to define campaign issues in its own way or by the interpretation of its own current affairs broadcasters. It has gone so far at times as to get reactions from outside the United Kingdom to a speech by the prime minister during an election campaign. When Prime Minister Harold Wilson delivered an address on Britain's attitude toward the Common Market detailing the methods which would be used by the Labor Party to seek British entry, BBC queried the representatives of four common market countries—Holland, Germany, France, and Italy, as to whether the terms as outlined by Prime Minister Wilson would be acceptable to those foreign countries. The answers in each case, turned out to be a resounding negative. But there were no recriminations against the BBC. The BBC tried one American device that was quickly throttled. News personnel asked citizens how they planned to vote and whom they thought would win the election. This device was later ruled out-of-bounds as an attempt to influence the election.

Independent Television News also tried a tactic which resulted in a reprimand. Alex Douglas-Home was involved in a by-election in 1963. His Liberal opponent sought to restrict him from gaining any publicity on television by refusing to be interviewed for television broadcast purposes. He felt that if he were not to accept any air time, then any news agency which gave its time to the Prime Minister would be in violation of the 1949 Representation of the People Act. ITN devised a stratagem to circumvent the plot of the Liberal. They showed a still picture of the Liberal candidate while one of their broadcasters off camera read from the Liberal Party Manifesto. Cox and his associates felt that, in this manner, they had given the Liberal Party Candidate ample display on television and thus ITN would be able to report on Alex Douglas-Home's campaign. Later this tactic was made illegal by a revision of the Representation of the People Act.

Intensive television coverage of British election campaigns is now standard operating procedure—in straight news broadcasts, current affairs programs, interviews and discussions, and in the regular party campaign broadcasts which have consistently been a feature of British elections. In accordance with tradition developed over the years on BBC radio, each party is granted time for campaign appearances based on a formula roughly reflecting the relative strengths among voters of the three parties. The standard procedure apportions time on a 5-5-3 ratio, with the weaker Liberal party on the short end of the stick. Time and facilities are granted free and the parties pay any special production costs.

In Germany, television was a relatively inconsequential force in party political campaigning prior to the 1961 election, largely because there simply were not enough television receivers to make it worth the expenditure of any major effort by the political parties. German elections take place every four years, at a date established by the Bundestag. In 1961, considerable attention was paid to television, but 1965 marks the beginning of major television participation.

There are a number of differences between Great Britain and Germany which govern the manner of political campaigning, the attitudes of political parties toward television and the attitude of the broadcasters toward political parties and campaigns. In the first place, there is very little tradition in Germany. The German government and political system are post-war creations, and even the present boundaries of Germany did not exist until after the Second World War.

There is a vastly different broadcast structure. Whereas British broadcasting is dominated by the powerful British Broadcasting Corporation with its two television networks and the Independent Television Authority with its regional program contractors frequently linked together to form a network, Germany has no national network as such. The power in the ARD group of German stations resides with the governments of the German Lands, or states, rather than with the federal government. The broadcast organizations are created by the governments of the Lands, their executive personnel and boards of directors appointed by those governments and each State broadcast organization maintains a considerable degree of autonomy.

The second German network ZDF does function as a full national network, but it derives its powers from states rather than from the federal government. Since it operates on ultra high frequencies, rather than VHF and is a relatively late starter, it has taken time to achieve anything near parity with the ARD stations. The stations in the first network each operate satellite regional stations, but these regional stations are not linked together into a national network and operate only as local carriers. Support for the state, or Länder, stations is derived both from license fees and the sale of commercial advertising and for the second network from the sale of advertising only. Neither operates, as does the BBC, a world-wide short-wave propaganda broadcasting function on contract for the government.

Because of this considerable difference in structure, German broadcasters are in many respects unlike their British counterparts. They are more politically oriented. They normally reflect the coloration of the party in power in the state where they are chartered. They are less self-restrained, due presumably in part to the lack of a tradition comparable to that which exercises constraints over British political broadcasting, and in part perhaps to the more boisterous nature of the West German Republic.

The German political parties have caught some of the same unrestrained, aggressive and boisterous atmophere. They lay great emphasis on campaign methodology, television production, image-building, and responsiveness to voter attitudes as indicated through public opinion polls. They also rely more heavily on advertising techniques. The ultimate impact of their use of television is highly professional and extremely sophisticated.

Germany operates on a parliamentary basis. Candidates for ministerial positions run only in their own constituencies as candidates for Parliament. German parties, however, emphasize campaigning throughout the nation as a whole, and in projecting the image of the party throughout the country, rather than limiting the campaign to a specific candidate in a specific constituency. In the United Kingdom party leaders and a few chosen associates campaign nationally, but not on the scale practiced in Germany where the campaign more nearly resembles one in the United States. The national campaign puts a premium on a high degree of sophistication in the use of late twentieth century appeals to voters, more perhaps than in any country except the United States.

Campaigning for public office by television in Japan didn't occur until December 1969. In a complete reversal of the pattern in Great Britain, there had been broadcast news coverage prior to that year, but there was no campaigning as such on the television screen. An act of Parliament had been passed in Japan in 1949 which made it possible for candidates for the Japanese Diet to campaign on radio, so there was a precedent for broadcast campaigning. However, no serious effort was made to pass a similar act for television until the spring of 1969, twenty years later, when a bill was introduced in the Diet and finally passed in June. The legislation made it possible to set up a complicated and detailed program for the election campaign period, culminating with the election of December 1969.

Japan's broadcasting structure differs widely from both the United Kingdom and Germany. It might be described as something comparable to a cross between the British and the U.S. systems. It is dominated by a large, powerful license-fee-supported radio and television network, Nippon Hoso Kyokai. NHK was established by the Japanese government and functions as a government corporation. It is the only genuine network operating in Japan and covers approximately 96 percent of the entire Japanese population. Competing with the NHK system is a vast potpourri of commercially oriented stations which are linked together in smaller informal networks, but are not able to achieve the full nationwide coverage which is obtainable by NHK. In Tokyo, NHK has two channels. These compete with no less than five commercial channels, at least two of which consistently command large shares of the total audience.

Because of NHK's close relationship to government, it became the major outlet for political broadcasting, even though the commercial stations also participated in making time available to candidates for their representations to the electorate. It is notable that the commercial stations were compensated by the government for the time given. In all, some 950 candidates availed themselves of the opportunity to speak to their constituencies through the medium of television. In contrast with England, Germany and Japan, Italy has only one television ssytem, but its one company operates two channels. The company is Radio Audizioni Italiana, known as RAI-TV and pronounced as if it were Rye. RAI is a subsidiary of a government-sponsored corporation Istituto Ricostruzione Italiana. IRI was established by the Italian government after the war to operate a number of Italian businesses, including shipping and communications in addition to broadcasting. Some IRI stock is held by private shareholders and the whole complex is expected to operate at a profit, notwithstanding the fact that the corporation is subjected to a heavy degree of governmental control.

RAI-TV has played a significant part in political campaigning in Italy since the early 1960s. Systems for allocating time are essentially the same as in the United Kingdom, Germany and Japan. There is a limited amount of news-coverage, and it is severely restricted in form and content. Even in the highly volatile political climate of Italy, however, RAI-TV has had considerably more experience in covering political campaigns than most of its counterparts elsewhere in the world.

Sweden, as in the case of Italy, has only one broadcasting organization, Sveriges Radio or the Swedish Broadcasting Corporation. The corporation operates two television networks, supported by license fees. It is a government corporation with a large minority of private investment, but it operates with a minimum of government restraint. Its role in political party campaign broadcasting does not vary significantly from the general European pattern. It furnishes opportunities for representatives of the parties to make campaign speeches and provides time and facilities for interview, debate and expanded news coverage. The corporation in its semi-autonomous position is able to control its own policies and procedures, and it largely sets down its own rules and regulations for political broadcasting; but it is bound by a fairness requirement and a strong tie to government tradition.

While the structures and approaches to politics vary, the types of opportunities made available to political parties and candidates for the use of television air time in the United Kingdom, Germany, Italy, Sweden and Japan are essentially the same. There are two principal threads which run through all five countries. Time for campaign presentations is provided to the candidate without charge. The burden is assumed either by the network in question or by the government through subsidy. Program production is a responsibility of the candidates or parties and except for special debate or discussion features, not of the distributing network. The parties have essentially the same freedom to operate that they have in the United States, but they have avoided the enormous burden of television time costs which have become so important a factor in American campaigning.

The election period in the United Kingdom is so short, only approximately seventeen days of actual campaigning, that there isn't time for any very elaborate campaigning programming. The main feature is a series of regular reports by the leaders of the three major British parties. There are thirteen such reports set up in a 5-5-3 ratio with the Conservatives and the Laborites each having five appearances and the Liberal Party three. The duration of these programs is ten to thirteen minutes, and they are carried simultaneously by all three networks, BBC 1, BBC 2 and ITV. Production is either done by the parties themselves or contracted for by the parties with whatever facilities the parties see fit to use. Production costs are paid by the parties.

There is only one other regular election feature, the two major party leaders are given the opportunity to appear in 45-minute programs, in which they are queried on the basis of questions submitted by members of the electorate. British citizens are encouraged to submit the questions which are then examined by a group of journalists who select what are presumed to be the most pertinent ones to be put to the party leaders. This cannot be properly called a debate, since the party responses are scheduled at separate times and produced in separate studios. There are normally three or four such programs during the course of the campaign.

Both the BBC and ITN gear up for specialized coverage of the campaign. In the case of ITN, the additional time for campaign programs is added on to its half-hour "News at 10." BBC is able to devote much more time because of its plethora of current affairs programs. The principal regular news feature of the British campaign, except for the coverage of party rallies, is the daily morning press conferences held by the parties at their headquarters. The conference may feature the party leader himself or the party secretary or a selected representative. Television covers, just as newspapers, with pencil and paper, but cameras and microphones are barred. Following the conclusion of the conference, the party representative who presides makes himself available to cameras for a special follow-up summary conference for television release.

In the United States there would be a hue and cry from the television reporters that would shake the very foundations of the American political system as a result of this sort of treatment, but BBC and ITN executives take it with equanimity. They explain that they would question whether television broadcasters have the right to use newspaper reporters as actors and use their questions on the air. They further believe that they obtain a more effective presentation by filming or taping the summary. The film summary is taken to the regular news center for editing and inclusion within regularly scheduled news broadcasts.

The BBC furnishes considerable additional election coverage on its regular current affairs programs, "Panorama," which runs for forty minutes on Monday nights and "Twenty Four Hours," which runs thirty-five minutes Monday through Friday. These two programs frequently feature interviews relating to the election and, in some cases, to analytical news items covering the election or reactions from outside the United Kingdom.

In addition, the Independent Television Companies also put out during elections a considerable number of special election programs, and there is a long and complicated history of argument with the political parties about the exact shape which these should take. Any discussion of political coverage in Britain would be incomplete without reference to the Granada "Marathon" programs in which three minutes of time is given to every candidate in the Granada area, in each constituency, to put his case; and to the series of confrontations between party leaders on Rediffusion's (now Thames') "This Week," and to local coverage by regional companies.

There is one other facet of British political coverage which is technically not a part of the campaign broadcast schedule, but is nevertheless a significant element in year-round broadcast coverage of politics. This is the annual series of party appearances by the leaders of the parties or their representatives.

Normally there are six to ten of these appearances during the year scheduled as during campaigns on a 5-5-3 ratio. These are frankly political appearances, even though Ministers of the Crown may be involved in them, and their sole purpose is to support party programs and party activities. This is in distinct contrast to the American system which provides no formal opportunity for this sort of political outlet during the off-campaign period. Separate provisions are made for official reports by Ministers of the Crown on such occasions when such reports are required, and machinery has been set up for opposition parties to reply.

The German election campaign, which occurs every four years, permits greater flexibility because of a considerably longer period of time over which the campaign is scheduled. Length is set by a party agreement, but usually runs to about six weeks, more than double the British time period. The allocation of time for party appearances on television is arranged on essentially the same basis as the British system. Each party gets an allocation based on its strength in the last election. Under these terms the Christian Democrats and the Social Democrats get essentially equal allocations and the weaker Free Democrats get 40 to 50 percent as much as either.

Official election broadcast periods are scheduled just before or just after the regularly scheduled early evening television news programs which are carried between 7:00 and 8:15 P.M. Running time is usually set at five minutes, although some of these appearances run for only two-and-one-half minutes. Production of the programs is done by the parties themselves. Frequently they are very carefully, elaborately, and expensively produced in the manner of the American commercial announcement. The usual practice is for the party to employ a producer with broad experience in German television. Services of an outstanding advertising agency are engaged to furnish ideas, themes, and creative support for the producer. Party programs appear on both German networks, with time contributed by the network. The maximum allowable number of performances is seven, or thirty-five minutes total time on each of the two networks for each of the two major parties.

The Japanese were the last of the major free countries of the world to enlist television on an official basis in their election campaigns. In doing so, by necessity they set up by far the most elaborate campaign schedule. Every candidate for the 635 seats in the Japanese Diet has an opportunity for two four-and-one-half-minute presentations, plus a half minute of biographical data on each for a total program length of five minutes. One of these is released on a local NHK station, and the other on one of the commercial stations covering his own constituency.

In the December 1969 election no less than 965 candidates took advantage of this opportunity. The result frequently was a considerable degree of confusion, particularly in densely populated cities such as Tokyo, Osaka and Kyoto, where there are a great number of candidates representing an equally large number of constituencies. There were so many candidates booking time that voters found themselves confronted by a baffling maze of political talk out of which they had the puzzling problem of selecting the specific broadcast they most wanted to see. Apparently, however, the system worked. As of now it is expected that it will be repeated in the next election.

The 1969 campaign also featured a number of special election programs, plus a general election preview which was more an extended news report than an opportunity for candidates to push their programs. The six special programs scheduled for the pre-election period included one entitled "The Future Course for Japan," which involved six fifty-minute debates running from 10:10 until 11:00 o'clock at night. There were two members to a team. Various combinations of teams were recruited from the five principal Japanese parties.

The second of the special programs was entitled "The Party I Support." It ran for an hour and twenty-five minutes and featured ten prominent Japanese citizens who discussed the five political parties, their aims, objectives, personnel, and chances for winning the election.

The third was called "Questioning the Parties." Participants included party representatives and guests. The format called for discussion of the issues of the campaign. Running time varied from an hour and twenty minutes to an hour-and-a-half. The first of this series concerned itself with Japanese security problems, the second economic problems, and the third educational and social problems. A fourth series of election features carried on NHK was called "The Party Leader's Appeal." Party leaders in various parts of the country appealed to voters for support of specific party programs. Running time was eighty-five minutes. Program number five, running for an hour and one-half, was titled, "Crucial Questions." Featured guests were the five Secretaries General of the principal parties. There were two programs in the series. The first featured the Liberal Democratic and Socialist Parties. The second the Democratic Socialists, Komeito, and the Communists. Two regular NHK commentators interrogated party leaders. Program number six was called, "You Are the Leading Players." It ran the day before the election for a duration of one hour. Fifty voters were invited to an NHK studio. Various data, culled from the campaign appeals of the five parties, were introduced and analyzed before the fifty voters. Included were a poll of the views of the candidates and a survey of voter attitudes.

Italy's system for television coverage of campaigns differs from the other countries described here largely in the fact that it has more parliamentary parties. A total of eight are eligible to participate in an election campaign. The principal outlet for party campaigning on the RAI television networks is a series of appearances by party leaders, spread out over the eight weeks of the campaign, with one leader assigned to each week. Each leader is granted a specified number of minutes for a single appearance. The order is set by lot, leading to some skillful Italian jockeying for the last two or three spots immediately prior to the election. Time for each of the parties, irrespective of how many votes they may draw in a popular election, or how many seats they may occupy in Parliament, is exactly the same. The decision as to who may speak for the party is determined by the party leadership.

A second feature of the Italian election campaign is the scheduling of inter-party debates. Two are scheduled during the course of the campaign. Four parties are invited to each, and an effort is made to achieve a balance between left and right. Two parties from the right side of the center are balanced with two from the left for each program. Formats for the appearances by the party leaders or their representatives are set by an interparliamentary commission which has a changing membership from year to year or from election to election. Even though formats are specified by the commission, there is a good deal of ingenuity demonstrated by the parties in arranging for maximum impact in the one appearance by the leader or his representative.

In the matter of news coverage RAI-Television's news teams are much more restricted than those in Germany, Japan, or the United States. There is one quirk that would be anathema to any American television news executive: RAI editors are permitted, in coverage of the campaign, to use only silent footage of performances by candidates at rallies or public meetings. Absolutely no synchronous sound is permitted.

The system prescribed by the interparliamentary commission prevents news crews from using their sound-on-film equipment. While the lips of the speaker move soundlessly on the screen, an announcer in the studio reads script previously selected by the speaker in question. Programs of this type are presented every Sunday night during the election period and frequently during the off-election period as well. Editors and reporters are prevented from covering political affairs except for official government ceremonies which, of course, are usually not political. On the other hand, official reports from ministers are permitted, and the Prime Minister can always make a speech during an election campaign, a privilege which is his in fact at any time, although there is no formal provision for the opposition to reply. Some current affairs discussions are scheduled during the election period, but they too are tightly controlled by the interparliamentary commission. As one Italian described it, teeth are pulled by regulation, and all participants in these current affairs discussion programs are courteous and polite.

In sharp contrast, the Swedish system for furnishing time for election campaigning is flexible, relaxed and designed to stimulate free discussion. The campaign is limited to three weeks, so there can be no protracted campaigning. In contrast to many other countries, time on television is allocated on a basis of tradition rather than on any specific legal formula. Responsibility for allocating time is accepted by the Swedish Broadcasting Corporation in consultation with the parties. Each party in Parliament, of which there are five, gets equal time, except for the fact that a few special privileges are granted to the party in power so that it may have reasonable opportunity to defend itself from the other four parties who are constantly on the attack. There are no special governmental provisions guiding the Swedish Broadcasting Corporation in setting up its regulations, except there is a general requirment for the maintenance of impartiality.

There are essentially three types of programs. The main outlet for party campaigning is the five-minute program. Each of the parliamentary parties gets one of these five-minute segments, except for the party in power, which gets two. The parties set up their own formats, select their own speakers, and generally take the full responsibility for production. All are scheduled in prime time.

The second feature is a series of interviews of party leaders by the staff of the Swedish Broadcasting Corporation. Each of these interviews runs for forty minutes, and they likewise are scheduled in prime time. The third is a series of debates of which there are three during the campaign period. The first runs 90 minutes, the second 120 minutes, the third 180 minutes. Subject matter for the debates is selected in consultation with the leaders of the parties. Normal practice is for six contestants to appear, one each from the four out-parties and two from the government which is again given the opportunity for double representation in order to better defend itself from attack. The second network operated by the Swedish Broadcasting Corporation adds to the above series an additional program, a 45-minute interview of party leaders by Swedish broadcasting personnel.

There are no current affairs programs of the BBC type, but there is a substantially extended news coverage. News crews cover party rallies, speeches of party leaders, and additional party functions during the three-week period of the campaign. The length of regular news programs may be somewhat increased during the course of the campaign in order to accommodate the additional public interest in the election. Normally stories covered in the campaign are covered on motion picture film, but on occasion a candidate will come to the studio live.

There is no specific demand that the Swedish Broadcasting Corporation maintain absolute balance regarding the five parties in its news broadcasts, but there is a general mandate that the corporation be fair. No effort is made to count minutes and seconds of coverage for one party or the other, but an endeavor is made and enforced by executives to maintain at least a rough balance. There is no system of enforcing such a balance, but the management assumes that the parties tape record all broadcasts during the campaign. The wealthier of the parties, it is assumed, make video tapes in addition to sound records. By so doing they are able to keep accurate records and grounds for protest, should protests be in order.

The patterns established in the five countries detailed above generally reflect patterns for political broadcasting in the countries of the world where television plays a substantial role in public affairs. The other Scandinavian countries—Denmark, Norway and Finland—follow patterns similar to Sweden, including television debates. Holland has to wrestle with a mulitparty system but succeeds in furnishing some exposure for all. In France during the de Gaulle regime, the general himself always arranged to occupy the most favorable campaign time periods, notably the last speaking opportunity immediately before election day. But the representatives of the other parties were likewise given an opportunity to state their cases before the French voting public over the facilities of the French ORTF networks.

French broadcasting is an anomaly in the western world. While no two countries of Western Europe support broadcasting organizations that are identical in nature and responsibility to government, they are, with the exception of France, operated as government corporations. Governmental charters generally give them considerable degrees of autonomy. Dedicated taxes free them from the necessity of petitioning parliaments each year for operating funds. Independent boards of directors enable them to set their own rules and procedures within a broad mandate from government.

French broadcasting, on the other hand, is operated as a branch of government. Executives are appointed by government and responsible to it. Policies are established by government and transgressions can be punished by government. The problems faced by the news executive are obvious. He can schedule news concerning views of the opposition parties and candidates, he can arrange for air appearances by opponents of the regime in power, but he is always under pressure, whether theoretical or real, to treat the government more favorably; and during the de Gaulle years the pressures were very real indeed. News coverage with some exceptions was a tool in the hands of the majority and it had lost the trust of the audience.

Dissatisfaction with government control of broadcasting in France came to a head during the street riots of 1968. Headstrong members of the news staff who had been restive under governmental restraints suddenly felt liberated and proceeded to use their new freedom until order was restored. Mass firings and a major reorganization followed.

Following General Charles de Gaulle's departure from office, a less restrictive policy prevailed. A new chief executive for news, Pierre des Graupes, set about to establish a more objective policy and, although he has met a number of set-backs, he has been persistent in his efforts to present a report which more nearly meets standards of fairness and balance as practiced in the other western European countries.

As Michel Gordey, foreign editor for *France Soir*, put it: "There were ups and downs and difficulties which des Graupes had to face, but he faced them." French government officials since the departure of de Gaulle have been less demanding in their request for favorable treatment.

News executives were given added protection by an administrative order which gave them tenure during a two-year contract period, unless they were found by the Administrative Council to be deficient in the exercise of their functions. But France still has a long way to go before its television will be able to play as significant a role in the political process as do the television broadcasters in England, Germany, Sweden or Italy. Gordey believes there is a permanent danger to this newly acquired freedom to publish in France.

In Australia and New Zealand practices are quite similar to those in the United Kingdom. In South America, where privately owned and commercially supported television has taken a stronger hold than elsewhere in the world except in North America, provision is made for electioneering by television. Parties are well aware of the hold of the television broadcast on the voter.

A delineation of the varying methods of granting time to parties and party leaders, the formats of the programs in which they participate, and the systems used for maintaining balance among the parties in various countries, gives only a fragmentary and rather superficial view of the methods by which the parties operate. But the degree of sophistication in the employment of television techniques, while it varies from country to country, in some areas very nearly measures up to the high degree of professionalism practiced in the United States, if it is not in fact equal.

Perhaps the most sophisticated in the use of advanced

techniques for campaigning by television is Germany. There are a number of reasons why the Germans should have developed the technique of television campaigning to a high degree of artistry. Campaigns in Germany are generally longer; there is less rigid application of rules and regulations than, for example, in the United Kingdom; and there is less tradition restraining party campaigners and television executives alike. Finally, Germany has been remarkably prosperous in the post-war years, making more campaign funds available.

Except for the language barrier, an American citizen interested in political party campaigning by television, would have seen much in the German campaign of September 1969 that would have reminded him of the American campaign of 1968. Both the major parties employed the services of advertising agencies; both carried film and television advisors on their campaign staffs and both employed opinion research companies to keep a constant finger on the public pulse. In their public opinion polling the Social Democrats used an extraordinarily large sample of 10,000—much larger than usual—in order to break down Germany into valid geographic and demographic units. The motive was to ensure that voter appeals could be so designed as to reach all major elements of the population. The most competent technical experts were employed for the production of party programs which were aired on the two German television networks. Production itself was assigned to the most innovative and creative German television and film studios.

Public opinion research was not only contracted for, but was put to good use. The Christian Democrats, for example, discovered that while the party was declining somewhat in prestige, it had one enormous asset in the person of its chancellor, Mr. Kiesinger. Out of this discovery the slogan was coined: "It's the Chancellor that counts." The chancellor was set up as the leader and spokesman for his party, and became the symbol of the campaign.

On the other hand, the Social Democrats discovered that their party leader, Willy Brandt, had little of the charismatic appeal of Chancellor Kiesinger, but that the party possessed in its ranks a substantial number of attractive, progressive, alert, bright, young men, who created an image of progressivism and confidence. Consequently the Social Democrats put their emphasis on this team of young Social Democrats rather than on the party leader.

The Free Democrats, on the other hand, had a much more difficult problem. It was touch and go whether they would be able to achieve the five percent of the popular vote which would permit them to occupy any seats in the Bundestag. They had thus bent their efforts toward achieving that five percent level. In order to do so they developed a theme which they drove home with extraordinary vigor. They suggested that the German voter split his vote: that he should first vote for an SPD candidate, then give his second vote to a Free Democrat. In a system which employs proportional representation this meant that the party could build enough secondary strength to assure itself of remaining in the running for some parliamentary seats. By supporting the Social Democrats they were detracting from the strength of the Christian Democrats, who appeared to be the stronger opponent.

Party leaders were carefully trained by film and television experts for their appearances on the regular party-produced television films and for party rallies which would be filmed by television news crews. The CDU, for example, used closed circuit filming as a training device. A half dozen closed party meetings were set up in which Chancellor Kiesinger appeared. These were recorded on videotape, studied carefully, and eventually the Chancellor was invited in to observe them and listen to criticisms from experts.

Such films as were commissioned by the party were carefully planned to use the most effective available techniques and thoroughly screened before release to assure maximum impact. Rallies were staged in a manner to make the most efficient use of cameras and lighting. Speakers were trained in methods for most attractive presentation. Efforts were made to furnish news clips of party rallies to television news crews and to help the crews obtain footage of important messages.

The Social Democrats had a relatively easier time in 1969 planning their campaign than the Christian Democrats because they had been junior partners in a government coalition with the CDU. This put the CDU at a disadvantage in that it couldn't boast of its accomplishments in the last two years of its government without implying credit to the SPD. On the other hand, as junior partner, the SPD was free to attack.

Through its extensive polling processes the SPD discovered that it should concentrate its television spots on international reforms which it believed were required and on the solution of problems in traffic, health, education and social security. The SPD strategy was to identify carefully its target groups, write off those voters who couldn't be won, and those who were safely committed to the SPD. It then was able to concentrate on those areas where there was a geniune possibility for party growth.

The party, during the last few months before the election campaign started, realizing that it was necessary to build a record for itself, planned certain items of legislation which were introduced in the Bundestag with a full recognition that the bills would never be passed. SPD strategy was based on the theory that such legislation would furnish opportunity for the SPD to call attention to the recalcitrance and obsolesence of the CDU party and to furnish campaign ammunition which could be effectively turned into television programming.

The CDU on the other hand was forced to change its strategy somewhat from its 1965 campaign because of its coalition relationship with the SPD. In 1965 it had stressed three points: the past success of the party, the economic boom which it had stimulated, and the personality of Chancellor Ludwig Erhard, the economic miracle worker who had steered the country into an unprecedented economic boom. In 1969 it could still concentrate on past successes but its identification with those successes was diluted by the necessity of sharing them with the

SPD. The economic boom, in the meantime, had flattened out and could no longer be pointed to as a magnificent accomplishment. So the party machinery concentrated on building the already favorable image of Chancellor Kiesinger. Television spots were built around "Kiesinger, the man"; "Kiesinger, the reformer"; and "Kiesinger, man of peace", which is strangely reminiscent of the 1952 Eisenhower campaign.

While the British election campaign is not nearly as free-wheeling as its counterpart in Germany, British campaign managers are no less knowledgeable about the use of television than their German counterparts. Intensive studies have been made by both major British parties to determine how television best meets the requirements of the British election campaign. Careful attention is given to the most effective use of the media once the campaign is in motion.

The two principal targets of the British campaign strategists are the regular television appearances on the three British television networks and regularly scheduled news coverage.

Since the campaign of 1959 primary attention has been given to the staging of the party leaders' appearances on television. In that year Prime Minister Harold Macmillan elicited a good bit of surprise among his audience when he appeared in his final broadcast standing beside a large and attractively designed globe. It was generally considered that the Prime Minister was more at ease in this performance than he ever had been previously. He had been notorious for feeling stiff and uncomfortable before television cameras, in contrast to his reputation in face to face or small group conversation, where he was regarded as one of the brightest, most articulate and knowledgeable men on the British political scene. The production and staging of his 1959 appearance were carried out in such a way that it was possible for the Prime Minister to make a formal presentation but still retain an attitude of informality and direct communication to viewers.

It may be signficant that Chris Chattaway, one of the British track stars of the early 1950s who succeeded in running a mile in less than four minutes, and later a BBC commentator, member of Parliament, and Minister of Communications, was sent to the United States prior to the campaign to examine American practices in the use of television as a medium for political party campaigns. Macmillan was also supported by advice from British commercial broadcasters in the production of his highly successful broadcast.

There is little evidence that British parties have selected party leaders on the basis of charisma or favorable image potential during the age of television. None of the conservative candidates, including the leader in the 1970 election, Edward Heath, has demonstrated a particularly favorable television personality. On the other hand, former Labor prime minister, Harold Wilson, is credited with having that undefinable charisma; but it is generally assumed that he was picked for his leadership qualities and his political capabilities rather than for the image he might create on television.

The Liberal party leader, Jo Grimmond, was one of the most attractive figures on television to appear on the British campaign screen in recent years. He succeeded in giving the Liberal party a big lift, and there are experts who believe that Liberal party strength in the 1964 election derived largely from the image created by Grimmond in his television appearances.

While the leadership may not be picked for its attractiveness on television, it is likely that many of the younger candidates for Parliament are selected by the leaders because it is hoped they will prove to be effective television performers. Technically the candidate for a seat from a given constituency has to be selected by the residents of that constituency. He is not permitted formally to declare his candidacy until the opening of the election campaign. As a matter of common practice, however, central party headquarters in London frequently makes a selection several months in advance of the dissolution of Parliament. The prospective candidate then begins to meet voters in his constituency as a "prospective candidate for Parliament." By the use of this device, central party headquarters exercises control over the selection of candidates who will be presented during the actual election campaign and is able to do so with an eye on possible television capabilities of the man chosen.

Advertising agency contributions to the British election campaign are quite different from those in the United States. Since there are no spot announcements, and since media placement is not a factor, there is little for the advertising agency to do in connection with formal public speeches or question-and-answer sessions. Consequently, the advertising agency function is largely limited to placing advertisements in the press, calling attention to local political rallies, and supervising the production of billboards, posters, leaflets, and campaign buttons, all non-television functions.

Aid in the production of the party leaders' appearances on the three television networks can be obtained from professionals working for the BBC or for one of the independent television program contracting companies, rather than from the agency field. Public opinion research is extensively used prior to the three-week course of the campaign. Once the campaign is underway, there is very little opportunity to shift campaign strategy or to modify the television approach. The time span is too short.

The main influence that television may have exercised over the general conduct of the British election campaign is to concentrate strategic direction in the London area and to focus on the party leader as a symbol of the party. This does not necessarily reduce the efforts of the run-of-the-mill candidate in his selected constituency, but it has increased the importance of party headquarters. The new emphasis on the regular television news broadcast, the 8:50 P.M. BBC program and the "News at 10:00" on ITV, has reinforced the trend.

The morning press conference was an important vehicle of the British campaign prior to the 1959 election. Television coverage beginning that year, however, gave the event new significance in the political spectrum. This was especially evident to political leaders as they watched their pronouncements on subsequent news programs. Moreover, the briefing officer, whether the party leader himself, party secretary, or some other representative, has become a major figure in an election campaign. The first person to achieve stature in this role was Morgan Phillips, the Labor party secretary, who conducted morning press conferences in September and October of 1959.

Both the Labor and Conservative parties are able to draw for advice concerning television techniques on leading figures from British independent television. Sidney Bernstein, the chairman of Granada, for example, has long been identified with Labor causes. Norman Collins, deputy chairman of Associated Television, and formerly a program controller at BBC, has similarly been identified with the Conservative side and played a significant role in connection with Harold Macmillan's performances in the 1959 election. He is credited with having suggested the set, featuring the large globe, that Macmillan used with such great success.

Political campaigning on television in Japan is too new for any significant techniques to have been developed or for the Japanese parties to have been more than introduced to campaigning on television. The use of television in the 1969 campaign, however, engendered enough interest and enthusiasm, and played a sufficiently significant role, that party leaderships are beginning seriously to consider the manner in which television will be used in the next Japanese election.

Some thought is being given to the possibility of using agency-produced sixty-second spot commercials during the next campaign. Such spot announcements would be placed on the commercial television stations. Since the private sector of Japanese television is in many respects similar to that in the United States, the next Japanese election may bear a striking resemblance, at least in the use of political advertising, to a U.S. campaign.

There undoubtedly will be conflict, as a matter of fact, there has been controversy already as to how it will be possible to reconcile the desire of the parties to have a hand in the production of the television programs. Television management is insisting that production is a prerogative of station owners. The government agreed in large measure, specifying in 1969 that all political party programs were the sole responsibility of the broadcasters. But NHK is not likely to take kindly to the growing role of its commercial rivals. It is most unlikely that the government broadcasting corporation will willingly give up any of its jealously guarded prerogatives, unless forced by government to do so. It seems likely however that the commercial spot will ultimately come to Japan and that advertising agencies will eventually begin to play a significant role in political party and candidate propaganda efforts. When the commercial spot is introduced, station management's role will inevitably be diminished and production control will begin to erode.

The influence of television on politics throughout the world has grown in direct ratio to the density of receivers, and the relative freedom accorded its coverage. The trend so far has been upward at an accelerating pace. Unless unforeseen controls are imposed, we can expect that trend to continue. While the impact of television on government will probably continue to grow at a uniform pace from country to country, the shape and form it takes may vary widely. It is unlikely, for example, that the spot commercial will ever dominate the political campaign in Western Europe as it has in the United States. Europeans are too wary over the television commercial, too distrustful of it, to allow its intrusion. Publicized antagonism to the use of the spot commercial in the United States will inevitably reinforce opposition.

The advertiser-sponsored commercial message has found a place in European television but Europeans have a tendency to take a snobbish attitude toward American hard-sell. In England, commercials on ITV stations fall only in natural breaks in program content. In Germany, Holland and Italy, they are all confined to a specific hour in the early evening broadcast schedule. In Scandinavia, there are no commercials, and in the United Kingdom, the BBC seems unlikely ever to relent and permit advertising to invade its sacred schedule. It seems natural in this environment that the free-wheeling, hard-hitting insistent sell of the American commercial will be restricted. There is too much traditional antagonism against it. But there are few other devices used by American political managers, which haven't already been adapted to use in other sections of the world.

Candidates are now being chosen in some instances because they show promise as attractive television personalities, capable of using the medium to communicate to the electorate. Television producers, directors and scriptwriters are beginning to assume positions in campaign organization charts, and lighting experts, stage designers and make-up men are joining campaign entourages. Film documentaries, short carefully produced talks, question and answer programs, and rallies staged for television are becoming commonplace just as in the United States.

European political television will probably never be a carbon copy of the American system. Differences in television structures are too great. The European television operations are tightly controlled, usually through government corporations. In contrast with the United States, there are very few of the brash, independent stations which make their own decisions and join networks only as voluntary affiliates, rather than as cogs in a government corporation. The only stations to operate largely without restraints are those in Luxembourg and Monaco, and their coverage is not sufficient to upset the conservative patterns established elsewhere.

It is unlikely that in this controlled environment political leaders will make unrestricted war on each other by means of television, as in the United States. It is unlikely that one candidate or party will monopolize the airwaves and saturate the electorate with television signals of the hard sell variety. Europe and Japan will undoubtedly go forward to use television more intensively in future campaigns. There will be more speeches, interviews, debates, discussions, short film documentaries and events staged for news cameras in the hope that they will wind up as items on a regular news program. But unless a major change occurs in the method of broadcast regulation, appearances will be balanced on the 5-5-3, or 3-3-2, or 1-1-1 ratios. Film clips may verge dangerously near commercial spots, but they won't go quite that far. Speeches may be vehement, insinuation and innuendo may be barely concealed, but politeness ultimately will prevail.

Whether the influence of television over the political process will be as great as in the United States, or even greater, remains to be seen. But the simple fact that candidates for public office and their managers are building elaborate professional machinery to exploit television's virtues as a communications link to the people is evidence enough that the television camera is a dominant factor on the political scene—in the United States, in Western Europe, in Japan and in the remainder of the world.

GOVERNMENT AND TELEVISION

7

While it is the relationship of television with campaigns and elections that furnishes color, drama, excitement, and the thrill of a contest, it is the day-to-day contact between the government and its citizens, and among the various components of government, that demonstrates the day-to-day workhorse role of the medium.

In the United States, this relationship is carried on in a number of ways. The President communicates to the people by presidential messages, statements and press conferences; Congress reaches the people through interviews, discussions, coverage of committee hearings, and reports to home constituencies. The Congress makes it wishes known to the President through building pressures among the electorate by these same devices —and the President attempts to influence Congress in the same way.

The various administrative departments, agencies, and bureaus of government are no less adept. Through carefully constructed and often costly public information departments they explain their policies to the people and build support for new policies. Sometimes, cynics point out, as much effort goes into justifying their own existences as in informing the public.

Policy makers at all levels use television to communicate to the people. They use a myriad of devices: trial balloons, leaks, explanations of policy, press conferences, and interviews when the broadcasters are sufficiently interested to approach them. People, on the other hand, communicate to the various agencies of government through political campaigns, in which the television camera plays a significant role. But generally it is the average citizen—except at election time—who has the most difficulty in making his views known to government. There is no established mechanism which will allow him to communicate. The frustration which results from this inability to achieve access to the channels of communications is surely one of the major factors in the popularity of the action-demonstration technique. The demonstrator can at least exorcise his frustrations and at best be seen on television violently espousing his cause. The person not inclined to demonstrating can join clubs, organizations, societies, pressure groups, political parties, and special interest groups, and thus use the power of the group to gain access to television, in an effort to make his voice heard by persons in authority.

What is true of the federal government in its relationships with the public is likewise true of state, county, city, and even smaller administrative units. But television, as a matter of record, is much more frequently seen in the meetings of city councils and boards of education than in the halls of the Congress of the United States. And mayors of major cities frequently are granted more time on their local television stations than the President of the United States on the national networks.

The mechanism which establishes this inter-relationship is a delicate one and there is a constant danger that it will get out of balance. The Federal Communications Act of 1934, which established the Federal Communications Commission, specified that fairness and balance must prevail in the broadcast spectrum; but it is much easier to legislate fairness and balance than to enforce it. The office of the President, backed by all the powerful paraphernalia of the nation's highest office, has a natural advantage in commanding the media. But it frequently isn't necessary to command. The great degree of public interest attending virtually every word the President utters, every step he takes, every decision he announces, focuses attention on the man and the office and makes the presidency the most intensely covered office in the world.

The intensity is reflected in the constantly increasing volume of manpower and equipment asssigned by television to the White House. The networks prior to 1952 usually stationed one man to do double duty as radio and television reporter. Now at least one correspondent, frequently two, backed up by full film crews is the standard. Station groups are beginning to show an increasing interest in White House activities and in the number of assigned fulltime personnel to the White House news corps. In addition, the wire services have personnel on duty to watch out specifically for broadcast needs. As recently as 1955, CBS News, in an economy wave and assuming that President Eisenhower would make little news during his September vacation in Denver, failed to send a correspondent with the presidential party. It was thirty-six hours after the president's serious heart attack before the regular White House reporter arrived on the scene. This is a gamble which has not since been repeated, nor is it likely to be.

It is little wonder that the leaders of the opposition rail at both media and the White House and the machinery of the party in power. It is no wonder they complain to the Federal Communications Commission that fairness and balance is not being maintained. It is no wonder that they clamor for new restrictions on the White House and new mechanisms to measure fairness and balance.[1]

The fact is that there are no yardsticks, no scales, no meter that will indicate when fairness and balance have been achieved or when they are out of line. It is quite possible that if fairness and balance were to be rigidly enforced on the basis of some kind of formula, that broadcasters and politicians alike would be forced to devote more time to making reports and measurements than to covering and conducting the business of government. This is one of the weaknesses of the American system of broadcast regulation, but it is another case where the cure might be worse than the illness.

What is true of the White House and the presidency is true in lesser measure of other office holders of the government in power. Broadcast facilities of equal magnitude are available to members of Congress and to the heads of administrative agencies, boards, commissions, bureaus; but without the magic of the White House at their fingertips, the facilities are less responsive to call. There is comparatively less access to communications facilities available to persons outside the power structure. People can't talk back to big government any more than they can talk back to big business, except by banding together into well-financed pressure groups, or by demonstrating and threatening violence. They have little opportunity to achieve access to communications channels, which are efficient for downward communication but blocked for communications upwards.

It is largely the responsibility of the representatives of the media themselves to maintain the delicate balance between the various competing factors within government; between the political parties; among the racial groups; between rich and poor; business and labor; agriculture and industry; supporters of education and those in favor of cutting educational costs to the bone; between residents of urban areas and those who live in small towns and on farms; and between youth and age.

The television executive sits in the middle, exercising his judgment in an effort to maintain a tenuous fairness and balance, and the middle is not always a comfortable position to occupy, for the man in the middle is subject to pressures from all sides. The attack by Vice President Agnew against the television network news divisions exemplifies the manner in which the Administration can bring pressure to bear to get a better hearing for the Administration point of view and to stifle the opposition. On the other hand, demonstrations—many of them leading to riots—in Chicago during the 1968 Democratic National Convention, at Kent State University in Ohio, at Jackson State in Mississippi, and on the streets in New York, Detroit, Watts, Chicago, Washington, New Haven and Cambridge —many of them carefully designed to obtain television coverage—indicate the lengths to which some elements of society feel they have to go to attract attention or to create a framework in which they can be seen and heard.

The balance has been upset in the past by experts in the use of the broadcast media. Franklin Roosevelt, during the thirteen years of his administration, used his radio fireside chats and his regular press conferences in such a way as to keep the programs of his administration constantly before the public. This influence was somewhat offset by widespread opposition from the daily press, but the success of the Roosevelt administration in winning wide public support in order to obtain favorable action in Congress is testimony to the success of the FDR radio broadcast policy.

President John F. Kennedy, with masterful skill in the use of television, stimulated howls of rage and pain from the Republican party representatives, who felt that he was misusing the power of broadcasting. But in 1969 the shoe was on another foot. The Nixon administration came into power with a taut, efficient, well-oiled public relations machine that was geared to exert maximum pressure on all fronts.

As an election nears, an alert, tough-minded Administration can put the entire government propaganda apparatus into motion with a concentrated power that is almost an irresistible force, without violating any formal rules governing allocations of time. This is the type of force the opposition is confronted by. The broadcaster is forced into the unenviable position, particularly unenviable for a licensed business, of serving as referee, restraining the Administration from getting out of bounds, occasionally giving the opposition an opportunity to reach a point a little closer to balance.

This is not a new problem occasioned by the presence of television; as many questions were raised during the era when radio was paramount. Television, however, has greatly increased the dimensions of the problems, for, like radio and unlike privately owned advertising-supported print media, it is a licensed institution, and thereby subject to various undefined pressures from government or political party. It is a particularly attractive target because of its well-documented ability to attract viewers and its assumed capability to persuade them.

Radio was a target but not nearly so large. It had a little more freedom because it was not regarded as being so mighty a political force. It was a household medium, but it didn't ever quite suffer from being in the intense spotlight that plagues every move television makes.

Within radio there was a greater diversity of opinion. Both CBS and NBC paid lip service to objectivity, but permitted the Edward R. Murrows, Elmer Davis's, H. V. Kaltenborns, Joseph C. Harshs, and Cecil Browns, a degree of latitude in shaping public opinion, which has never been permitted on television, except perhaps in the early days of "See It Now." Both the ABC and Mutual networks gave free-range to so-called "commentators," among them Fulton Lewis and Gabriel Heatter, who were editorialists rather than news broadcasters.

Today, news broadcasting is a tightly controlled art with emphasis on hard news and objectivity. Eric Sevareid, David Brinkley, John Chancellor and Howard K. Smith regularly comment on the news, but in short, and usually polite, skillfully written essays on the current scene. There is none of the bombast of a Heatter, the ire of a Lewis or the incisive scalpel of a Davis.

Today's television reporter is a much less flamboyant individual. The sheer size of the required staff and the complexity of fitting the component news elements into a logical pattern for broadcasting call for an "organization man" rather than a solo performer. But the television "anchorman" is hardly anonymous. Not even the most glamorous stars of the home screen command as much exposure day in and day out and few have the durability of the Cronkites or Brinkleys, who have remained on center stage for almost two decades.

A most commonly traveled route to stardom for the network television news correspondent or anchorman has involved substantial reporting experience, frequently on newspapers or wire services but sometimes only in broadcast news organizations.

Walter Cronkite came into broadcasting as a seasoned veteran of wire service reporting and editing. By the time he joined the CBS News staff in 1950 in Washington, he had edited a regional wire report for the United Press, covered the United States Eighth Air Force in England and on the continent during the war, established a post-war bureau for the United Press in Amsterdam and spent two years as U.P. bureau chief in Moscow.

John Chancellor had worked on the editorial staff of the *Chicago Daily News* before joining NBC in that city, and Harry Reasoner had been a reporter for the now defunct *Minneapolis Times* before entering broadcasting as a reporter/writer for a news oriented radio station in Minneapolis and St. Paul. He was later news chief for a Twin Cities television station before moving on to the CBS News staff in New York.

The three analyst-essayists who appear regularly on the early evening network news programs also used newspaper or wire service experience as a stepping stone to radio and television stardom; Eric Sevareid on the *Minneapolis Journal* and *Paris Herald Tribune,* Howard Smith on the wartime United Press staff in London and David Brinkley on a Washington newspaper.

William H. Lawrence of ABC News achieved a national reputation as White House and political correspondent for *The New York Times* before he moved to ABC News. John Scali of the same staff was a widely respected diplomatic correspondent for the Associated Press, and Sander Vanocur prior to assuming a news staff position at NBC had been a reporter for *The New York Times.* Charles Kuralt caught the attention of network news chiefs when he won an Ernie Pyle award for feature writing on a Charlotte, North Carolina, newspaper.

How to measure the potential for success in attracting audiences is one of the great mysteries of television. There are no guidelines, no aptitude tests, no mathematical skills that can be applied to the individual's competence as reporter, writer or presenter to predict his talent at attracting or holding an audience. The only successful predictor has been intuition on the part of the news executive in charge.

Cronkite received his chance at fame and fortune as a result of a series of happenstances and my own pretty solid hunch that he would be a knowledgeable, confident and durable link between viewer and event. He joined the CBS News staff in mid-summer of 1950 shortly after the opening gun in the Korean War. Largely because no one else was available, he was assigned the 11:00 P.M. news spot on Washington's television station WTOP. He demonstrated sufficient talent in building and holding an audience in that program that I selected him to anchor the network pool coverage of the Japanese Peace Conference in San Francisco in September 1951. When the time came to select a correspondent to anchor the 1952 political conventions, CBS television executives expressed a strong preference for using the skill, experience and reputation of Robert Trout, who had been covering national political conventions since 1936. I balked at the recommendation, arguing that Cronkite belonged to a new breed, the reporter who could interpret the picture and give it meaning and perspective. Trout, I contended, was a magnificent ad libber who could create word pictures with consummate skill, but in television the picture was already available and needed no description. Cronkite, I suggested, could better elaborate on it. Persistence paid off and Cronkite won the assignment. The wisdom of the choice is now self-evident. The name which most viewers immediately identify with political coverage is that of Walter Cronkite.

Cronkite has maintained his preeminence because he works at it, and he works at it because he is interested. Consequently the audience recognizes him as an expert political observer, just as they regard him as an expert on rocketry and space exploration. The confidence, born of detailed knowledge, shows through the screen.

John Chancellor had much of the same vital interest in the news and the capacity to absorb great volumes of information. He is a thorough going reporter whether working the floor of a political convention or the central news desk of NBC's nightly news. Harry Reasoner hasn't yet had the opportunity to demonstrate the same vital enthusiasm for politics but his chance will undoubtedly come, and it will be his skill at absorbing the intricate threads of political maneuvering that will give him the same loyal response from the public if, in fact, he is going to obtain that response.

Television news has attracted and provided outlets for the inferior reporter just as have newspapers, magazines and wire services. The hazards on television are greater because of the significant role played by showmanship. It is conceivable that the vacant mind speaking through an attractive appearance, backed up by a dramatic delivery, could capture the loyalty of millions of viewers. It has in fact happened on local stations. It is possible that image could play as great a role in creating star quality in news broadcasters as in politicians. There is no assurance that television's theoretical x-ray eye will unmask news broadcasting charlatans. But the fact is that network news performers have generally been chosen with care and with an eye to their competence to report, capacity to understand and will to be fair. And even if the charlatan should achieve a position of eminence, the enormous complexity of television's news editorial function must by its very nature impose constraints that make it virtually impossible for an irresponsible anchorman to delude the public.

The homogenizing process involved in the multitude of steps leading from event to screen will almost certainly continue to blunt the efforts of the reporter who approaches his task with a burning desire to promote a personal point of view.

It is in the selection of the story to be covered and the choice of the picture to support it that distortion is most likely to creep in, and it is in connection with this innate weakness in television reporting that the news executive seeking to obtain reasonable objectivity must be most concerned.

There are good reasons for the trend toward reasonable objectivity. The power of the television network is so great, it is doubtful whether any one individual should be granted facilities to advocate a point of view. But, conversely, the public is deprived of the broad range of opinions which characterized radio. The average individual's opinion leadership now comes from members of the government or special pleaders for a cause, or from members of the opposition, who are likewise special pleaders. This is the environment in which the average citizen must make his decisions. No wonder he is frequently frustrated; no wonder he pays attention to the Vice-President of the United States, when he attacks the networks' news divisions as being dominated by a dozen members of the Eastern establishment, who have no right to filter the news for the individual.

There is room for criticism, however. There is considerable reason to question whether our television system, as now constituted, provides sufficient range of information, analysis, opinion and leadership to justify its enormous power. The three-legged stool of Administration, opposition and broadcaster must be re-designed to assure the public some voice, if only to avoid frustration and the violent consequences which frequently follow frustration. One leg or another is generally being called to account.

The sturdiest of the three legs, the most powerful voice, and the repository of the greatest power is the presidency. The president has enormous advantages in going before the public on the television screen. He can reach very large segments of the entire population in an informal manner in the quiet of their own homes. He is able to make his case without running the risk of being subjected to questioning, rebuttal, or analysis. There is no filtering process. He has the advantage of choosing the site, decorating the set in the most effective way and lighting it to his best advantage, and making his presentation in a manner judged most suitable for his own style of performance.

Newspaper copy is obviously different. Before appearing in print, the news story of the president's speech has gone through the filtering processes produced by the reporter's brain, background and experience, and by the brains, backgrounds and experiences of a battery of editors. It has been subjected to modifications, deletions or additions. It has been trimmed and polished and sometimes given added perspective by relating it to other stories before it appears in print.

There are many avenues of access to television available to the White House. Even if requests to utilize those facilities are not accompanied by pressure, a television operator will think twice before turning them down. He has to be aware of the subtle power of the nation's highest office and can always justify his decisions to carry White House messages on the basis of news value. There are scores of methods by which the president can appear on television or see to it that his program and ideas are given adequate play. These opportunities are not limited to presidential messages, press conferences or White House press briefings. They also include ceremonial events, appearances on camera before and after meetings with congressmen or public leaders, statements read before and after trips, televised conversations with network television correspondents, and even escorted camera tours of the White House, as carried out so effectively by President Harry Truman, when the presidential mansion was re-opened after extensive renovation. Indirectly, the president is in a position to communicate to the people through third parties. Virtually every visitor to the oval office is queried by television reporters on the White House ground after his visit with the president.

A formal presidential message is obviously the most direct device. President Roosevelt developed the fireside chat on radio to a high degree of artistry; but it was President Truman who made the first formal presidential speech on televison, his State of the Union message to the joint houses of Congress in early

January of 1949. This speech also marked the first occasion on which television cameras were permitted to enter the sanctuary of the chamber of the House of Representatives. Since then, the president's report to the people on television has become commonplace. President Eisenhower used the device 49 times in eight years in office, an average of about six times a year. President Nixon made 12 formal addresses plus 10 live televised press conferences during the first seventeen months of his administration. The Nixon total compares with 32 appearances by President Johnson in a similar period, and 18 by President John F. Kennedy.

During the Eisenhower administration it was rarely suggested that all three networks carry a presidential address simultaneously. The president and his press secretary, Mr. Hagerty, felt that they could get more exposure, overall, if the message were carried live on one network and delayed to later times on the others. They also made it a point that if they hurt one network severely by costly preemption at one time, they would try to redress the balance on the next request by easing off on that network and asking another one to accept the principal burden.

Television executives came under vigorous criticism during the Eisenhower administration for relying on Hagerty's evaluation of presidential speeches before they made their plans to accept, reject, schedule live, or delay. It was on the basis of the press secretary's evaluations, however, that they were able to make relatively straightforward decisions. Only the press secretary, the president, and the speech writers and advisors knew the contents or the importance of the proposed message, and only they could suggest its relative merits. The only alternative would have been to accept all offers.

With the arrival of the Kennedy administration, the White House was firmer in its appeals for time and the networks more willing to accede to presidential requests. By the time of the Johnson administration it had become common practice for all networks to accept all presidential requests for time on a live and simultaneous basis. President Johnson also converted the

State of the Union Message from a noon-time broadcast from the House chamber into a night-time event in order to capture the much larger audience available during the mid-evening hours.

While presidential messages have increased in number, and the impact on the public grown as the number of television homes in the United States increased to an almost saturation level, the fairness and balance problem has never been solved. There is always the question following a presidential speech as to what constitutes fairness and balance; who is authorized and empowered to speak for the opposition? If an authorized spokesman can be identified and given the power and authority by the various contesting elements within a given political party, how is it possible for him to get an equal opportunity? Does it mean that he should be given the same time period on a subsequent night over the same facilities? If so, how can he be relatively certain of the same size of audience?

It should be pointed out that the often referred to Section 315 of the Federal Communications Act does not apply in a fairness and balance situation. It is applicable only in the case of an election campaign when an opportunity to use the facilities of a television station or network is granted to one candidate for public office. Then it is mandatory that equal time and equal facilities be granted to all other candidates for that same office. The president would come under the jurisdiction of Section 315 during an election campaign if he were to use the privileges of the White House to make a purely partisan speech in his own behalf. But this is a rare occurrence.

The networks have experimented with several varieties of devices for maintaining balance following presidential messages. Some balance is furnished by analysis by network news personnel immediately following the presidential message. Ironically it was such analysis immediately following President Nixon's November 3rd speech that so angered Vice-President Agnew and presumably others within the Administration that it impeled him to deliver his bitter speech castigating the networks. The vice-president's talk made before a group of middle-western Republicans was considered by broadcasters the most vicious attack ever made in broadcast journalism by a high government official. The vice-president charged that television reporters had subjected the president's carefully planned message to "instant analysis and querulous criticism," that the president's audience "was inherited by a small band of network commentators and self-appointed analysts," and that the majority of the analysts "expressed in one way or another their hostility to what he had to say."

Then the vice-president went on to strike at the heart of the television news broadcast organization. "The purpose of my remarks tonight," the vice-president said, "is to focus your attention on this little group of men who not only enjoy a right of instant rebuttal to every presidential address but, more importantly, wield a free hand in selecting, presenting and interpreting the great issues in our nation."

He complained that " a small group of men, numbering perhaps no more than a dozen anchor men, commentators and executive producers, settle upon 20 minutes or so of film and commentary that is to reach the public. . . . They decide what 40 to 50 million Americans will learn of the day's events in the nation and in the world." Then came the hint that sent broadcast executives scurrying to their typewriters to prepare rebuttals. "Perhaps it is time," the vice-president said, "that the networks be made more responsive to the views of the nation and more responsible to the people they serve."

Nothing strikes terror into the hearts of broadcasters so quickly and leaves so profound a hurt as a hint of government action. The threat of license cancellation, even though subtly delivered, is a deadly weapon aimed directly at the pocketbooks of licensees. Without a license there can be no broadcast.

The vice-president raised visions of another type of penality, restrictive congressional legislation. Congress has rarely passed bills restricting broadcasters' freedom, but the threat is constantly present and warding off the threat is frequently a costly exercise for a network which may spend literally hundreds of thousands of dollars preparing for a legislative hearing.

There obviously was some truth to the vice-president's charges. No institution, no matter how hard it tries, particularly when it is as complex as a worldwide television news organization, can wholly avoid mistakes. It is likewise conceivable that there are persons in the network news divisions who are attempting to use the facilities to which they have access for expressing their own opinions. By the same token, the vice-president was guilty of gross exaggeration when he referred to the dozen members of the Eastern Establishment who "filter the news." The whole process of news gathering is so complex, involves so many individual decisions at so many geographical points remote from news headquarters, and demands so much individual effort in order to mold a variety of disparate elements together in one tightly constructed news broadcast that anything but highly generalized supervisory and policy control is largely out of the question.

CBS president Frank Stanton went on the offensive two weeks after the November 3rd Des Moines talk, when he told the Radio & Television Executives Society in New York City on November 25: "The ominous character of the vice-president's attack derives directly from the fact that it is made upon the journalism of a medium, licensed by the government, of which he is a high-ranking officer. This is a new relationship in government press relations. This all-important fact of the licensing power of life and death over the broadcast press brings an implicit threat to a government official's attack on it—whether or not that is the intention, and whether or not the official says he is speaking only as an individual."

CBS News division president Richard S. Salant, speaking at Phoenix, Arizona on December 5, elaborated on the repression theme. "What makes the vice-president's speech so disturbing, so unprecedented, is that for the first time in the history of journalism there was a comprehensive, angry attack by the government on licensed journalism."

Other broadcasters pointed out that many of the vice-president's "tiny and close fraternity of privileged men who live and work in the geographical and intellectual confines of New York and Washington" actually came from the Middle West and Far West. Even though there were quips about the vice-president's presumed inaccuracies; however, there still was an undercurrent of uneasiness in the broadcast news fraternity.

It is very clear that the vice-president's attack on television news focused new attention on the entire process of gathering, editing, and broadcasting of news and the relationship of television news to government. There is undoubtedly truth to the charge that there is generally a homogeneity of political attitude among most of the news executives and correspondents. A large majority would probably subscribe to what is called a "liberal" view of government. It is likewise true that three networks enjoy a virtual monopoly in the presentation for broadcast purposes of national news. Hence, their correspondents and analysts have access to audiences greater than their counterparts in daily press and magazines. It is also true in some cases that the broadcaster analyst may be selected for his role more on the basis of his ability to communicate than on his skills as a reporter and analyst.

A test, however, is found not in the power that could be assumed, but rather in how the responsibility is discharged. On that basis, television has done very well. Correspondents generally have followed an admonition handed down to the CBS News staff in 1954 from CBS chairman William S. Paley, in which he asked them to maintain "the will and intent to be objective." The number of journalists on network television, who in any way practice "advocacy journalism" is miniscule.

The main purpose served by the vice-president's attack on the media was to focus attention on the role of the television news broadcaster as a check on the president and as part of the national mechanism for maintaining fairness and balance among political parties. In the weeks following the Agnew speech, the issue continued to attract public attention. Critics of the Nixon administration charged that the president was monopolizing the airwaves and making improper use of the presidency to support political goals.

The Democratic national committee was particularly outspoken in denouncing the Republican party and exposing its own frustrations. It had no money to buy time, and it was so fractionalized that it had difficulty selecting a spokesman who could reply to the president on behalf of any substantial majority of the Democratic party.

President Stanton of CBS instituted a new plan in the summer of 1970 by which he had hoped that it might be possible to limit the Republican advantage or the natural advantage of any party holding the power of the presidency. He announced that CBS television would schedule a program called "Loyal Opposition" four times a year to help reduce the imbalance arising from presidential appearances on network television.[2] Democratic chairman Lawrence O'Brien appeared on the first, which also turned out to be the last, of these half hour programs, when he represented the Democratic National Committee in a "Loyal Opposition" appearance on July 7.

As was to be expected, the Republicans cried out in pain when they were attacked by chairman O'Brien and argued that he was not answering the president directly, but enunciating a general Democratic party policy. The Federal Communications Commission decision, handed down on August 14, caused the quick demise of the series. The Commission ruled that CBS would have to "afford some reasonable time" to a Republican spokesman to reply to chairman O'Brien, thus creating an absurd situation in which answers to answers could go on indefinitely. CBS promptly cancelled the program, leaving the whole matter as confused as it had been at the time of the Agnew speech.[3]

Former FCC chairman Newton Minow has informally suggested another plan that might succeed where predecessors have failed. He proposes that the opposition party delegate on an annual basis, probably through a mechanism of an annual convention, an official spokesman for the party. The official spokesman would then be in a position to claim air time as a matter of oppositional rights, following each presidential speech. The pattern would be much similar to that used in the United Kingdom, where political parties regularly designate their leaders, whether in or out of power.

The United Kingdom has solved the problem of fairness and balance in what appears to be an effective way. The prime minister has the right to command time on the British television networks—two BBC networks and ITV—for what is described as a "ministerial broadcast." This device is usually used only a couple of times a year, a recent exception being the Rhodesian crisis when Prime Minister Wilson gave several reports to the public. When the prime minister requests such a ministerial broadcast, the opposition party automatically gets the same time segment on the next night, and on the third night there is a discussion, usually among members of Parliament representing all shades of opinion. This simple but effective plan for achieving balance in the United Kingdom was accomplished by an aide-mémoire, issued in 1957 by the chairman of the board of governors of the BBC in respect of its relationships with the prime minister and the head of the opposition party.

No such machinery existed prior to the Suez crisis of 1956. Prime Minister Anthony Eden, during the height of that crisis, asked for time to make a report to the British people on the urgent nature of the crisis. BBC was then forced to make a decision as to whether to give the right of reply to the Labor opposition. After considerable internal discussion the BBC management decided to furnish time for Labor Party leader Hugh Gaitskill, who was known to have taken up a position opposing the government regarding the Suez matter. The Gaitskill speech set the precedent which was later converted into the aide-mémoire.

An updated version of this aide-mémoire published by the chairman of the board of governors of the BBC in 1968 specifies that when a minister claims or is offered an opportunity to make a policy statement of a politically contentious kind as distinct from a truly administrative statement (which is one, for example, on traffic problems), the right of the opposition for equal time and equal facilities is automatic and is not dependent on the discretion of the BBC. Broadcasts of this type, however, are relatively rare and normally develop on an ad hoc basis.

Sweden handles the problem in quite a different way. The prime minister of that country never asks for time, but the Swedish Broadcasting Corporation may decide that special circumstances exist in which they believe that a statement from the prime minister is in order. Under these conditions executives of the corporation extend a special invitation for use of SR facilities. If the prime minister accepts, equal time with similar facilities is divided among the opposition parties.

A more informal device available to the head of state or chief of state for communicating to the public is the formal press conference. There is nothing new about the press conference as such, but the fact that many such conferences are carried live on television is a relatively new development.

The first American president to permit a press conference to be covered live with television cameras and microphones was President Kennedy in January 1961. The way for this dramatic step, however, had been carefully paved during the preceding two administrations of President Eisenhower. During the period intervening between the November 1952 election and President Eisenhower's inauguration on January 20, 1953, the President-elect and his press secretary, James Hagerty, discussed on several occasions the question of the manner in which they would participate in press conferences. Both, according to Hagerty, had agreed that at some time it would be in order to permit live radio and television coverage; but they felt that television technology was not ready. Rather than approach it in a piecemeal way, they felt they should withhold a decision on radio until television could participate.

They were also concerned regarding the possible repercussions which might result from an erroneous statement in a live press conference and decided it would be much more advantageous to experiment with motion picture film until such time as they were certain that they and the country were both ready for the live performance.

The traditional presidential press conferences rules permitted attendance by pencil-and-paper reporters representing newspapers, wire services, and radio and television alike. No one was permitted to leave until the "Thank You, Mr. President" signal, whereupon there was a mad rush to the exits to file their stories. Later in the day those who wished could obtain a transcript of the conference which was prepared by a White House stenographer. The transcript, however, was not available until five or six hours after the conference's conclusion. No direct quotes were permitted except on special occasions, and everything had to be reported in the third person.

Hagerty's first step was to speed the process of making transcripts available, and once they were, to permit correspondents to use direct quotes. This could be done, though, only after Hagerty had had an opportunity to check the transcript for errors of fact.

The first conferences of this type were conducted in the Indian Treaty room in the Executive Office Building across the street west of the White House. The room was small and dark and shaded so that it would have been difficult to light. Manufacturers of film in the early 1950s had not yet found the secret of the high speed emulsions which were later to permit a drastic reduction in the light values required for making 16 mm motion pictures. Consequently, as Hagerty explains it, it would have been necessary to light the room with strong spots—so strong that the president, having an aversion to strong light anyway, wouldn't have been able to see the correspondents in the first row.

By late 1954 two separate delegations called on Hagerty to discuss the possibility of running a test filming of a presidential press conference. The network committee arrived first to report that members had heard of a new fast film which manufacturers would shortly be able to distribute. The committee representing Eastman and Ansco next visited the White House to report that indeed it was true that there was a fast film which would shortly be available. Hagerty expressed interest and suggested that as soon as sufficient quantity could be delivered for a test run, he would see to it that such a test would be made.

Approximately three months later the representatives of the film manufacturers returned to report that they thought they had solved the problem and the test would probably work. When the new high speed film arrived, Hagerty went to the Indian Treaty room to play the role of the president. Members of the network committee, Julian Goodman, now president of the National Broadcasting Company for NBC, Lewis Shollenberger of CBS, and Robert Fleming of ABC, later an assistant White House press secretary, were to serve as reporters. The film was thought to be sufficiently fast that no spot lights would be needed, so lighting was limited to a number of floods.

Following the completion of the test, the film was rushed to a laboratory in northeast Washington for processing and returned to the White House for screening by a number of Hagerty's colleagues on the personal presidential staff, including Sherman Adams, General Wilton B. (Jerry) Persons, and Thomas Stevens. Approval was unanimous, so Hagerty arranged to show the test film to the president himself. The president gave his approval, and the decision was then made to permit film cameras on a pool basis into the next presidential press conference. Hagerty informed the television representatives immediately but asked them to keep it quiet in view of the fact that the decision would probably meet some opposition from the press. On the day prior to the press conference which was to be held on January 23, 1955, members of the White House press corps were informed that film cameras would be permitted at the press conference. The reaction, according to Hagerty, was negative and sarcastic. Three of the most vociferous complaints came from representatives of the three wire services: Marvin Arrowsmith for the Associated Press, Merriman Smith for the United Press International, and Robert Clark for International News Service.

Noting that opposition would continue to be strong from the wire services, Hagerty called the three television representatives and asked them whether they didn't pay substantial sums of money in subscription fees for services from the three wires. He suggested that perhaps a call from their New York headquarters to wire service headquarters, in view of the size of the fees, might somehow reduce the vehemence of the opposition from the three wire service members of the White House press corps. A half hour later, as Hagerty tells the story, Arrowsmith, Smith, and Clark came to his office waving white handkerchiefs and announcing that they had received the message.

With that, plans went forward. Hagerty insisted on the right to screen the film before it went out in order to correct any serious misstatements the President might make. Fortunately, there was only one error that had to be deleted. The French military, at this time, was getting into increasing troubles in Indochina. The President was asked concerning circumstances there. He replied that "the situation in Indonesia is rapidly deteriorating." Permitting this statement to go out, Hagerty felt, would have done irreparable damage to our relationships with the Indonesians; but he was able to effect an editing change eliminating the damaging word "Indonesia." There was no further editing and the film was released for broadcast. After the first three or four press conferences filmed in this manner, it was decided that editing was no longer necessary, so the word was given: "Gentlemen, use it all."

The live Kennedy conference on January 29, 1961 was a logical step in the evolution begun by the filming in 1955. Again there was a chorus of complaints, but not nearly as vociferous as those which followed the announcement of the filming. James Reston of *The New York Times* described the live press conference as the "goofiest idea since the hula-hoop." And other critics took the position that it was either dangerous or an example of excessive showmanship or demeaning to the press. But the conference went off without any untoward circumstances and has become a standard part of White House relations with the press and public. The only major change that has occurred in the intervening years involved changes in the location. President Kennedy took his press conference to the auditorium in the State Department building but President Nixon and his advisors found a site much closer to home in the East Room at the White House. The East Room has proven itself well adapted to the purpose.

While the physical environment has been steadily improving, serious questions concerning the usefulness of the televised press conference have been gaining in volume. The optimistic hopes expressed by Hagerty that the presidential press conference might become an American counterpart to the interrogation of the British Prime Minister in the Parliamentary Chambers proved to be an empty dream. There has been criticism of the conference as an extension of show business, as a vehicle for the president to use a supporting cast from the press while he lays down White House policy, as a device for the president to build political support, and as a presidential tour de force rather than an honest give and take.

It is difficult to say where the responsibility lies. Individual members of the press are frequently guilty of using the conference as an opportunity to achieve personal publicity. Too often they do not vigorously follow up on questions which are answered in generalities. But the White House is equally at fault for scheduling conferences too infrequently, using them and the correspondents who attend as backdrops for laying down party policy, and for making the event a game of skill rather than a forthright attempt to inform the public.

In any case, television may have killed the spirit of the old press conference. Questions to a great extent have lost the hard-hitting, fact-seeking cast of the pre-television area and are frequently short speeches directed at the television audience.

Posing and elbowing for position on camera have become commonplace. The follow-up question is virtually non-existent. As Peter Lisagor of the *Chicago Daily News* once put it: "If one guy gets up and asks, 'Mr. President, do you think the war will end tomorrow?', the next one may ask, 'Are you going to the football game this weekend?' "

It doesn't seem likely at this late stage that the free give-an-take of Franklin D. Roosevelt, Harry Truman or Dwight Eisenhower with the Washington correspondents can be restored, short of exiling cameras and microphones. President Nixon intends to continue to schedule future interviews on camera with selected network representatives. But these are conversations rather than press conferences and subject to the same shortcomings that characterize the conferences in the East Room. The president promises he will also initiate conversations with press representatives without benefit of camera and microphones. But these also can hardly take the place of the old press conference. The ground rules will be set by the president, and it is difficult for a correspondent, accredited to the White House, to probe very deeply in private conversation. The traditional respect of the Press for the office inhibits potentially embarrassing questions, and the reporter who cherishes his White House assignment is timid about jeopardizing his position. Hagerty and Pierre Salinger, who opened up the first press conferences to television, can be credited with the best of intentions and great courage in breaking tradition. But they may have killed the press conference rather than make it the vital institution they had hoped.

The televised interrogation of the Chief of State or the head of Government is by no means an exclusively American institution. President de Gaulle of France from time to time reported to the French people and the world in press conferences. It was generally conceded that he never seemed very much surprised at the questions asked and the resultant performance was closer to an orchestrated speech than a lively give-and-take.

In both Germany and Japan the live televised press conference featuring the head of the state is a frequent occurrence. Within his first six months in office, Chancellor Willy Brandt of the Federal Republic of West Germany had already conducted four conferences. They were free and open with a lively give-and-take. The Japanese government-supported network, NHK, likewise carries live press conferences with the Japanese prime minister within its framework of intensive coverage of governmental activities.

The situation in Sweden is considerably different. There the press kept the Swedish Broadcasting Corporation out of the prime minister's press conferences for many years. In the mid-1960s, however, Swedish television was able to disregard the opposition and started scheduling live coverage from time to time as they thought the conference might be worthwhile. Once having established the privilege, however, Swedish television news executives resumed sending pencil-and-paper reporters or requested the prime minister to summarize his comments for film cameras following the conclusion of the conference.

In the United Kingdom there is no provision for a formal televised press conference. The closest approach occurs when the prime minister appears perhaps once a year on one of the current affairs programs scheduled by the British Broadcasting Corporation. He is then interviewed by a single television reporter.

The most effective regular contact between the White House and the news corps is achieved through the daily or several times daily press briefings conducted by the press secretary. The president himself doesn't appear, but the device is an effective method of explaining the Administration's point of view or announcing new programs. Reporters from all media are welcome. Normally the briefing begins with a standard report from the press secretary, but on occasion, when he has a statement from the president to read he will permit himself to be filmed and thus have direct access to television networks and stations.

Members of the Congress of the United States have virtually

no power to command attention by requesting airtime. Television appearances usually are available only to senior members and even then only at the invitation of the broadcaster. As a result, no member of Congress obtains the almost constant exposure that accrues to the president. But Congress, nevertheless, is well covered by television. The fact that since 1960 no candidates other than former senators have been serious contenders for the presidency of the United States is evidence enough.

Members of the Senate of the United States and the House of Representatives were alert enough to the powers of broadcasting as early as 1939 to recognize that some system should be devised to aid in radio coverage of the two chambers. Press galleries to facilitate wire service and newspaper coverage had been established at an earlier date, but in 1939 the decision was made to add radio galleries. These radio galleries continued to function until the advent of television in the late '40s when they were expanded to embrace television.

The galleries accredit correspondents; furnish studio space for recordings made in the Capitol building; provide working space and communications for members of the gallery; serve as information clearing houses concerning news developing on the floor and in committees; and represent broadcasters in negotiations with the House and Senate leadership. In national convention years they represent broadcasters in negotations with the management of the conventions. In short, they furnish a base of operations for reporters from the broadcast media on Capitol Hill. They also in a sense serve as a liaison between members of the two representative bodies and their leadership with the members of the broadcast news corps.

Network film crews have been covering both the House and Senate since the early 1950s. Film cameras are not permitted access to the floor of either the Senate or the House, but they are enabled to work in the corridors outside, on the steps of the Capitol building and on occasion, when they are invited, to the offices of individual senators or congressmen. The Senate will also permit coverage either on film or live of Senate hearings upon invitation of the chairman of the committee. Similar privileges covering House committees have consistently been denied, except for two sessions of the Congress when the Republicans were in power: the first one in 1947 and 1948, and the second in 1953 and 1954. In both instances the Speaker of the House of Representatives was Congressman Joseph Martin from Massachusetts. The long-time Democratic Speaker of the House, Sam Rayburn of Texas, however, was adamant in his refusal to permit television coverage either in committee rooms or on the floor of the House itself. The sole exception in the House takes place on the occasion of joint sessions of the House and Senate when they are addressed by the President or by visiting heads of state; or, in 1951, by General Douglas MacArthur after his firing by President Truman.

In order to facilitate service of radio tapes and television film and tape to home television stations, both the House and the Senate have established what they call the Senate and House "facilities." These facilities are, in fact, complete studios for radio and television purposes. Space is allocated by the leadership of the two bodies and equipment has been purchased with Senate and House funds. A congressman or senator who so desires is permitted to go to the facility and record, either on audio-tape or motion picture film, messages and reports to be sent back to his home community. In some cases this has become a supplement, or even a substitute, for a printed newsletter. The facilities would theoretically be available for use by television networks or individual stations, except for the fact they are manned by non-union government employees. Since most stations operate under union contract, they are prevented by such contracts from making use of the facilities and personnel. The television networks normally keep a minimum of two crews on Capitol Hill on a daily basis when Congress is in session—one to cover the House, the other to cover the Senate. The Senate crews are also available in the event that hearings of general public interest are in progress in one of the Senate committee rooms. Since the House has constantly refused to permit coverage of its hearings, there is no such strain on House facilities.

Generally, the old hands in covering Capitol Hill for television will point out that there are few congressmen who are not attracted like bees to honey by the sight of television camera and microphone; however, there is usually a considerable difference between a senator's degree of interest in a television film camera and his aptitude as a subject for the camera. The older members have frequently been suspicious of the new device and have lacked confidence, so they have been disinclined to push themselves toward television reports or interviews. On the other hand, the newer members, with a feeling of greater confidence and enthusiasm, have been willing to take the time and the trouble to learn best how to use television and film as a means of keeping in touch with their constituencies at home.

The more experienced hands point out, for example, that when Joe Martin from Massachusetts was replaced by Gerald Ford from Michigan as the House Minority Leader, the Republican leadership suddenly took a new and increased interest in television. Ford himself asked many questions of the network regulars who had been covering the House, arranged for members of his leadership group to go to television studios to test their capabilities with the medium and to check tapes made while they were experimenting. Ford's eager students learned by a process of trial and error that it was necessary to have something of significance to say to command space in one of the principal early evening network television programs. They found that calling a network representative at five o'clock in the afternoon with a suggestion for a filmed piece on the Huntley-Brinkley show that night was not very likely to yield results. If they had something of genuine importance to say, and if it was regarded by news executives in Washington as being of genuine national interest, and it could be filmed by noon or shortly later, they found network personnel cooperative, and sometimes saw results on the early evening news programs.

Frustrations are prevalent among members of the two bodies with relatively less seniority and inferior committee assignments. Some members in these categories have expressed dissatisfaction with their lack of exposure. They are constantly being bypassed on behalf of the Senate and House leadership and more senior members. This is less true in the Senate, with 100 members and six-year terms, than it is in the House with 435 members and two-year terms.

There is, however, a developing television outlet for members in this category through the mushrooming growth of regional bureaus in Washington which represent groups of television stations or individual stations scattered throughout the country. Time-Life Broadcast representing, at that time, four television stations, established an independent Washington news bureau in 1960. Two staff members, a reporter and a combination reporter-cameraman, set up offices in the Time-Life News bureau in Washington and started to cover news from the four states of Indiana, Michigan, Minnesota, and Colorado, in which the company owned stations.

The Time-Life bureau was not the first of the broadcast bureaus in Washington. Westinghouse had established a bureau to service its radio stations two years earlier. WCCO in Minneapolis-St. Paul had employed a part-time Washington reporter from the CBS Washington news staff as early as 1947 to cover the congressional delegation from Minnesota and members from neighboring districts in Wisconsin. It was Time-Life Broadcast in 1960, however, that set the pace for the growth of news bureaus supporting television stations. There are now a dozen such bureaus and each year sees the addition of one or two more.

The functions of the bureaus differ in direct proportion to the type of constituency which they represent. The Metromedia bureau, for example, represents a number of television stations which have no network affiliations. The same is true of RKO General. Staff members in those bureaus cover not only news of special interest to their stations but also general national sources, including the White House, and government departments and agencies; whereas the bureaus representing stations which have network affiliations are concerned almost exclusively with representatives of districts within the coverage area of the stations represented. The Time-Life bureau, for example, devotes approximately 60 percent of its time to covering members of Congress and Senate from the states where Time-Life owns stations. The principal focus is on the House, but in the case of Indiana and Colorado, senators also receive thorough coverage, since the Time-Life stations are located in the capital cities of Indianapolis and Denver, which are also the most populous cities in the respective state and state capitals. Less emphasis is put on senators from Michigan and California, since the Time-Life Broadcast stations are located in the relatively lesser cities of Grand Rapids and San Diego.

From the point of view of the junior member of Congress, the station or group news bureau is a God-send because it furnishes a ready-made outlet for statements and reports to his home constituents. He may not be sufficiently important to command network exposure, but he is of sufficient significance to command time on the television stations in his home district.

The main network question-and-answer shows—"Face the Nation," "Meet the Press," "Issues and Answers"—and the nighttime talks shows—Johnny Carson, Merv Griffin, Dick Cavett—are also treasure lodes of opportunity for the members of Congress with sufficient marquee value and presence as communicators to win invitations to appear. Few members of the House, however, except the top leaders, have achieved sufficient national stature to obtain such invitations. Members of the Senate who have had more opportunity to project themselves onto the national scene are invited in far greater numbers. It has been suggested that appearances on these programs have projected Senators, including John Kennedy, Lyndon Johnson, Stuart Symington, Hubert Humphrey, Barry Goldwater, William Fulbright, Richard Russell, Eugene McCarthy, George McGovern, and Edmund Muskie into positions where they have been regarded as serious contenders for either the presidency or the vice-presidency.

Except for a very few of the real old timers, television has become a major concern for almost all members of Congress when they plan support for programs, establish procedures for maintaining good relations with voters in their constituences, and organize to campaign for reelection. Almost all of them recognize the value of television as a campaign instrument. Representative Mark Andrews from North Dakota, for example, spends virtually all of his campaign budget on one-minute announcements on North Dakota television stations. Representatives from the large cities—New York, Chicago, Los Angeles, Philadelphia, Detroit—on the other hand, are frustrated because of the large number of congressional districts within the range of the television transmitters serving their areas. Their opportunities for exposure are consequently sharply limited.

Broadcasters are curious as to how soon the new enthusiasm for television will lead to relaxation of the rules against the presence of television cameras within the House and Senate chambers. New, unobstrusive television cameras with substantially reduced lighting requirements may make it possible to furnish full coverage in both the House and the Senate. Legislation has been introduced permitting such coverage, but so far without favorable action. The standard arguments used against television, include the charges that the camera will make actors out of members, and that the congressional bodies are not ready to suffer the embarrassments which will surely develop when only three or four senators are sitting at their desks reading newspapers while one member of the body is addressing a limited number of disinterested colleagues.

Germany permits live coverage of the Bundestag now. Very often German television will cover a complete debate. During early 1970 it covered up to three full days of hearings on German foreign policy. Japan, too, permits live coverage of its parliament. NHK cameras have frequently furnished live coverage of debates in the Diet and of meetings of Diet committees.

The British Parliament, however, has yet to see the presence of a television camera, except in an off-hours experiment, and it seems unlikely that the electronic camera will ever invade the sacred precincts of the House of Parliament. One overwhelmingly important reason is that the Parliamentary Chamber itself is so constructed that it would be almost impossible for television coverage to be arranged there. There is simply no place to put cameras where they could focus on members speaking from their seats, which is traditional in Parliament, and from the podium where the ministers of the crown sit. The Houses of Parliament are, in fact, off limits to any type of recording equipment—television or radio.

Reporters who cover Parliament have the privilege of plying their trade with pencil and paper in the precincts of the House of Commons and the House of Lords, but any filming for television must be done outside the building itself. The general BBC procedure is for its reporters to prepare summaries of the action as if they were producing copy for a newspaper, and walk across the street to a studio where they feed their sound reports into BBC headquarters for inclusion within the regularly scheduled news programs. Independent Television News lacks a recording facility or a studio in the vicinity of the Houses of Parliament, so its reporters must either call in stories by telephone or return to ITN headquarters to make their reports.

Interviewing of members of Parliament for inclusion within regularly scheduled news broadcasts is rarely done. One of the reasons for this absence of parliamentary interviews on regular news may be that the BBC has considerably more outlet for talk programs involving political topics than do the American networks. One night a week in a period between 10:00 and 11:00 o'clock BBC broadcasts a well-known program, "Panorama," which runs for forty minutes, of which up to one-half is frequently devoted to political topics. Five nights a week the corporation carries a 35-minute program called "24 Hours," which also includes a heavy dose of political content. It is estimated that up to 100 separate interviews broadcast during the course of the year will feature one or more members of Parliament. Some of these discussion programs take the form of personal confrontations which might be described as debates. The BBC moderator sits between representatives of opposing factions, opens the discussion, calls for opening statements, and then by cross-questioning eventually leads into a free and open discussion between the combatants.

There is no coverage of committees of the House of Parliament, largely due to the fact that the British have, for the most part, avoided the investigatory type of hearing that has been so attractive to American television viewers. Most committee meetings are designed to sharpen and perfect legislation, rather than to focus on investigatory proceedings; so they are concerned mostly with detail and rewriting. Even in view of the heavy exposure given to members of Parliament on the BBC current affairs programs, there is no real problem with maintaining balance. There is no formal system prescribed for British television, but it is assumed that something like a balanced schedule will be maintained on an informal basis. BBC current affairs chief, John Grist, keeps his own records and, as he puts it, if he finds that there are any deviations from reasonable equalization, he will "ring up" his producer and suggest that something be done quickly to redress the balance.

Even though cameras and microphones are not permitted within the corridors of the Houses of Parliament, or even on the exterior grounds, BBC and ITN officials both maintain that the coverage which they furnish to Parliamentary activities is roughly comparable to that furnished by the London printed press, with the possible exception of the *Times* of London which functions as a newspaper of record, printing verbatim accounts of Parliamentary debates.

West German television also furnishes an outlet for parliamentary opinion in an extensive schedule of current affairs shows. There are three such programs on the first German network, "Panorama," which originates in Hamburg; "Report," which originates in Munich and Baden-Baden; and "Monitor," which originates in Cologne. Each of these programs gives extensive coverage to parliamentary affairs and general governmental activities. There are studio facilities available in Bonn, so it is unnecessary for a member of the Bundestag to go to his home constituency or to the main studios of the originating station in order to appear. The second German network, ZDF, also carries a program of this type and likewise has studio facilities in Bonn.

Critics charge that the German programs are not as scrupulously fair as those conducted by the BBC and ITN in the United Kingdom. Politics is a much more pervasive factor in the conduct of the affairs of the German television stations and networks. The chief executives of each of the Länder stations have staffs rounded out with political appointees. What balance is maintained is maintained largely by strict surveillance of the stations by the parties, who keep detailed records and probably actually record a good deal of the program material. Evidence gained by such checking is available for complaints and for fulminations against unfair programming.

Given this great volume of political news, what of the public? Does the public care? The proliferation of independent station and group bureaus in Washington furnishing individualized coverage to subscriber stations and the growing enthusiasm of members of Congress for using the bureaus reflects a high degree of public interest in affairs in the national capital.

The interest of the executive departments of the United States government in encouraging use of television facilities has at best been spotty. The Department of Defense and the Department of Agriculture have been leaders. Others have shown varying degrees of enthusiasm, but all at lower levels.

The Department of Agriculture came into the television era with a long record of experience in producing programs for radio and in assisting in independent production of radio programs. An active and agrressive film production unit had long been making product for both theatrical and 16 mm usage.

The Department of Defense had similarly been producing radio programs and supported a competent film unit staffed by persons who had substantial experience in commercial film production. The move into television was relatively simple and painless. Upon its creation in 1948 the Department of Defense acquired the rather substantial film libraries of its three component services, Army, Navy, and Air Force, and the personnel to staff those film units. The extraordinary success of DOD's television and film activities and the size of its public relations budget made it a natural target for CBS News's controversial "Selling of the Pentagon."

Many of the other departments had had extensive experience in print, notably Commerce and Interior. But both were slow to make the move into television.

One of the major factors in making the executive departments in the Nixon era conscious of television is the work of the Director of Communications, Herbert Klein. Klein, from the moment he moved into the Executive Office Building, started an educational program with the Secretaries of the various departments. One of the benefits resulting from the Klein program was improved liaison between the reporters covering Washington for television and the Secretaries, Undersecretaries, and Assistant Secretaries and bureau heads in the various departments.

Klein has been working assiduously to discover methods of going over the heads of the Washington broadcast news corps to reach directly to television personnel in the home communities. One of the devices he has used has been to enlist the support of White House staff members and cabinet members who frequently travel widely throughout the country for speeches and public appearances as a result of Klein's careful training program. Such emissaries of the Administration are prepared to hold airport news conferences, appear on local television, carry on conversations with local editors, and brief various key groups in the community. This is an added burden to the traveling cabinet members, but considered well worthwhile by the Administration's director of communications, who is skeptical of what he regards as the filtering process through which Washington news goes before it reaches out into the hinterlands.

A number of cabinet members had set high standards at an earlier period. Robert McNamara, when he was Secretary of Defense, was considered one of the most skilled at the use of the television medium. His press conferences were models of precision, information, and effective use of charts, graphs, blackboards, and pointers. Ramsey Clark as Attorney General was likewise considered one of the star performers among the cabinet members.

One of the first to face the television cameras in a formal press conference was Secretary of State John Foster Dulles. Shortly after President Eisenhower participated in his first filmed press conference in 1955, the networks started extending enthusiastic invitations to the Secretary of State to participate in similarly filmed press conferences. The advisors resisted for some time, but finally agreed to bring the Secretary to the camera for a summary, after the conclusion of a regular non-televised press conference. These summaries were standard operating procedure for a time but gradually dwindled off into vacuities. Finally, on one occasion, the only statement which the Secretary was willing to read before the television camera related to a telegram he had sent to the government of Paraguay congratulating that government on celebrating the anniversary of its independence. When it was revealed that this would be the substance of the news from the Secretary, the television cameras were immediately pulled out, leaving Mr. Dulles with an empty room.

The Secretary, when his press conference was completed, came out to the anteroom looking for the television cameras and was astonished at not finding them. It was explained to him that television network programs had very little use for soft news items and that it was hardly worthwhile to carry on with the filming program if this was all they were to get. It would make much more sense, they argued, if they were permitted to move their cameras into the actual press conference itself. The Secretary went home, thought about it, watched television programs for a while, and finally decided to permit cameras in. This had a profound effect upon the State Department all the way from the top executive level down through the ranks and was a significant turning point. From that day executives throughout the entire department were alert to the possibilities for reaching the public through television and planned methods for its utilization.

The increasing warmth in relations between television editors and program producers on the one hand, and representatives of the governmental departments on the other, has come about in part because of the increasing importance of television throughout the world reflected in vastly higher set density, but also in part because of the enlistment into the government public relations ranks of public relations advisors more attuned to modern communications and understanding of the requirements of television. Thus, when Herb Klein assumed his post as Director of Communications, he was able to work with a cadre of relatively well-equipped and experienced personnel.

Outside the United States, some of the most extensive efforts to promote government activities on television broadcasts are evident in West Germany. The West German government carries out a substantial program of film production involving virtually all departments of government. The focal point is the Bundespresse, the German press and information office, which reports directly to the chancellor. This office coordinates and synchronizes the press policies of these departments much in the manner of communications director Klein in the United States. Film programs produced either by the department directly or coordinated through the Bundespresse are made available to German television for use at their discretion. They are likewise used for German overseas propaganda purposes.

The role of the cabinet minister in the parliamentary system is considerably different from that of the secretary of the department in the United States, who has no parliamentary status. The cabinet minister, on the other hand, is both a member of Parliament and head of a government department. In this dual role he has frequent opportunities to appear on regularly scheduled television news broadcasts and interview and discussion programs. This is particularly true in the United Kingdom, where many of the 100 or more discussion programs broadcast each year featuring members of Parliament, involve one or more cabinet ministers. The activities and policies of the ministry are thus exposed through the appearances of the cabinet minister himself, who usually has developed a thorough acquaintanceship with television through numerous appearances.

Some of the smaller agencies, bureaus, and administrations, particularly those which must keep in close touch with the public, or which are dealing with topics of intrinsic public interest, have developed effective policies for dealing with television. Notable among these are the Internal Revenue Service, the Federal Aeronautics Administration, the Civil Aeronautics Board, the Bureau of Census, the Weather Bureau which is now a part of the larger National Oceanic and Atmospheric Agency, and perhaps the most sophisticated of all, the National Aeronautics and Space Administration. The most dramatic television of the decade of the '60s developed through NASA projects and was stimulated and aided by NASA professionals.

NASA felt a compulsion to carry its program intensively to the public for two reasons. In the first place it was felt that United States' national prestige had suffered a vicious blow when the Soviet Union succeeded in becoming the first nation to project itself into space. The second factor was the requirement for enormous sums of money in order to launch the vast research and development projects which would be required in connection with putting an American citizen on the moon during the decade of the 1960s.

The two objectives complemented each other. The vigorous public relations effort to make every small American step into space look like a major victory was designed to increase interest in the whole program and presumably encourage a more favorable attitude in Congress from which appropriations had to come. On the other hand, the vast expenditures of money had to be justified; and what better justification could there be than play by play television coverage of the thrill, excitement, anxiety and suspense involved in another mission in space.

In a sense the NASA public relations men gave the American people bread and circuses. The race for space furnished enough thrills and contest elements to keep the budget rising when it was essential that NASA have virtually limitless sums to spend. The funds were essential to assure success of the moon landing to which Preident Kennedy had pledged the country at the opening of the decade. NASA's beginning efforts were inauspicious. It was that administration's director of public relations who had to issue a cover-up story when Francis Gary Powers disappeared over the Soviet Union in May 1960. It was he who was blamed for misleading the press when Powers showed up in the possession of Soviet army personnel only two days after the NASA story had confidently said that he had disappeared on a weather flight over the Turkish border.

It didn't take NASA long, however, before its public relations personnel were among the most sophisticated in the business. Some of its motion picture films have been masterpieces of production. Its capability for interesting the American networks in devoting hundreds of hours, millions of dollars, and almost limitless ingenuity to coverage of the space flights is testimony to its skill in obtaining media support.

All of the gigantic propaganda apparatus of government, whether it be in the United States or elsewhere, diffused as it is by department, sub-department, bureau, agency, administration, or commission, serves a vital function as a link between the policy makers and the administration and the citizen voter.

The functioning of a democracy depends in large part on this link. It is obvious that at times, perhaps many times, its aims are political rather than informational; self-serving rather than in the public interest; narrowly partisan or even defensive, rather than designed for the greater good of the greater number. But in its information disseminating and policy exposition roles and in its contacts with the media, it serves as an essential arm of government. Without its efforts to search out facts, synthesize policies, serve as go-between and arranger, the media would be hard put to function simply because of the magnitude of the job.

It is undoubtedly true that television news is reaching elements of the public who never read newspapers, and if they did, only glanced at headlines or read the comic strips, either because they were illiterate or uninterested. Radio has the same capacity as television to reach the illiterate and semi-literate, but it lacks the easier-to-follow, easier-to-understand, more entertaining, illustrated story for which television is particularly adept. By reason of its capacity to convert news into simplified, illustrated stories, television has broadened the base of democracy to the extent of bringing former dropouts to at least a minimal level of understanding and interest, and thus likewise enlarged the base of communication between policy maker and voter.

The process of intercommunication between policy makers and public is reflected in the desire of policy makers to shape policy in such fashion that it will get favorable notice in the media and thus greatly improve chances of gaining public support. It has long been true that the policy makers create new policy with one eye on the policy itself and another on the syndicated columnists and the editorial pages of the major national newspapers. Now veteran observers in Washington are beginning to suggest that the reactions of Walter Cronkite, David Brinkley, John Chancellor, Howard K. Smith, Harry Reasoner, and Eric Sevareid, are similarly taken into account before decisions are made.

Looked at from the public side of the spectrum, television

has played a significant role in creating issues of such urgency and importance that agencies of government have been forced to act on such crucial issues as civil rights and the Vietnamese war. In each case an often reluctant government has been forced to take action because public sentiment reflected in the communications media has made such action mandatory.

It cannot be said that television has revolutionized the relationship between government and the public, but it has certainly added another dimension to that relationship and opened up a new and frequently purer channel of communication—one which sometimes functions in both directions.

FACE TO FACE:

THE TELEVISION DEBATE

```
┌─────────────────┐
│  ┌───────────┐  │
│  │           │  │
│  │     8     │  │
│  │           │  │
│  └───────────┘  │
└─────────────────┘
```

One of the most controversial elements in the 1960 presidential campaign was the series of confrontations between the two major candidates, which have been given the romantic, and highly misleading title: "The Great Debates." These appearances by Senator Kennedy and Vice-President Nixon have been more talked about, written about, discussed, researched, analyzed, and generally worked over than any political innovation of the television era. They were subjected to more than thirty public opinion research projects to determine their influence on the outcome of the election. They were the subject of a noisy—if not acrimonious—argument about production, lighting, and makeup after the first confrontation. The question of whether it was permissible to use notes was a subject of a bitter argument between the two candidates after the second debate. These confrontations have been condemned almost hysterically by some critics for not being "great debates" at all. But more than 100,000,000 persons saw and heard some part of one or more, and the average audience ran somewhat in excess of 60,000,000 for the four appearances, a figure much higher than for the combined entertainment programs which were replaced.

Perhaps most importantly, the debates are credited by many experts with having been a decisive factor in the campaign.

Many experts credit John F. Kennedy's election to the presidency to his success in the first of these encounters. At the conclusion of the first debate on September 26, 1960, it was being confidently predicted that similar joint appearances would henceforth be a traditional feature of presidential campaigns; 1960 had set a pattern that would prevail into the indefinite future. President Kennedy reaffirmed, on a number of occasions after his election, that he would participate in similar face-to-face discussion sessions in the 1964 campaign. Two presidential elections—1964 and 1968—have now come and gone without a repeat of the 1960 confrontations. And the evidence seems clear that a repetition of the 1960 series in future presidential years is most unlikely. If similar confrontations are ever scheduled again, it appears certain that incumbent candidates will not participate, thus limiting the device to those presidential campaign years when neither candidate has occupied the White House.

The 1960 debates, however, engendered so much excitement and their repercussions have been so widespread both within the United States and elsewhere in the democratic world that they justify a close look. Although the debates were billed as an innovative phenomenon of the electronic age, they were new only insofar as major presidential candidates in the final stages of a campaign had never before participated in similar face-to-face sessions. Candidates Kennedy and Hubert Humphrey had debated in West Virginia in the April 1960 primary; candidates Kennedy and Lyndon Johnson at the Democratic convention in Los Angeles during July; and Kennedy and vice-presidential candidate Henry Cabot Lodge during the senatorial campaign in Massachusetts in 1952. Many political experts credit the debate between New York Governor Thomas E. Dewey and Harold E. Stassen in Portland, Oregon, in April of 1948, carried on national radio networks, with being a major factor in Dewey's victorious campaign for the Republican nomination in that year. Candidates for lesser offices have frequently argued their cases before television audiences since the advent of television. In the pre-television period the same Richard Nixon owed in part his election to Congress for his first term there in 1946 to a debate with incumbent Jerry Voorhis.

But 1960 was the first year that presidential candidates were willing to enter the same studio, occupy the same rostrum, and discuss the same issues for a nationwide audience provided by television. The first suggestion for such an electronic confrontation came in 1952 from the late Senator Blair Moody of Michigan during his participation in the CBS television discussion program "Peoples Platform." [1] Moody was a former *Detroit News* Washington correspondent who had recently been appointed to the Senate following the death of Senator Arthur Vandenburg. It was only a matter of days before the Moody suggestion became the prize in a CBS–NBC internetwork public relations contest. The network rivalry to claim credit for stimulating debate between presidential candidates was to last more than eight years and was not culminated until candidates Kennedy and Nixon accepted telegraphed invitations from NBC president Robert Sarnoff during the last week of July 1960 to participate in a series of "Great Debates." NBC's alertness in getting the telegrams off to the two candidates almost immediately after Nixon's nomination in Chicago at the Republican convention won the day temporarily for NBC.

It was only ten days after the Moody comment on "Peoples Platform" that CBS president Dr. Frank Stanton wrote to Senator Moody expressing interest, if not enthusiasm, for his idea.[2] Stanton, however, pointed out that the suggestion would be very difficult to implement in view of the existence in the federal statutes of Section 315 of the Federal Communications Act of 1934. Section 315, the frequently misinterpreted equal time clause, specifies that if a broadcaster gives times to one candidate running for office during the period of an election campaign it must provide similar time for all other candidates running for the same office. In many local situations this is not a particularly serious hazard, since there are freqently only two candidates and seldom more than three or four. In presidential election campaigns, however, there have consistently been from twelve to sixteen candidates and sometimes more officially and duly qualified on the ballots of one or more states. The hitch in scheduling a series of debates between the two candidates of the major parties would have been that each other candidate running for the presidency in that same year would have had to have been given similar, if not wholly equal time. Obviously this would have been totally out of the question—which Dr. Stanton pointed out to Senator Moody.

Notwithstanding Section 315, however, Dr. Stanton did get in touch with the Eisenhower forces to suggest an Eisenhower–Stevenson debate. General Eisenhower deferred to the president of the Batten, Barton, Durstine & Osborn Agency, Bernard C. Duffy, who gave the suggestion a flat and abrupt turndown. NBC's president, Sarnoff, in the meantime, also saw the interesting possibilities involved in the Stevenson–Eisenhower debate and fired off letters to both, offering NBC facilities. The answer was the same as in the case of Stanton's invitation—a flat rejection.

Stanton and Sarnoff, then, going their separate ways, launched an eight-year campaign to obtain the repeal of Section 315, at least as it applied to presidential candidates of the two major parties, a goal which was finally achieved in August 1960. The two presidents used a number of other arguments concerning the harassment that broadcasters were often subjected to by minor party candidates; but always the principal objective, as explained to congressional committees, was to make it possible to schedule a series of confrontations between the presidential candidates of the two major parties. There had been enough indication of support for such a move during the spring and summer of 1960 to enable both Stanton and Sarnoff to move forward with confidence in extending specific invitations to the two candidates, even before legislation suspending Section 315 as it applied to presidential elections was passed. Final sus-

pension came August 24, 1960; by by that time it was a foregone conclusion that Congress would act favorably. Both candidates had agreed a month earlier to participate, thus defusing
any lingering opposition.

The 1960 year was a particularly favorable one to renew the
campaign for repeal. Neither candidate would be an incumbent
president, so the "dignity of the office" would not be at stake.
It was true that neither candidate was an incumbent in 1952,
but television was still in an infant stage as a campaign medium
and was taken seriously only after the national conventions.
In 1956 General Eisenhower had not the slightest interest in
the debate idea and, although some tentative feelers were extended, they were extended without much hope of success.

Section 315 was still on the books on July 27, 1960, when
delegates to the Republican National Convention balloted at
the International Amphitheater near the Chicago Stock Yards
in the city's southwest side. There wasn't much doubt how the
balloting would come out; it was a foregone conclusion that
Richard Nixon would be their overwhelming choice, which indeed he was by a vote of 1531 delegates to 10 for Senator Barry
Goldwater of Arizona. On that night Robert Sarnoff's wire of
invitation was despatched to Vice-President Nixon, and just
before he went before the convention on Thursday night, July
28, to deliver his acceptance speech, word was leaked through
some of his aides that he intended to accept.

There was brief consternation in the CBS ranks until telegrams were framed extending similar invitations to the two
candidates. It should be noted that the Sarnoff invitation specifically suggested that Nixon and Kennedy participate in a
series of confrontations which were to be called by the formal
title: "The Great Debates."

Kennedy accepted first and Nixon's formal acceptance spelling out his terms and conditions arrived in Sarnoff's office three
days later.[3] There was one significant line indicating that the
performances were to be "conducted as full and free exchange
without prepared texts or notes, and without interruption, and

with time for questioning by panels of accredited journalists." The two points, "without texts or notes," and "panels of accredited journalists," were both to be points of contention during later negotiations. After CBS had despatched its invitations, the American Broadcasting Company and the Mutual Broadcasting System Radio Network did likewise, so that all seven networks (three television and four radio) had by that time extended invitations. But this was only the beginning.

Members of the Nixon staff, except for the vice-president's closest advisors, Robert Finch and Herbert Klein, were as surprised as CBS at the NBC coup. The candidate had told his campaign staff at a May meeting at the Statler Hotel in Washington that he would not participate in any debates at any time. "There will be no debates," Nixon had said then. "There can be no conversation about debates. I won't tolerate it," he added. President Eisenhower had given him similar counsel in precise and unmistakable terms. A shock wave ran through the members of the Nixon staff, Leonard Hall, Carroll Newton, James Bassett, James Shepley and General "Jerry" Persons. Rumors indicated that Leonard Hall had briefly threatened to resign his position as Nixon's campaign manager as a result of his disappointment over the vice-president's decision.

No one on the Nixon campaign staff, however, believed that the debates would actually ever come off. Staff members felt that negotiations between the representatives of the candidates would pose so many obstacles to agreement that they would make it virtually impossible to arrive at mutually acceptable terms and conditions. They were confident that stalemate and abandonment of the plan was inevitable. They might very nearly have been right. The big problem was not getting an acceptance in principle from the two candidates; it was hammering out a formula acceptable to both sides.

Negotiations started in a suite at the Waldorf-Astoria Hotel on the afternoon of August 9, 1960. Representatives of all the networks involved were in attendance, as were representatives of the candidates.[4] There was a good deal of sparring over some of the issues which were pertinent and some which were extraneous. Each of the networks, for example, had offered, if Section 315 were to be deleted from the books, a total of eight hours to be used for free coverage of the presidential campaign, with a specification that at least four of these hours were to be devoted to direct confrontation between the two principal candidates.

At the opening of the Waldorf-Astoria session, the candidates' representatives probed for a while to determine whether it would not be possible to obtain all of the eight hours free for use as they saw fit. Or, in the event that there should be some confrontation program, whether they could use the additional hours in any way they desired. They were quickly disabused of the notion by the network representatives who specified that free time would be provided only on the basis that the networks would set the formats. Nothing conclusive came out of the August ninth meeting, except an agreement in principle that there would be direct confrontations between the two candidates, with the details to be worked out at a later date.

On August 24th the repeal of Section 315, as it applied to candidates for president and vice-president, was finally enacted. On August 31st the representatives of the candidates and the networks met again.[5] This time the meeting room was a dark, low-ceilinged, interior suite at the Mayflower Hotel in Washington, D.C. By the time the network delegation arrived, the candidates' representatives, including Leonard Reinsch and Theodore Sorenson for Senator Kennedy, and Fred Scribner, Jr., Under Secretary of the Treasury; Herbert Klein, the Vice-President's press secretary; and Ted Rogers, a television specialist, for Vice-President Nixon were seated.

The first part of the meeting was essentially a rehash of the session at the Waldorf-Astoria three weeks earlier. There was one evidence of softening of attitudes, however. The candidates' representatives were ready to commit on three or four confrontation-type programs, provided they would then have free access to four open hours to use as they wished. Reinsch, representing the Democrats, was more enthusiastic about this point than Scribner, probably because the Democratic Party was, as usual, seriously short of funds.

It was soon obvious, however, that the representatives of both candidates had given considerable thought to plans for direct confrontation and were prepared to talk specifics. Scribner, as the principal spokesman for the group, suggested that the conferees aim generally at four confrontations, the first and the fourth to be in the nature of debates, and the second and third, press conferences. The representatives of the candidates were interested only in broad topics covering general areas. They refused to consider framing a specific proposition which would limit the areas of discussion. Their desire was that one of the two debate type programs be devoted to domestic policy and the other to foreign policy.

The network representatives were opposed to the press conference format and made a strong case for formal debate. CBS particularly argued for the Oregon plan in which the two debaters, after making their opening statements, cross interrogate each other and then go back to concluding summary speeches. Scribner and Reinsch were adamant and wouldn't budge an inch. They insisted that there be a panel of interrogators, preferably four at all four shows. If they were to be forced to accept the press conference format, the network representatives specified that all panelists would be selected by the network personnel from their own staffs. This demand led to another quarrel with representatives of the candidates, who insisted on the inclusion at some point of representatives of wire services, newspapers, and news magazines.

Notwithstanding the bickering over detail, it appeared at this point as if an acceptable compromise would eventually be reached. The optimism was shattered a moment later when Scribner again raised the question of the eight hours. If there were to be four debates, the parties would program the other four hours as they wished. Network representatives insisted that the offer of four hours for the debate-type programs was firm, but that the additional four hours would either be used for appearances on already scheduled discussion programs or abandoned. CBS offered four hours of appearances on its "Face the Nation" panel interview program and additional exposure on "Person to Person," featuring Edward R. Murrow, who interviewed celebrities in their homes. "Person to Person" was a highly rated nighttime program. CBS, in addition, offered another hour for a joint appearance of the vice-presidential candidates. The NBC offer was for four multi-network programs of the type previously discussed plus an additional four hours, two to each party: one to accommodate the vice-presidential candidates, and one the presidential. That left NBC with two hours still to be discussed.

Both networks insisted they would control the non-debate hours. Scribner, noting an impasse developing, suggested a recess. Network personnel left the room and wandered aimlessly in the corridors for fifteen minutes awaiting an invitation to return. When the signal came it was apparent that the Kennedy-Nixon forces were sufficiently impressed by the firm network stand that they were ready to abandon their claim for the four clear hours on their own terms and start talking specifically about four joint appearances. Scribner then redirected attention to the four confrontations. He had previously specified that there could be a one-hour debate sometime on September 26 originating in Chicago. This would be devoted to domestic policy. Another debate would be scheduled for October 21, originating from New York City and relating to foreign policy. It was obvious that Scribner and Reinsch and their associates had tried one last gamble to try to pry loose the additional four hours on their terms. Having been rebuffed, they were willing to get back to the original objective. It became evident that their planning had been much more detailed than network personnel suspected. Without any delay Scribner started spelling out the format on which both sides had apparently agreed. He said that on two programs there would be eight-minute opening statements from each of the candidates, a question-and-answer period for thirty-four minutes and three-minute summaries.

The other two programs, as spelled out by Scribner, called for a news conference format, with the two candidates answering in tandem questions put by a panel of four representatives of the working press including wire services, newspapers, news magazines, radio and television. These two programs were to be booked on October 7 and October 13.

This led to two further points of contention: who should moderate the programs; and what should be the composition of the panel and who would select the members?

The network delegates proposed that an outstanding jurist, college president, or person widely known in public affairs, be selected as moderator. The representatives of the candidates demurred and insisted that it be a television professional. They argued that any person other than broadcast professionals would be inclined to impose his own attitudes and personality on the debates. They felt that a network professional would be in a much better position to maintain absolute neutrality. This argument was accepted with some reluctance.

The question of the composition of the panels was a stickier problem. The network group insisted that since these were network programs, all panelists should be network representatives. John Charles Daly of the American Broadcasting Company was particularly firm in this point. The Kennedy point of view suggested it would be satisfactory for the networks to designate all four of the panelists on programs 1 and 4—the debate type programs—but that there must be some representation of newspapers and wire services on programs 2 and 3. This point was not resolved when the meeting broke up and became the subject for considerable controversy at a later date.

It was decided to issue a press release designating the four dates as being acceptable to all parties concerned with the possible exception that a change might have to be made in the October 8 date because of a possible conflict with a football game that ABC had scheduled. There was some fear that a run-over into the debate might be irritating to the football fans in the event the game were cut off.

It was left then to the networks to offer specific times for each of the broadcast dates and to allocate production responsibilities. By a draw of numbers CBS won responsibility for the first broadcast, NBC for the second, and ABC for the third and fourth. The network representatives then decided that CBS, as the producing agency for debate number 1, would designate the chairman. Likewise, NBC would designate the chairman for number 2, and ABC for 3 and 4. Specific program times were selected within a few days; the major hurdles had been overcome much more easily than anyone had anticipated.

The question of an overall title for the debate series was left to the networks. Robert Sarnoff's letters and telegrams had described the series as "The Great Debates"; but there was considerable resistance within the network group to this title, since it didn't seem to be appropriate in view of the format selected. It was decided that the title card to be shown on the screen, introducing each debate, would carry the words: "Face-to-Face." In the body of the program it would be referred to as a "Joint Appearance." Even in view of this decision, which was apparently unanimous among the network personnel, NBC did not completely abandon its favorite "Great Debate" title. On the first program, a title card appeared on the NBC screen prior to the official debate opening, carrying the series title originally used in the Sarnoff telegram. All publicity, however, from all networks referred to the scheduled programs as "Joint Appearances."

The general tendency among critics following the series was to condemn the networks for permitting or encouraging the use of the press conference format. They were also chided for having introduced show business into the contests by insisting on the presence of reporters. The critics had been badly misinformed. The networks had held out until the very end for a formal debate concept rather than the press conference version upon which the candidates insisted. The reason for the network collapse at the Mayflower meeting on August 31 in Washington, D.C., was that they believed that it would better serve the public interest to compromise in the interest of getting firm candidate acceptance rather than run the risk of a suspension of negotiations.

The first of the joint appearances took place in the studios of WBBM-TV, a CBS-owned station in Chicago, on Monday, September 26. The set had been designed in New York by a graphic arts specialist on the CBS corporate staff, Louis Dorfsman. CBS president Frank Stanton had consulted with Dorfsman from time to time before the original design was drawn and while Dorfsman was experimenting with several approaches. His role was significant. The set was built in New York and shipped to Chicago to be set up in WBBM-TV studio No. 1 on Sunday, September 25.

The furniture was contemporary Danish and the lecterns from which the two speakers would work were not much more than music stands. (Men's locker room modern, some critics said.) The set itself turned out to be somewhat lighter in its gray scale than anticipated, so it was repainted to darken it a little on the day of the broadcast. Finally a scrim was hung over the set in order to soften it somewhat and intensify the gray. After the lighting had been carefully set by a lighting specialist from CBS headquarters in New York, the Nixon advisors insisted on placing two additional flood lights on the floor in front of the vice-president. This was standard operating procedure in lighting Nixon in order to lighten up some of the darkness under his eyes and soften his features.

The WBBM building had been carefully checked out by security forces, including Secret Service, FBI, and the Chicago police force. The building lent itself admirably to segregating press from the participants and the technical crews required to produce the broadcast. The interest in this first confrontation between two presidential candidates exceeded the expectations of any of the principals involved. While 200 were expected in the press delegation, some 380 actually appeared with credentials. Members of the network negotiating team had assumed that the top managements of the networks involved would be somewhat less than enthusiastic about making the trip from New York to Chicago to observe a program which could better be seen in their offices or homes in New York. As it turned out, when Senator Kennedy, the first of the participants to arrive, drove into the building, he was greeted by a receiving line that included the chairman and president of each of the four companies involved.

The candidates went directly to the production studio, posed for test camera shots and audio tests, chatted amiably with CBS representatives who were responsible for the production of the broadcast, and retired to designated waiting rooms until shortly before the starting time.

At precisely 8:30 P.M. CST a card appeared on television screens of all affiliated stations throughout the country with the words: "Face to Face." It was a few seconds earlier that NBC had projected the "Great Debate" card. The voice of Howard K. Smith, then a CBS News correspondent, broke the silence to say that the radio and television networks of the United States were bringing the public this "joint appearance," and the broadcast was under way. Senator Kennedy opened with an eight-minute speech. It was clear that he had no text or notes.

The opening statement from Vice-President Nixon left persons in the studio in a state of stunned surprise. They had expected the vice-president, with his reputation for pugnacity, belligerence, and toughness as a debater, to pounce on the senator from Massachusetts. Instead he was soft and conciliatory, and the blandness and conciliatory attitude persisted throughout the remainder of the hour. Following the program's conclusion the two candidates shook hands, chatted for a moment, and withdrew to return to their respective hotels. In the meantime, the press, released from the adjacent studios in which they had observed the proceedings, swarmed into the production studio to see for themselves an area which had previously been restricted to them. WBBM-TV continued with a special half-hour of programming, interviewing persons who had been in the studio for their impressions and political experts concerning their attitudes toward the debate as a new art form in political campaigning.[6]

The general attitude that night was that personal confrontations had become an essential part of United States political campaigning; that any candidate in the future would find it difficult to resist participation in a continuation of the "Face-to-Face" series. There was jubilation among network executives that everything had come off without a hitch, and a general state of euphoria prevailed. A secondary benefit of the programs came from the press coverage: banner headlines appeared in newspapers all over the country. The major newspapers carried complete texts; television critics devoted their columns to analysis of the event; editorial writers had a field day. In short, debate No. 1 turned out to be the most publicized single event in the entire campaign and later proved to be one of the highest rated television shows ever produced. More than seventy million persons, it was discovered through the rating services, watched the program, and most of them stayed through most of the entire sixty minutes program time.

CBS, however, was soon on the defensive following charges from the Nixon camp that the Nixon staff had been misinformed on light values and the gray scale of the set and that there were problems with the lighting. Newspaper columnists suggested the vice-president had been sabotaged by CBS makeup personnel, since the vice-president had looked pale and gray throughout most of the performance. Kennedy, on the other hand, appeared with a deep tan, probably a hold-over from the time prior to the campaign he had spent on Cape Cod and in Florida. The vice-president had recently been released from a hospital where he had been treated for an infection, and he was naturally pallid in contrast to his ruddy opponent.

It was later discovered that an inferior type of easy-to-apply makeup had been applied to the vice-president by a member of his own staff; thus, if anything, adding to the contrast between the two candidates. It was also soon discovered that the excessive light which upset the carefully achieved balance in the studio derived from the flood lights which had been placed in front of the vice-president by his own television advisors. The light suit he had worn was judged to have been a mistake. The error stemmed in part from misinterpretation of the description of the gray-tone scale of the set. The controversy was eventually put to rest on the other three programs, one of which involved an electronic confrontation with Vice-President Nixon in the studios of ABC on the west coast and Senator Kennedy in ABC studios on the east coast.

During the intervening period and continuing far beyond election day, a battery of public opinion analysts, content research specialists, television and radio head counters, social psychologists, and behavioral scientists had a field day with statistics, hypotheses, scripts, and reactions.[7] They finally surfaced with a variety of assumptions and some conclusions.

The evidence suggested that the appearance in the confrontations had given the Kennedy candidacy an enormous boost. Whether this stemmed from having "won the debate" or from stimulating new interest in himself and his campaign is still disputed. It is certain, however, that audiences for his personal appearances grew and, following the September 26th campaign, funds were easier to obtain. Voters who had previously thought that the vice-president was a sure winner began to regard Kennedy as a potential President of the United States.

Reactions from radio listeners, as opposed to television viewers, furnished an entirely different picture of the results. Television viewers seemed to be generally of the opinion that the edge, if any, went to Senator Kennedy; radio viewers, on the other hand, were more inclined to believe that the vice-president had been a clear victor. This was small consolation to the vice-president, however, since the radio audience represented only a fraction of the number of persons who watched the programs on television.

Behavioral scientists who did a careful analysis of the entire series of confrontations came to the conclusion that the Kennedy "victory," if such it really was, probably stemmed much more from the response to the images of the two candidates than to the contents of the programs or the debating skills exhibited.

An analysis of the texts of the four confrontations would reveal very little in terms of new approaches to campaign problems, sparkling diction, brilliant ideas colorfully stated, or even anything very new. Correspondents who had been traveling with the two candidates were convinced that all four confrontations consisted largely, on the part of both contestants, of paste-up jobs taken from the speeches they were accustomed to deliver several times a day before audiences at airports, supermarkets, parking lots, city hall plazas, and hotel ballrooms.

There was one specific result, however, which is still affecting politics and political campaigning in the democratic world. It wasn't very long after the conclusion of the 1960 campaign before the technique of the debate, largely copied after the format as agreed upon in the Mayflower meeting of August 31, began to appear in other countries around the world. The debate has become standard procedure in Germany. In the West German election of September, 1961, the candidates of the major parties appeared a few days before the election in an hour-long discussion session in which they were given an opportunity to outline their programs on the German television network. The program was chaired by a television commentator. In September 1969 the four major parties in the running, including the Bavarian wing of the Christian Democratic Party, were invited to send their leaders to Bonn to appear in a confrontation, also of sixty-minute duration, in which they would be queried by prominent television news and public affairs personalities.

Debates involving all parties are regular features of the

Swedish political campaign. The procedure there is to conduct three debates during the campaign. There are six contestants in each—one each representing the leadership of the five parties and a second representating the party in power. The reason for this concession to the party in power is that it is felt that the four opposition leaders will all be attacking the government, and the government, thus, deserves a bit of extra time to protect itself.

Three confrontations running 90 minutes, 120 minutes, and 180 minutes respectively, are spread out over the three weeks of the campaign. Subject matter is chosen as a result of consultation of the parties with representatives of the Swedish Broadcasting Corporation, which serves as referee. If there is any disagreement, the Swedish Broadcasting Corporation decides. There has been so much controversy concerning the role of the chairman in Swedish political debates that it has now become standard procedure for the Director-General of the Swedish Broadcasting Corporation to moderate the 180-minute confrontation which occurs during the last few days before the election.

The problem in Finland is somewhat complicated by the fact that there are seven parties in the running in that country. The procedure adopted by the Finnish Broadcasting Company is to permit each of the seven parties to assign two of its personnel—so the Finnish confrontation includes a total of fourteen persons. In the 1966 Finnish election both the Prime Minister and the Minister of Foreign Affairs participated for the party in power, and four party chairmen represented minority parties. The program took up a good part of the evening, running from 7:40 P.M. until 11:55, with an hour and twenty minutes intermission between 9:15 and 10:35.

Italy's debates are even more complicated than Finland's. In Italy eight parties qualify to participate in inter-party discussions. The Italians solved the problem by scheduling two debates of four parties each. By carefully drawing a line down through a theoretical political center, it is possible to balance each program: two parties from left of the center and two from the right.

The last country to commit itself to the use of this device in political campaigning was Japan. In the December 1969 election the Japanese Broadcasting Corporation, NHK, scheduled six separate fifty-minute confrontation programs on six consecutive days leading up to the election. The parties were paired off in six separate combinations. The two parties which had gained the most votes in the previous election, the Liberal Democrats and the Socialist Party, each were assigned three appearances; and the other three, the Democratic Socialists, Komeito, and the Communist Party, were each given two.

It is noteworthy that each of these confrontations follows a formula more nearly comparable to that employed by the 1960 Kennedy-Nixon debates than to a formal debate routine. It is also notable that all countries cited developed the debate format after the wide publicity given to the Kennedy-Nixon performances in 1960.

So, as the post mortems continued between the conclusion of the first Kennedy-Nixon joint appearance and the second scheduled for October 8th in Washington, the impact was felt throughout the world. As it turned out, the United States was one of the few countries in the democratic world which was not to carry on with the confrontation device in subsequent national political campaigns.

The second of the Kennedy-Nixon confrontations was to have taken place in Cleveland, Ohio, on October 8th; but it was discovered by NBC personnel that the NBC-owned station in that city lacked the studio facilities to meet production requirements. A careful inspection of other possible debate sites in the city proved similarly frustrating. As a consequence, the venue was moved to the NBC facilities in Washington, D.C., and both candidates agreed to go there. There were a number of items, however, that had not been settled. The most perplexing remaining topic of controversy was the composition of the panels of newspaper men for the second and third of the confrontations. The networks had insisted that the interrogators on programs one and four be selected exclusively from network news staffs and picked by the networks themselves.

It was understood by network personnel from Fred Scribner's statements at the Mayflower meeting that the two press conference-type confrontations, programs No. 2 and 3, would have panels of interrogators made up of two persons selected by the networks and two from press, wire services and magazines. Both Press Secretary Herbert Klein representing Vice-President Nixon and Pierre Salinger for Senator Kennedy were under considerable pressure from members of the press corps traveling with them, however, to get greater newspaper exposure. The two press secretaries took the offensive and insisted that no agreement had been made to limit the panel to four and to limit the press, wire service and magazine contribution to two for each of the two programs. In the meantime, another problem arose. Representatives of special interest groups, including civil rights supporters and labor union members, began clamoring for representation on the panels. The civil rights proponents were particularly difficult to reject, because neither of the two candidates was willing to incur the opposition of civil rights supporters. Network representatives were adamant in insisting that only representatives of press, radio, television, were able to function as true reporters—eliciting information from the two candidates, not delivering impassioned pleas for their own causes in the guise of interrogation.

Network representatives also held firm to what they considered to be a firm stipulation from Fred Scribner at the Mayflower meeting that only two press representatives would be selected for the second panel and two for the third. Salinger and Klein, while giving in reluctantly, sought to disengage from the responsibility of selecting the two press delegates. Their strategy was to shift the burden to the network committee. Network personnel resisted, however, and suggested that Klein and Salinger select print media representatives from the slate of reporters who had been traveling with them and the candidates they represented. Support was finally won for this point of view, and the two press secretaries went ahead to arrange for drawings to select personnel from their groups.

Klein's selection came from the bar of the hotel in which the Nixon party was staying one night a few days before the October 7th debate. Each person in the vice-president's party was given a number, the numbers were placed in a hat, and a barmaid was asked to select two numbers from a hat. So a barmaid is credited with the selection of Alvin Spivak of United Press International and Donald R. Levy of *Newsday*.

The rule barring notes and text which had been stipulated by Vice-President Nixon in his wire of acceptance during the Republican convention in July, and reinforced by Fred Scribner in subsequent meetings, became a subject of controversy immediately after the Washington encounter. Senator Kennedy appeared bearing a sheaf of papers which he placed on his desk. Following the conclusion of the program, according to observers in the studio, Vice-President Nixon protested violently over what he regarded as a breach of the agreement between the two contestants.[8] No notes, texts, or sheafs of paper were in evidence at the final two confrontations.

The only other element of controversy that marred the equanimity of the negotiating groups was the question of a fifth debate. Three Democratic senators in mid-October had recommended that since the fourth and last confrontation was scheduled for October 21st, a good seventeen days before the election, that there should be one more meeting at a date closer to the election. The three, Senators Mike Mansfield of Montana, Mike Monroney of Oklahoma, and John Pastore of Rhode Island, were obviously aware that the Nixon entourage had requested conclusion of the debate schedule at a relatively early date in order to give the vice-president an opportunity to campaign with all the vigor at his command and without necessity for being held directly accountable for statements made during the concluding days prior to the election.

The recommendation from the Senators, however, was enough to set in motion another series of negotiating sessions to determine where and when a fifth debate might take place, what its format would be, and who would be the participants. There was a good deal of feeling at this time that Democrat vice-presidential candidate Senator Lyndon Johnson and Republican candidate Ambassador Henry Cabot Lodge should somehow or other be brought into the programs.

The Nixon negotiators, as a counter proposal, argued that an additional hour should be added to the fourth of the confrontation series, thus running it from 10:00 P.M. until midnight. The additional hour, Nixon supporters argued, should be rounded out with questions from citizens appearing before cameras and microphones set up at various points around the country. The Democrats were dissatisfied with this device, however, since their principal objective was to force the Nixon people into a date closer to the election. Network representatives also resisted the plan on the basis that there was insufficient time to arrange the complicated mechanism which would be required.

It is doubtful, however, that either the Nixon or the Kennedy groups seriously wanted to have the fifth debate. Scribner and Reinsch continued sparring right up to Saturday, October 29, and then broke off their negotiations with an exchange of angry telegrams. In the meantime, CBS had won the draw for the fifth debate and had prepared security arrangements, printed admission badges, and was busy creating the stage set for a debate which was to have taken place on Monday night, October 31. But as of noon on Saturday, the 29th, the issue had been put to rest, probably to the relief of both candidates and their negotiators, as well as the network personnel who were relieved of the burden of arranging another confrontation.

There are a number of significant results which almost certainly stemmed from the debates. Not only were the audiences exceptionally large in contrast with the numbers of persons who normally tuned in for the pre-empted entertainment programs, but they were huge in terms of expectable ratings for political campaign speeches. The most significant difference between these confrontations and the standard political address was the fact that viewers were able, at one time and place, to watch both candidates and listen to arguments from both sidess of the political spectrum. It is assumed that persons inclined toward the Republican side will usually watch and listen to Republican candidates and, similarly, persons with Democratic inclinations will be tuned in for the Democratic candidate. In this case there was a very significant cross-over. Whether the cross-over was a factor in stimulating a better informed electorate is a moot question. Most behavioral scientists suggest that it was not. But there can be little doubt that the opportuntiy to see and hear two candidates at one time and in one place stimulated additional interest in the election. The additional advantages of the heavy newspaper follow-up plus intensive coverage by radio and television in subsequent news broadcasts must have substantially heightened the impact.

The effect on political party campaign methods in countries other than the United States has already been noted, but it is noteworthy that there was a similar impact on campaigns for lesser offices in the United States as well. Some form of debate, discussion, or confrontation involving candidates has since become commonplace in many sections of the United States. The device had been frequently used prior to 1960, but evidence suggests that there has been an upward surge since that time. The confrontation technique has been used since 1960 at all levels of government office in both primaries and final elections. A classic case is the contest between Senators Eugene McCarthy and Robert Kennedy, prior to the California primary in June 1968.

The Minnesota senator had been clamoring for weeks for a direct confrontation with the late President's brother. Kennedy had been skillfully dodging and delaying. His intention was to avoid at all costs a face-to-face meeting with his surprisingly strong opponent. McCarthy's unexpected victory in the Oregon primary on May 28th, however, forced a reassessment of the Kennedy strategy. The decision was finally made out of desperation, on the day after the Oregon loss, to accept the McCarthy challenge.

The day selected for debate was June 1, a Saturday. The occasion was to be an ABC television panel interview program called "Issues and Answers"; the site was to be an ABC studio in San Francisco. The format called for interrogation in turn of each candidate by a panel of ABC correspondents: Frank Reynolds, William H. Lawrence, and Robert Clark. Following each response, the opponent was to be given a chance for reply.

From the ABC point of view the event was an outstanding success. More than 32 million persons, according to rating data, watched the contest, which outrated entertainment programs on both competing networks.

Kennedy had canceled a meeting with 600 labor leaders to go into seclusion with his advisors, to prepare for the contest, much as his brother had prepared for his first confrontation with Richard Nixon in 1960. But McCarthy, too, took preparation seriously and briefed himself thoroughly before proceeding to the ABC studio at 6:00 P.M. on a Saturday night. Some 300 reporters packed into the two adjacent studios and a throng of pro-McCarthy supporters jammed the streets outside.[9]

The program proceeded exactly as planned. But the results were less than decisive. McCarthy called it a "no decision bout." "We were," he said, "wearing 16-ounce gloves." One observer described it as a "milk toast discussion"; another called it "tepid." Each side's supporters claimed victory, but it was Kennedy who was the victor in the California primary by a narrow margin.

It is possible that Section 315, which has consistently inhibited face to face confrontation in contests with large numbers of candidates, may be repealed either for presidential and vice-presidential races only or for all offices. But repeal will come only after vigorous opposition has been suppressed. Very few incumbent office holders will willingly create an opportunity giving their opponents a level of theoretical equality. It is this spirit of "let's-not-help-the-opposition" that has largely been responsible for keeping the Congress of the United States from voting campaign reforms for national elections in the past years. The office holder feels he has a special position and sees no reason why he should yield any of his advantages to the opposition.

It is conceivable that the debate form may be used again in a national presidential election in the United States at such time when two non-incumbents are contesting for the presidency. This could happen in 1972, if President Nixon is defeated in the 1972 convention or decides not to run for a second term, both of which seem unlikely possibilities. But it is more likely to occur in 1976. Perhaps by that year, marking the 16th anniversary of the Kennedy-Nixon confrontations, and the 200th anniversary of the Declaration of Independence, the United States may see a repetition in 1976 style, and with 1976 technology, of the "great debates" of 1960. But odds are against it. Few candidates will be willing to run the risk of an uncontrolled campaign environment that may have defeated Richard Nixon in 1960.

POLITICAL CONVENTION COVERAGE

The 1968 Democratic national convention was a shock to millions of Americans. Convention viewers, who constituted more than half of the entire American public, had been accustomed to viewing televised reports of political conventions with a mixed bag of varied reactions including party loyalty, enthusiastic candidate support, love of the game of politics, dislike of the opposition party, and fascinated boredom—all stirred in with a mild amusement at the curious antics of grown men on the convention floor. In 1968 they were stunned to see something vastly different.

Normal political rivalries, which at times become intense but hardly violent, gave way to a cold, hard bitterness that appeared irreconcilable. Whereas NBC's John Chancellor had been carried off the floor of the 1964 Republican convention in San Francisco in a good-natured effort to enforce an edict from the chairman, with Chancellor on camera talking into a microphone all the way, there was nothing good-natured about the blow that struck CBS's Dan Rather, also on camera with microphone in hand, on the convention floor in 1968.

As chaos, turmoil, anger, and bitterness dominated the convention floor, riots broke out on Michigan Avenue, and coverage of convention proceedings was interrupted to show police charging into ranks of demonstrators.

Divisions among delegates have rarely been so intense: war supporters versus anti-war; segregationists versus integrationists; urban dwellers versus rural; blacks versus whites; the young versus middle-aged and old; and new voters versus "the establishment." Supporters of Senator Eugene McCarthy for the Democratic nomination, who had been working so intensively since they began the New Hampshire campaign in early winter, and supporters of Senator Robert Kennedy, who had seen their candidate assassinated after winning the California primary, were totally frustrated. They were frustrated at the loss of the nomination; frustrated at convention procedures; and frustrated at the whole electoral process, particularly the delegate selection system which made it possible for Vice-President Hubert Humphrey to win the nomination without campaigning in the primaries.

When the convention was over, a badly-split, bitter, and impoverished party remained. There was little enthusiasm for the candidate who only twenty years earlier had been the courageous young spellbinder prepared to challenge the forces of conservatism and segregation; now he was reviled and condemned by the new liberals as a tired lackey of the discredited policies of the White House and totally out of touch with the times. The vice-president himself was disspirited and had little enthusiasm for the campaign in which he had to start almost immediately. The treasury was empty; normal sources of funding for the Democratic Party were pessimistic about the results of the election and hence unwilling to open up their checkbooks; no detailed campaign plans had been drawn; and the party was torn and divided as even the Democratic Party, notorious for it deep schisms, had rarely been divided before.

All of this led to some genuine soul searching regarding the whole convention process. The Democratic Party set up two commissions: one to study the convention procedure; the other the delegate selection process. The public, which had previously tolerated the foibles of the convention system with curiosity and a tolerant amusement, wondered whether some drastic revision should not be considered in order. The vice-president in private conversations, condemned the television camera as a major factor in causing the disarray of the convention. "It [the camera] just adds to the disorder," he said. "It adds to the confusion, promotes a kind of bizarre behavior. It slows down the work of the convention, and, more importantly, the convention's got some business to do."

Choas was really nothing new in conventions. The 1932 Democratic convention was considered by observers just about as chaotic as 1968. Bitterness became intense during the credentials battle at the 1952 Republican Convention in Chicago, and was relieved only when a member of the Puerto Rican delegation, Judge Marcelino Romani, in a heavy Spanish accent, called for a polling of the delegation. The dialogue between Judge Romani and the chair became so absurd that the whole audience roared with laughter.[1]

But the fact is that the 1968 Democratic convention focused attention anew on a political institution that seems an anachronism in this modern age. The convention process has been condemned as raucous, irrelevant, archaic, undemocratic, servile to the bosses, an adolescent bore, and an outrageous television network extravaganza. People began to ask again: Why use the convention system? Why not go to a direct primary? Why is the convention like it is? Why is there so much network coverage? And, particularly following 1968, they asked, "has television distorted the convention process?" or, conversely, "have the parties distorted the convention process for television's benefit?" These were questions well worth asking.

There are a number of important answers. From the television network point of view, the convention is a spectacle, a gigantic pageant; it carries a certain element of suspense, even though the identity of the presidential candidate is sometimes a foregone conclusion. It is one feature of government with a strong suspense element that broadcasters can cover. Importantly, for the broadcasters, it provides an opportunity for head-to-head competition so the networks can prove themselves in combat. This isn't true in the usual rating battles between programs in the prime evening hours, because the programs are usually of widely varying formats and types. It isn't even true when Walter Cronkite, the NBC Evening News, and Reasoner and Smith are in direct competition, because the news programs are built of different ingredients. During a political convention, however, the ingredients are precisely the same; the time devoted is essentially the same, except for some deviation on the part of the American Broadcasting Company in 1968, and it is possible through the ever-present rating services to measure the success of one network against another. Only national elections offer similar opportunities for direct competition.

The history of television coverage of political conventions is relatively short but longer than one who first saw televised conventions in 1952 might suppose. There was some coverage of the conventions of 1940, but only 100,000 homes in the United States were equipped with television receivers in that year and able to watch the Republican convention from Philadelphia. There was no television coverage in 1944 because of the war; but in 1948 the networks were out in full force. There still were, however, only 400,000 homes equipped with receivers in the seven Eastern seabord cities interconnected by network lines. This meant that only residents of a few areas in the northeast could watch the proceedings as Governor Thomas E. Dewey of New York was nominated by the Republicans, President Harry Truman by the Democrats, and Henry Wallace by the Progressives.

The real beginnings of television coverage of political conventions occurred in 1952. By early July 1952 between seventeen and eighteen million homes in the United States were equipped with television receivers and some sixty-seven cities from coast to coast were interconnected. Television was thus available to nearly one third of the total of United States public. The television networks started preparing early in 1951 for 1952 political coverage. CBS took the lead by approaching the two national committees in May 1951 to determine the possibility of commercial sponsorship of convention coverage. These conversations were undertaken because of the anticipated high cost of television compared to radio coverage in preceding convention years. It was assumed then that all costs, including equipment, manpower, production, travel, and the loss of revenue from preemption of programs, which would have to be cancelled in order to make way for convention coverage, would impose a financial burden of between $3 and $4 million on each of the networks reporting the conventions.

CBS personnel met with Republican National Committee Chairman Guy Gabrielson and Publicity Director William Mylander in late May 1951 and explained the nature of the problems involved. Gabrielson and Mylander inquired whether it might not be possible for the national committees of the two parties to obtain rights fees to the events in return for granting the privilege of commercial sponsorship. It was pointed out that payment of rights fees to the national committee probably would constitute a contribution to a national committee, and thus would automatically make the networks guilty of violating the "Corrupt Practices" act. The rights fees suggestion was quickly abandoned.

Reaching a decision on the question of so marked a deviation from previous conventions as to permit commercial sponsorship was not a matter that could be resolved immediately. Negotiations went on between the political parties themselves and between the parties and the networks, until, by fall, it was decided that sponsorship would be permitted, provided the networks lived up to a code. The code specified that whiskey and beer sponsorship were definitely forbidden, any sponsorship would have to be cleared with the national committees which would not arbitrarily withhold approval, and that commercials should come only at reasonable breaks in the program schedule.[2]

The first network to sign up a sponsor was CBS Television, which had a commitment from Westinghouse by the evening of December 26, 1951. About a week later NBC, operating under forced draft in view of the CBS sale, obtained a signed contract from Philco. ABC some weeks later succeeded in selling its coverage to Admiral. There was one clause in the CBS contract with Westinghouse that was later to stimulate coverage of pre-convention activities and also contribute to a decision on the part of the networks to cover all the proceedings of the convention from "gavel to gavel."

In the CBS-Westinghouse negotiations, Westinghouse had asked how much coverage they might expect. CBS, estimating very conservatively, indicated a minimum of approximately fifteen hours. This was predicated on covering highlights only, including opening ceremonies, keynote speeches, addresses by principal political figures and nominating speeches, demonstrations, balloting, and acceptance speeches, if any. The Ketchum, McCleod & Grove advertising agency, representing Westinghouse, then asked for a firm guarantee of twenty hours of coverage for fifteen hours of paid time. CBS ultimately accepted this compromise proposal which likewise became the basis of NBC and ABC contracts with Philco and Admiral, respectively. No thought had been given yet to "gavel to gavel" coverage.

Later on, however, as the network pool committee composed of the chief executives of news for the three networks began to investigate AT&T microwave and coaxial cable facilities which interconnected the country, it became evident that important areas including substantial segments of population and aggressive television stations were going to be served by only a single channel. This meant only one network could serve cities on these single channel lines. All of Florida, in addition to southern Georgia and Alabama, would have access to only one network service. Only a single microwave link extended southward from St. Louis to New Orleans and fishhooked back through Houston to Dallas, Forth Worth, Oklahoma City and Tulsa. And only a single service crossed the Great Plains to the West Coast. There were loyal affiliates of all three networks on these one-way single channel circuits. Some kind of an arrangement had to be worked out to provide equitable service for the three major networks. The ultimate solution was to make a firm decision that all networks would cover on a "gavel-to-gavel" basis. Service to single circuit areas would be furnished by the three networks on a rotating basis; each network would thus have an equal chance to serve its affiliates.

The next step in the procedure was the selection of the convention site. Fortunately for television, both national parties had agreed on Chicago as the convention city. This eliminated the necessity of setting up duplicate facilities. Network personnel were fearful, however, that party officials would select as the convention site the Chicago stadium, a building with inadequate space to install television facilities. The International Amphitheater would accommodate some 5,000 fewer persons than the stadium, a disadvantage of no little concern to functionaries of the national parties who were understandably more concerned with having adequate tickets available to meet the pressures from loyal party members than with accommodating broadcasters.

The Amphitheater, however, was almost perfectly adapted to the requirements of television. The building was so designed that it had two floors of exhibit space on either side of the arena itself. Each of the four exhibit areas had roughly the same square footage as the arena; thus for each square foot of space in the arena proper there were roughly four square feet for auxiliary and support space. The network committee decided to make a determined effort to swing the site selection committee's decision away from the stadium to the Amphitheater.

Network representatives set out to plead their case before party chiefs. Their argument was apparently a revelation. Party chiefs had not realized that the networks estimated that nearly

18,000,000 homes would be equipped with television receivers by July 1st when the convention preliminaries would start; they were not aware that some 67 cities would be interconnected by that time, and that the television signal could reach some 75 percent of the urban centers of the country. They hadn't realized that up to 50,000,000 persons might be able to look in—and probably would—on some portion of either or both conventions. They had not realized that this enormous audience bonus could be jeopardized, unless the International Amphitheater were selected as the convention site.

Television won its first skirmish with the high moguls of the political parties. It was only a preliminary skirmish—the main battle was yet to be fought; but at least the party leadership grudgingly recognized that a new force in political life was burgeoning. It is conceivable that no one—not even the network representatives—anticipated the revolutionary impact that television would demonstrate only seven months later in July, but the groundwork had been laid.

The networks kept up the pressure for cooperation. Since the Republican convention was to be held two weeks preceding the Democratic, the heaviest pressure was exerted on the GOP. A network delegation went to a meeting of the Republican national committee in San Francisco in early January 1952 with charts and tables to demonstrate to the party's arrangements committee what could be expected from television. It was felt that precedent set by the Republicans would quickly be adopted by the Democrats.

It was still necessary to fight for such privileges as removing blocks of seats in the balconies in order to place cameras in strategic positions, arranging for a center camera platform on the convention floor which would enable head-on shots of the speakers at the rostrum, and obtaining adequate support space in the wings to set up studio and control facilities. Party officials were aghast at the size of the staffs required to enable television to function effectively. They were baffled by the volume of floor passes requested in order to enable network personnel to move freely about the convention site, servicing electronic equipment, replacing tired crews, and exercising the same reporting privileges as the writing press on the floor of the convention. It is difficult now to realize that in the winter of 1952 it was essential that such a case be made. By 1956 the pendulum had swung over completely in the opposite direction: party representatives were falling all over themselves to cater to the requirements of television rather than resisting its demands.

Fortunately for television, the 1952 conventions turned out to be two of the most exciting of the twentieth century and the longest in terms of hours of deliberation between opening and closing gavels. Network personnel anticipated an interesting story, but were hardly prepared for the avalanche of news that poured out of Chicago as early as one week before the July 7th opening date for the Republican convention.

It had become obvious to the Eisenhower forces weeks earlier that the general could win the nomination only if the Taft forces were to be upset in meetings of the credentials committee. There were enough delegate votes in contested delegations —particularly in southern states— to swing the convention from the ostensible winner, Senator Taft, to the challenger, General Eisenhower. As a consequence, the focus during that preconvention week was on the deliberations of the credentials committee. The Taft forces in control of the party machinery decreed that the credentials committee should meet in closed sessions. The networks set up cameras outside the door of the meeting hall and buttonholed delegates as they left the hall for brief breathers. Eisenhower supporters, well instructed by their leadership, made use of this opportunity to state the Eisenhower case to the public through television facilities and used it to the hilt.

The networks, expecting a relaxing week prior to the opening of the convention in which they could set up their equipment, train their personnel, and tune up their machinery, found that the story was of such overwhelming interest that they started scheduling special programming. NBC was more alert than CBS because of its greater reserves of manpower and equipment and its more stable financial position. It was then clearly the number one news and information network. NBC's facilities were operating by Monday, June 30, one week before the official opening. CBS hastily swung into action and began its broadcasts on Tuesday, July 1.

The frustration of not being permitted into the credentials committee sessions induced two CBS staff members to look into the problem of installing a hidden microphone within the meeting room. A midnight scouting foray was successful in implanting not one but two microphones in well concealed positions where they could eavesdrop on proceedings. The CBS device worked. The signal was channeled directly to New York for recording so that tracing would be impossible; but Chicago reporters intercepted the signal to keep a running tab on proceedings. Only sixteen years later NBC producer Enid Roth was hailed into court on a charge of invasion of privacy for a similar bugging episode. In 1952, however, such ethical and legal considerations were a matter of slight concern.

Several precedents were set which were to persist through succeeding conventions, and to lead to some of the chaos, turmoil, and so-called circus atmosphere, which reached its climax at Chicago in 1968. The assumption had been made by network executives prior to the opening gavel that once the conventions were officially in session most programming, except for running news commentary from the "anchormen," would come from pool cameras. Interruptions of convention proceedings were regarded as rather unlikely possibilities.

The credentials committee, however, remained in session through much of the opening day and into the second day of the convention. Since the principal story of the convention remained in the credentials committee rather than with the cut-and-dried ritual taking place on the floor, the credentials committee became the main focus of attention. The rules committee, likewise, was involved in the Taft-Eisenhower dispute. Unlike the credentials committee, the rules committee **was** willing to permit the intrusion of television cameras. The networks enthusiastically took advantage of the opportunity, cutting in and out of official convention proceedings in a pattern that gave the viewer only a haphazard notion of what was actually transpiring on the convention floor.

Speakers who were looking forward to opportunities to appear before large national audiences discovered that they were speaking only to bored delegates milling around in the Amphitheater. The attractive woman Treasurer of the United States had made a thorough study of television and had determined that graphic arts would be a logical supplement to a successful speech on the rostrum. Her aides delivered carefully packaged charts and graphs to the network control rooms and to the pool, and a marked manuscript that indicated precisely when each of these visual aids should be employed. All her work was in vain. Only about one minute of her presentation was ever seen by the television audience, and none of her visual aids.

It had also been assumed that pool cameras would be adequate to cover the floor proceedings; that reports from correspondents on the floor carrying their walky-talky equipment would be broadcast in sound only, or that their reports would be used only for background purposes. NBC, however, had come equipped with small, portable shortwave cameras which quickly moved out onto the floor. To forestall the NBC advantage, both ABC and CBS quickly installed cameras of their own in their radio booths overlooking the convention floor. The cameras at first had difficulty spotting their reporters on the jam-packed floor as they buttonholed convention delegates and requested interviews. Ingenious but primitive flashlight signals were used to attract the attention of the cameramen high in the rafters above and behind the speaker's rostrum, so that they could zero in with zoom lenses. Wheeling cameras on pedestals onto the periphery of the floor was also attempted, but ran into stern opposition from sergeants-at-arms and security personnel.

All of this contributed further to disruption of convention

proceedings as observed by viewers in their homes, and also set a pattern for much expanded floor coverage in later convention years as portable cameras were to become more reliable and more compactly packaged.

Throughout both conventions television personnel were constantly discovering methods of flexing their muscles that they had not anticipated in advance. When General Eisenhower, after his nomination, left his suite at the Blackstone Hotel to descend in the elevator and cross the street to the Hilton where he took an elevator up to Taft headquarters to confer with the defeated Senator, television cameras followed him virtually every step of the way.

In 1952 the excursions away from the convention floor, while in a sense disruptive, did very little to divert attention from the main news story of the convention itself. By 1956, however, the experience gained, flexibility achieved, and the additional equipment available, made it possible for many more deviations from straight convention coverage, and the convention planners themselves contributed in some cases toward the disruption of their own proceedings.

The precedent set by planning authorities for the national parties in permitting the disruption of their own proceedings gave the networks all the latitude they needed to proceed to program on their own. Events occurring on the rostrum became fair game. If they were judged to be interesting, pertinent to the central news theme of the convention, and of some inherent dramatic value, they were carried; otherwise they were unceremoniously dumped and the network reporters went prowling around for more significant, more interesting, and presumably more important news.

It was evident by 1956 that the parties had switched from their rather mild curiosity about television prior to the 1952 conventions, to whole-hearted enthusiasm for what television could do for the parties, and this led to excesses by party planners. Party authorities began to regard the political convention as a gigantic pageant—an opportunity to show their most attractive features in the most dramatic way to an enormous audience of American citizens. The production of motion-picture films for screening in the convention hall in the expectation that a major party promotional effort would be seen by millions of television viewers was one device undertaken to squeeze more value out of what seemed a golden opportunity for free publicity.

The greatest extravaganza of them all occurred when the Democrats gathered in Atlantic City in August 1964 to nominate President Lyndon B. Johnson for his first full term in office. There wasn't very much business to transact. If any delegate arrived with a notion that any candidate other than the president would receive the presidential nomination, he kept that opinion carefully concealed. The only doubt about the vice-presidential candidate was not whom the delegates would select, but rather whom the president would advise them to nominate and when. Writing the platform was an interesting exercise, but there were few courageous souls who were going to insist on inclusion within the party's statement of creed of anything which would cause a negative reaction from the White House. As a result there was really nothing serious to do except extol the virtues of the Democratic Party, former Democratic heroes and the President of the United States.

Accordingly there were three films, one daily except the second day, all produced with the slick professionalism of Hollywood. The smash finale was reserved for the last day of the convention, August 27, which, by carefully planned coincidence, happened to be the birthday of President Johnson. After the president had been duly renominated and his annointed choice for the vice-presidential nomination, Hubert Humphrey, had undergone the formality of selection by the delegates, there was a gigantic birthday party for the president followed by a spectacular fireworks display on the Atlantic City beach. This crashing conclusion of a four-day meeting put to shame the lack of showmanship at the Republican convention, six weeks earlier—or any previous or subsequent conventions of either Democrats or Republicans.

There is nothing intrinsically wrong with a national political party enjoying itself, programming in an entertaining way, and making a serious attempt to sell its attitudes and program by means of the facilities offered by the television networks. Through this emphasis on showmanship rather than convention business, however, in trying to cater to the networks the parties have given carte blanche to the networks to go their own way to find news rather than frivolity and party promotion.

The parties were not really geared to television in 1952, and the business of the convention in that year was so inherently newsworthy that any deviations on the part of the networks from the proceedings on the convention floor were almost uniformly directly related to the business at hand, and, for the most part, involved committee meetings in downtown hotels.

Between 1952 and 1956, however, a number of significant developments occurred. Television broadcast equipment, particularly for portable remote purposes, became smaller, more efficient and reliable; communications improved substantially; and staffs were more experienced. Competition was tougher. Networks had discovered that prestige gained during a political convention rubbed off on the overall network image. Plans for the 1956 conventions were made on the same elaborate scale as for 1952, with the main difference being that more equipment was assigned and more personnel recruited for the job. Both conventions turned out to be relatively cut and dried affairs. The only really newsworthy element was the race between Senators Kennedy and Kefauver for the vice-presidential nomination at the Democratic meeting. The well-prepared, well-trained, and well-equipped news personnel did what they were trained to do: look for news wherever it might be, but there wasn't very much.

Prior to the 1964 conventions, the CBS News convention election unit made a detailed analysis of the coverage by the three networks of the two 1960 conventions.[3] The analysis revealed that the opening ceremonies, consisting of presentation of the colors, singing of the National Anthem, the pledge of allegiance to the United States, and the invocation, were usually carried by the networks without interruption. The keynote speech and addresses by important party figures with national reputations were usually presented in their entirety; nominating speeches were rarely cut. Seconding speeches, after the first two or three, were fair game. Demonstrations for leading candidates were covered for a few minutes and were returned to intermittently if no other news of importance was being made on the floor. Balloting was carried from beginning to end without interruption. Benedictions were usually carried, but not in all instances. Anything else that occurred during the convention was subject to interruption or total elimination. Speeches by women apparently were total anathema to network executives.

This is not to say that the items substituted for those taking place on the floor were of greater importance or of greater news significance. It simply illustrates that a news executive makes his own decisions, makes them almost instantaneously, and doesn't have any particular reverence for the bulk of the convention procedure.

Network news executives were mildly curious why the convention planners retained the archaic format and continued the traditional ritual in the same old way, when it was perfectly evident that much of it was not getting on the air. They also wondered why it was not realized that deviation from serious business simply encourages the networks to switch to their roving crews of reporters, cameras, and sound equipment. But programming was considered a party function. Coverage of the story was considered the network role.

The failure of party officers to distinguish between the two obligations derives in part from the part that most convention executives have been too busy with convention business to watch television screens. They assume that all of their well-laid plans to present the attractive members of the party faithful in such ways as to gain the most favorable exposure are actually being seen by television audiences.

A more significant factor, however, is the amateur status of the convention planners themselves. The Democratic national committee, since 1944, has left much of the convention planning procedure to Leonard Reinsch, a broadcast professional; but, as the president of the Cox Broadcasting Company which operates a number of radio and television stations and cable systems, he can spend only part of his time on convention plans and preparations. Reinsch too must work with the arrangements committee of the national committee and its host of subcommittees, all of which are composed of amateurs in convention planning or show business and most of whom serve only for one convention or two at the most, and then frequently on different committees.

The Republicans have had their counterpart to Reinsch in former Senator George Murphy of California. Senator Murphy has had many years of experience as an actor and as an executive of the Technicolor Corporation which functions closely with motion picture production. But Murphy is involved only for the last few weeks before the convention. The basic planning has been done long before his arrival by members of the national committee assigned to an arrangements committee and assorted sub-committees on program, theme, entertainment, decorations, housing, transportation, tickets, press credentials, and the like.

The easy way out for the committee chairmen and their members is to carry on with the same old routines. There has been some evolution since the advent of television. There has been a reduction in the length of the nominating and seconding speeches. Demonstrations are no longer permitted to run until demonstrators fall in their tracks on the convention floor or get bored with the quadrennial tribal dance on behalf of their candidates. Polling of the delegations which took so much time in 1952 has been eliminated. If a delegation now asks for a poll, the state is bypassed while it goes into caucus and reports back at the conclusion of the normal alphabetical calling of the states. Some attempt has been made to encourage speakers to restrict the length of their orations, but generally the format has changed very little. There still are speeches by the national chairman, the temporary chairman of the convention, the permanent chairman, a keynoter, and by elder statesmen of the party. Appearances are usually arranged for rising younger party members, and by candidates for governor, congress, or senator, who are either in trouble or stand a good chance of ousting an incumbent from the other party. Some of this could undoubtedly be dispensed with, but political expendiency calls for carrying on the old routine even though, as Mark Sullivan once pointed out, the standard keynote speech is a "combination of oratory, grand opera, and hog calling."

Political expedience is one key; the financial consideration is another. Financing of a national convention normally costs a minimum of three quarters of a million to a million dollars. This is exclusive of the expenses of individual delegates and the enormous costs incurred by the wire services, newspapers, magazines, radio and television networks, and the radio and television stations who send swarms of reporters, producers, directors, and technicians to the scene. Routine expenses are usually met by contributions from the host city; but the quid pro quo is a guarantee that the convention will last for at least four days. The four-day minimum makes it mandatory that convention planners devote the first couple of days to routine party business, rounding it out with assorted speeches from party figures who are either deserving of exposure or are believed to be effective in convincing the general public of the party's sterling qualities and its capacity to furnish the country with sound and progressive government.

Political expediency is equally important. The opening ceremonies furnish the party with an opportunity to pay off debts to American Legion and VFW posts and to party-oriented drum-and-bugle corps. The national anthem provides an opportunity to show off Republican-oriented singers and the invocation and benediction Republican-oriented clergymen. Sports figures, war heroes, young party leaders or representatives of minority groups get their chance by leading in the pledge of allegiance. Presentation of gavels, medals and convention badges furnishes an opportunity for brief appearances by members who have performed unusual services for the party, or to honor geographical areas in which additional party strength is desired. Sometimes the motivation is simply to show an attractive new face for the party. By this procedure it is possible theoretically to mollify all wings of the party, represent all geographical areas, furnish exposure to a variety of minority groups, and trot out for exposure some of the party elders. It is always assumed by the convention planners that all of this will be seen on television, but even if it isn't, it is still assumed that it is eminently worthwhile, particularly since the time is available.

The evidence would seem to indicate that television hasn't really had much effect on the national political convention. There has been some tightening up of convention procedures, some elimination of non-essential routine; and certainly a more cooperative spirit with regard to meeting television's requirements for working space, floor passes, camera platforms, and access for cameras and microphones to the convention floor. Republicans expect to complete their 1972 business in three days, marking the first break in the four-day tradition, and Democrats are debating substantial reforms, but it appears that the 1972 extravaganzas will still bear striking resemblance to those that have gone before.

The fact is that the television viewer has probably been more profoundly affected by television's coverage of the convention process than have the conventions themselves, or the delegates. Some 55,000,000 persons looked in on some parts of those early conventions in 1952. In 1968 cumulative audiences ran in excess of 100,000,000. Much of the adverse reaction to the 1968 Democratic convention in Chicago resulted not from the attitudes of the delegates themselves, but from a mass wave of anger and resentment that swept through the country among persons who had seen the chaotic performance on their television screens. Much of the clamor for change in the convention procedure doesn't come from the members of the arrangements committees who have been regular convention goers, but rather from the passive viewer who watches the performance in his living room. He is the one who can't understand why dignified adults behave like adolescents on the convention floor, the reason for mechanical demonstrations which they have seen form up outside the hall, march in on cue, and snake through convention aisles, until they disappear again on a second cue; why delegates mill about on the floor carrying on conversations, responding to requests for interviews by radio, television and newspaper reporters alike; why they read newspapers and munch on sandwiches while speakers drone on on the rostrum. He legitimately wonders how this process can possibly succeed with all its excesses of hoopla, hijinks, and folderol in selecting the right candidates for the highest offices in the United States government.

The picture of convention coverage, as seen by the television viewer, is a curious mixture of excitement, glamor, tension, sometimes irritation if not outright anger, mixed with ennui, boredom, and mild amusement at the antics of the politicans engaged in their tribal rites. The convention seems to be a chaotic and unmanageable circus that doesn't reflect the significance of the process. The public becomes cynical when it sees its presidential candidate selected in so disorderly a manner by a combination of apparent despots and over-aged adolescents parading in outlandish costumes with New Year's Eve noisemakers. The whole process on occasion looks like a parody. No wonder, when this process was accompanied by violence in the streets, and apparent repression in the hall during the 1968 Democratic convention, the public became disillusioned.

But still the convention is apparently the most efficient process for selecting candidates for the presidency and the

vice-presidency, even though it may not be of any great consequence in writing party platforms. There are excesses, obviously; there are childish hijinks; and there is an ample dosage
of outworn ritual that may have served its purpose in the pre-
television days, but is now useful principally to use up time
until the four-day or three-day commitment to the host city
is met.

Can anything be done to the convention to make it more
compatible with the interests of the public and the needs of the
American government without damaging its news value for
television? There are a number of steps that can be taken both
by networks and national political parties.

I have covered ten national political conventions, six as the
chief executive in charge of all CBS planning and coverage,
three as broadcast news reporter, and one as the salaried executive program director for the Republican National Committee
at the San Francisco Convention in 1964; additionally, I was
the official party spokesman for the American networks in
negotiation with the two national committees prior to the 1952
party meetings, when many of the patterns of television coverage that still prevail were originally developed. Inevitably I
have drawn a few conclusions of my own.

The role of the media should be to furnish the public with
news coverage of the convention; it should be to look over
the shoulders of the convention delegates and officials as the
convention proceeds with the party business. It should not,
on the other hand, in any way influence the convention in
either its procedures or its deliberations. Thus, it is the business of the national committee to go about its procedures in
an orderly and efficient way and for the media to report what
they see and hear.

This does not mean that the national committee should not
facilitate convention coverage. The deliberations of the national convention are surely an important part of the whole
process of American government, and, as such, deserve continuing intensive coverage. But there is an important dividing

line between creating a convention for television viewers and managing one to accomplish the convention's business in an expeditious manner. Within this framework there are certain changes which could be made to eliminate some of the chaotic conditions which developed around the 1968 Chicago convention and to assist in bringing the focus back to the business of the convention and away from some of the sideshows which have a tendency to obtrude.

The ideal convention should probably be held in a theater-type auditorium with wide aisles and comfortable seats. This would mean limiting the delegate roll to somewhere between 500 and 1,000, a substantial reduction from the approximately 6,000 delegates and alternates who jammed the floor at the 1968 Democratic convention and the roughly 3,500 who have consistently attended Republican meetings.

There should be rigid policing on the floor to bar everyone but delegates. All the paraphernalia of broadcasting on the floor should be operated on a pool basis in which all broadcasters would share a cooperative signal. The convention program could very well be stripped of all non-essentials. The budget for such a stripped-down convention could be held at a low enough level to forego the four-day guarantee to the host city.

Television could be adequately served as it is at the United Nations. There is adequate space for pool cameras surrounding the meeting hall of the General Assembly, and additional cameras can be set up in delegate lounges adjacent to the auditorium. Television executives might be expected to protest vigorously upon notice that such rules were being enforced, but complaints would subside somewhat as soon as they realized the rules were to be applied evenly.

As to the convention itself, convention planners would do well to realize that there are two audiences to which they must appeal: the one in the hall and the vastly larger one outside watching television and listening to radio. It would do well to keep the two separate. A bit of showmanship which is designed

to entertain the delegates and visitors in the hall—or the award-
ing of a gavel, a badge, a medal, or the convention organ, to a
deserving Republican for political purposes, should certainly
continue to have its place in the convention program so long
as it is fully understood that the television executive will
exercise his right to choose those items which he wishes to feed
out through the lines to his network, and reject those which
he doesn't believe have a place in his program. Likewise, if it
is important to introduce candidates for Senate, Congress, or
governors' positions, and it is politically wise to do so, there
is no reason for eliminating it from the program schedule so
long as it is fully understood that carrying or not carrying the
introductions on the television networks is a matter to be
left to the discretion of the television executive.

Demonstrations are an anachronism, particularly in their
present artificial form. They should be dispensed with except
on those occasions when the spirit in the hall becomes so
intense that delegates are moved by high emotion to demonstrate their feelings, in other words, when they are genuinely
"spontaneous." The problem is really not with the delegates
in the hall; the problem is with the paid marchers who are
imported, equipped outside the hall with signs, noise-makers,
banners, and costumes, and then ushered into the hall to
demonstrate on signal.

Interminable seconding speeches also belong to the past era.
Limiting the time for both nominating and seconding speeches
to a maximum of ten to fifteen minutes, and then granting the
candidate's supporters the right to divide the total up in any
way they see fit would be one device to put an end to this
impediment to convention efficiency.

Conventions could still be timed so that the most interesting
features, those features regarded as most important by party
planners, would occur at times when television audiences are
at their maximum. It would be easier to maintain rigid time
schedules if the chaotic conditions imposed by cameramen
wandering around the floor, demonstrations running overtime,

and seconding speakers taking too long, could be eliminated.

It seems self-evident that the parties should be concerned with the way they look to the general public.[4] One of the principal complaints of television viewers during the last few convention years has been that delegates seemed totally disinterested in the proceedings as they wander about the floor, sit at their seats reading newspapers, or chat amiably with neighboring delegates. One of the factors contributing to this disinterest in convention proceedings is the dullness which so frequently pervades the rostrum. If many of the long addresses, the interminable seconding speeches, or the never-ending demonstrations are excised from the program schedule, party planners could expect a higher attention level. Under the present system once a delegate's attention is lost it is almost impossible to regain it. The result can be the chaos we saw demonstrated at Chicago. If the convention can't hold the interest of the delegates on the floor, how can it hold the television audience?

The marriage of political conventions and television is potentially a useful one—useful for the political parties, useful for the candidates they select, useful for the American public in obtaining evidence on which it must later make its selection of parties and candidates, and useful to the television network in serving its function of informing the viewing public.

Even with the excesses which have occurred, even in view of the violence of some complaints about the whole convention process and their television coverage, there can be little doubt that television's careful attention to political coverage can serve the country well. The convention process is already much better understood than it was before television. Party leaders have become real flesh-and-blood human beings instead of shadowy figures who flit in and out of newspaper columns. The excitement engendered by the coverage of a political convention gives a running start to the subsequent campaign, and heightens interest in the process of selecting candidates for public office.

THE SOARING COST OF THE
TELEVISION CAMPAIGN

$$\boxed{10}$$

The desperate financial plight of the national Democratic party following the 1968 campaign and the rapidly accelerating curve of television costs for political broadcasts have forced new attention on an old problem. The problem—how, by some means, to establish an equitable system of campaign financing, a system that would provide relatively equal opportunities for candidates and major parties while at the same time enabling candidates and parties to remain free of those pressures from financial supporters that might adversely affect their capacity to make independent judgments.

The disparity between wealth and poverty has spiraled upward during the age of television. The enormous expense of television campaigning has raised some crucial questions we must face if we are to maintain our form of government at its best. As 1970 came to an end, the national Republican party was operating with a comfortable surplus while the Democratic national committee was struggling under the staggering burden of a $9 million deficit.

Hubert Humphrey's campaign for the presidency in 1968 almost failed to get under way because the treasury was bare. Only during the last six weeks were there sufficient resources in gifts and loans, mostly loans, to mount any campaign at all; and even then the Democrats were outspent by their Republican opponents on a two-to-one basis.[1] In the 1966 race for the governorship of New York, Governor Nelson Rockefeller outspent his Democratic rival, Frank O'Connor, by at least a ten to one margin.[2] In the 1970 Democratic senatorial primary in New York it is estimated that the successful candidate, Congressman Richard Ottinger, outspent his second ranking opponent, Paul O'Dwyer, at a ratio of between twelve- and twenty-to-one.[3] It is an interesting sidelight that Ottinger lost in the November election.

Other cases of shocking disparities have been numerous. It isn't always the candidate with the most money at his disposal who wins. Norton Simon dipped deeply into his very considerable resources in his campaign for the Republican nomination for governor of California in the June 1970 primary, while Governor Ronald Reagan restricted his total expenditures to only a fraction of Simon's. Reagan, however, won by a large margin. Similarly Milton Shapp, who campaigned for the governorship of Pennsylvania in both primary and run-off elections in 1966 was unable to defeat his Republican opponent Raymond Shaeffer, who spent only a fraction of Shapp's total outlay. Shapp's effort paid off, however, in the 1970 election when he was an easy winner.

Fears are growing that highly competent prospective office holders may be driven out of the political arena because of a lack of resources to fuel even a minimum campaign machine, and that parties may be so impoverished that even maintaining a minimal opposition to the party in power will be out of the question. There is growing evidence that running for political office has already become so costly that it is a luxury only a rich man can afford. And there is always the lurking suspicion that the candidate without personal resources will become beholden to his backers.

Restrictions applied by law are simply not working. They are not working with respect to primaries because state laws vary widely and are difficult to enforce. They are not working in national elections because there are too many loopholes. The $5,000 limitation on campaign contributions to any single committee supporting a candidate is easily side-stepped by the simple expedient of setting up another committee. Data gathered by the Citizens Research Foundation in Princeton, New Jersey, and printed in the March 1970 issue of *Fortune* magazine suggested that one Nixon supporter, W. Clement Stone of Chicago, donated at least $700,000 to the 1968 Nixon campaign, about a half million of it prior to the Miami Beach convention in July and another $200,000 thereafter.[4]

The Hubert Humphrey 1968 campaign, which was stalled through lack of funds through almost all of September, was finally able to sputter into motion because of loans to the campaign arranged by Democratic national treasurer Robert Short. The *Fortune* article indicates that two individuals, John (Jake-the-Barber) Factor, and MCA President Lou Wasserman, each loaned $240,000 to the Humphrey effort. Because of the $5,000 limitation, each loan had to be split into forty-eight separate packets which went to forty-eight separate committees. The committees had such varied names as "Doctors for Humphrey and Muskie," "Dentists for Humphrey and Muskie," and economists, conservationists, executives, sports stars, etc., all for Humphrey and Muskie. *The New York Times* in an editorial on March 17, 1970, pointed out that, in all, there were 97 committees accepting donations for the Humphrey-Muskie ticket. The Nixon campaign was forced to use the same device. The *Times* pointed out there were created for Nixon and Agnew such temporary organizations as "Victory '68," "Tennessee for Nixon," and another called "Thurmond Speaks," named for the South Carolina Senator.

The practice is not new, but television has turned the curve sharply upward—more sharply than if only normal increases in costs of standard campaign items such as travel, communications, printing and mailing, staff salaries and expenses, and billboards, campaign buttons, bumper stickers, and the like were to be included. The Citizens Research Foundation esti-mates that the overall cost of the 1952 election—national, state, and local; primary and final—amounted to about $150,000,000. By 1968 the figure had doubled to $300,000,000.[5]

Television expenditures alone rose from approximately $34.6 million in 1964 to $59.2 million in 1968; but this was for air time only. Former FCC chairman, Newton Minow, testifying before the Pastore committee of the United States Senate in the winter of 1970, using statistics derived from a study of campaign financing done by the Twentieth Century Fund, suggested that another twenty to thirty-three percent would have to be added to cover the costs of television and film production.[6] This would bring the 1964 total to approximately $42 million, and 1968 to at least $75 million—an increase of more than 50%. It may be significant that the national price index for the years 1964 to 1968 showed an increase of approx-imately 12%.

Even when the dramatic increase in population in the United States is taken into consideration, the impact of tele-vision costs is clearly evident. Minow, again using Citizens Research Foundation figures, estimated that the cost per voter in a national presidential campaign for all campaign expenses remained fairly constant in the 19 to 20-cent level from 1912 through 1952; by 1960 it had jumped to 29 cents; in 1964 to 35 cents; and in 1968 to 60 cents, a figure three times as high as in 1952.[7] The 60-cent figure includes about 10 cents for the George Wallace campaign, but 1924 and 1948 would likewise have to be adjusted to reflect the participation of third parties.

One other set of statistics is worthy of note. In 1968 candi-dates in the general election spent more than 75% of their television budgets on spot announcements, a percentage nearly twice as high as in 1964. Except for this sizable increase in expenditures on spots, total disbursements for television in the two campaigns remained at about the same level. It's evident that television has been the culprit soaking up the largest share of the total increase in campaign expenditures; and there seems little doubt that the trend will continue upward, unless decisive action is taken to control expenditures. As more candidates discover the effectiveness of the spot announcement, they will inevitably be attracted to this costliest but most efficient of campaign techniques.

Many critics have been focusing on the sheer size of the expenditure. They argue that waste and excessive pressure on candidates to do the bidding of their benefactors must stem from the efforts to raise campaign funds at these levels. Herbert Alexander of the Citizens Research Foundation, however, suggests that the $300 million spent in the 1968 campaign is not the real problem. Even $300 million, he adds, is a small price to pay for stimulating greater interest in an election, contributing to a more informed electorate, and for encouraging more people to participate in the democratic process—if, in fact, such results do follow.[8] Nor is Alexander worried about the upward spiral. The real problem, he suggests, is the inequitable distribution of the cost burden and the great disparity in funds available to competing candidates. The well-supported candidate is able to spend a disproportionate share of the available campaign funds, and thus an extreme penalty is imposed on the candidate who may possess the ability to govern, but has no independent resources to contribute to his election, nor access to affluent supporters.

The Democratic party has consistently had great difficulty obtaining campaign funds to match those of the Republican opposition. In recent elections it was only in 1964 that the Democrats were financed on a level comparable to the Republicans, and that resulted largely from the disaffection of many wealthy businessmen with the Barry Goldwater campaign.

The Democrats, however, have themselves to blame for part of their current problems. President John F. Kennedy, both during his campaign for the presidency in 1960 and after his assumption of office in 1961, relied largely on big givers to keep the Democratic national committee treasury fueled. It was Kennedy who established the pattern of the President's Clubs, with memberships selling for $1,000 each, thus enabling club members to attend social functions with the ruling elite and rub shoulders with the presidential family.

President Lyndon Johnson carried on the same tradition and very little effort was devoted to obtaining mass support from rank and file party members. As the party went into the 1968 campaign, it had forgotten how to solicit funds from the rank and file: its muscles had grown soft from relying on large gifts.

The impoverished status of the Democratic national committee treasury, however, doesn't necessarily mean that all Democratic candidates in subsequent elections will be starved for money. State and local committees gather resources of their own. Labor through its Committee on Public Education (COPE), is a powerful and frequently affluent source of support. But the impoverishment of the national committee means there is an impairment of the ability to enunciate and disseminate a unified party policy. Subsidies to local campaigns are restricted and research programs cut back. There is an inevitable diminution of the capability to react swiftly and surely to opposition attacks.

A national committee, as opposed to a local committee, has very little specific to offer contributors in non-national election years. Its function is to organize, conduct research, energize local parties, subsidize regional and local candidacies, and support a national political point of view. It provides national outlets for national committee policy, attacks the opposition, and arranges national exposure for party leaders. All the time it is preparing for national campaigns, but only in presidential election years does it have candidates to support nationally.

This leaves the Democratic national committee with a difficult dilemma: how do you erase the deficit when there is little specific to offer by way of benefits? Paying off old debts is not very attractive from the giver's point of view; there's not much excitement or thrill involved in supporting Hubert

Humphrey for the presidency in 1968 when the 1968 election is already several years past; nor should the contributors in the 1970s have to pay old debts for a campaign which was lost and is now recorded only in the history books. There's not much incentive for the big giver except party loyalty, which is a highly intangible commodity. A big giver would seem to have more to gain by donating his money to a specific candidate for office in an off-year campaign—a senator or a congressman, or a governor with a chance of winning—than by picking up the pieces for a presidential candidate who had lost two years or more earlier.

The Republican party during the 1960s had very carefully cultivated the small giver and had built up a surplus by exerting steady public relations pressure on the man with $10 or $25 to spare. In the process it created a mailing list that was yielding substantial returns. The Democrats had to build from the ground up. They had to create a mailing list, cultivate the habit of small gifts, and accomplish all of this while stalling off creditors and standing up to the immense power to command access to the media which is vested in the presidency.

In a move born largely out of desperation, the national committee decided in the spring of 1970 to try television advertising to stimulate loyal party members or persons disaffected with the Administration to start contributing in small sums or large to the opposition party. Obstacles were not only numerous, but sometimes appeared almost insuperable. Nothing of this sort had been tried before, and the party had few resources to spend on the gamble without some fairly concrete evidence that a reasonable return on the investment for advertising production and time on the air could be expected. This made test-marketing prior to launching a major campaign an absolute must.

In 1970 there was very little precedent in station and network policy for the acceptance of advertising to solicit funds as opposed to supporting candidates. CBS had had an outright policy against it. Stations and networks alike were accustomed to accepting commercial orders from candidates for office during campaign periods, but not for political commercials outside the limits of a formal campaign, and not at all for appeals for money between campaigns.

While it might be assumed that the relationship between the national committee and state and local committees might be warm and cooperative, when it comes to fund raising the local party managers keep a wary eye on any efforts to drain off funds which could otherwise be used to support their local candidates. A fund-raising campaign launched by a national committee during an off-election year would, by its very nature, have to siphon off some of the funds which would otherwise go toward enriching the coffers of local campaigns. This means that local candidates for governor, congress, United States senate, or for lesser offices, would be penalized to the extent that funds are drained out of their state and channeled into the national party treasury.

A fund-raising campaign based on solicitation through television advertising could yield significant results if it were successful. And in the summer of 1970 it appeared to be just about the only way the Democratic party could obtain resources to pay off at least part of its debt and build up some reserve to meet regular running expenses without forcing the treasurer of the party to scurry about at the end of each month to obtain the funds required to pay his bills.

There would be a number of subsidiary benefits to a successful campaign. It would aid in developing a mailing list, which the Republicans had but the Democrats sorely lacked. It would inform voters and local party functionaries that the party was vigorous and active and ready to take up the competition against the Republican party in the 1972 national election campaign. It would furnish an opportunity, while soliciting funds, to go on to the attack against the Republicans, and, if successful, it could furnish a base of both money and aggressive grass-roots support which had been lacking in the dispirited days following the 1968 loss.

The Democrats were faced with another crippling disadvantage. While the Republicans had resources adequate to employ consultants, the Democrats had to rely on voluntary help. Fortunately for the party, such help was available. The first logical step was to determine whether such a campaign would, in fact, yield results. Would people respond to a broadcast appeal for funds? Was there actually enough enthusiasm for the Democratic party to induce a person to take the trouble to write a check, address an envelope, affix a stamp, and take the letter to the post box? Could this be done without irritating the local party treasurers and candidates for office in the states, who, contrary to their Republican opponents, were getting no subsidies from the national committee and were forced to struggle to obtain resources to conduct their own campaigns? The logical approach was identical to that which was used by soap or cigarette manufacturer in trying out a new product—launch a test-marketing campaign.

But little emotional support, surely not enough to impel the voter to reach for his checkbook, could be engendered by telling him of the party's debts. While he might take pride in the party's past and its tradition, and would be happy to know that it was alive and well, this would hardly seem a likely approach to his pocketbook. On the other hand, if the attack on the opposition were vigorous enough; if the advertising themes were to touch sensitive nerves; if they were to stimulate genuine fears for the future of the economy, and for preservation of traditional American institutions and the country's position in the world community of nations, it would seem much more likely that pocketbooks would be opened and dollars forthcoming.

There was a risk involved. A vigorous partisan appeal would gain support from sympathizers, but it might drive the uncommitted into the hands of the opposition. On the other hand, without taking a risk there seemed little chance of success. The most likely target was the status of the United States economy: rising prices coincident with rising unemployment; high interest rates; a falling stock market; sagging profits and a resultant stagnating standard of living. The theme was finally set: "You don't have to wait until 1972 to vote against Richard Nixon." The next line read "Vote against him with your dollars now."

Media experts set out to determine where test markets could be found that would be reasonably sure indicators concerning the prospects for an all-out national campaign. Creative personnel were assigned the task of framing specific copy appeals and obtaining the necessary art work to illustrate the campaign, which was to emphasize the theme that the economy of the United States was in deep trouble, that no improvement could be expected unless the Democratic party were able to impose pressures on the White House, either through the Congress or by the force of public opinion.

The planning of this campaign occurred, coincidentally, with a surge of feeling that the White House was making excessive use of its inherent capability for dominating the television screens of the country. President Nixon had been making frequent and skillful use of television as an outlet for speeches, press conferences, and discussion sessions with television correspondents. The vice-president was continuing to obtain significant exposure in the regularly scheduled news broadcasts through the vigorous and aggressive speeches he was delivering at Repulican rallies throughout the country. All of this was leading to a revival of the uneasiness which accompanies the successful use of a communications medium by an articulate and strong-willed presidential leadership. Republicans had complained during the Franklin Roosevelt administration that the president was so thoroughly dominating the radio waves of the period that he had an enormous advantage in any political contest. Democrats complained during the 1950s about President Eisenhower's access to television. Now there was uneasiness about Richard Nixon's frequent and generally effective performances on the television screen.

First attempts to place the spot commercial campaign on a test-market basis were rebuffed by station managements. Managers argued that they would give time for the discussion of public issues but would not sell time for the solicitation of funds. The counsel for the Democratic national committee, Joseph Califano, took the matter to the Federal Communications Commission, but before the commission could take any action president Frank Stanton of the Columbia Broadcasting System struck the decisive blow that broke the barrier preventing the acceptance of commercials which solicited funds for political purposes. Stanton agreed that the CBS television network and CBS-owned stations would henceforth accept political fund-raising appeals in commercial form during non-presidential campaign periods. NBC had for several years been operating under a policy with sufficient flexibility that the commercials might have been accepted. ABC had announced a couple of weeks earlier that it was willing to broadcast commercials appealing for funds; but with CBS backing down there was no longer network opposition, and, as the networks go, stations frequently go as well.

At the same time, the CBS president announced that the network would as a matter of policy, hereafter, furnish the opposition party with a certain number of opportunities during the year to bring its case before the people on a free basis. CBS had from time-to-time in the past made time available on its own terms and conditions to representatives of the opposition party to respond after presidential messages which were considered, in the CBS judgment, as being political in orientation. This was the first time, however, that CBS had been willing to grant such opportunities to the opposition party as a matter of right. The decision was justified on the basis of the Federal Communications Act's "fairness and balance" clause which made it mandatory that licensees maintain fairness and balance in treating controversial issues.[9] With this CBS stand, all three networks were now operating for the first time under policies that conceded to the opposition the right to use network facilities without charge and at the discretion of the network authorities.

Thus in mid-summer of 1970 it seemed that progress had been made toward achieving a better economic balance between the national parties. Any optimism which might have been stimulated once, however, short-lived. The Democratic national committee's campaign to bolster its treasury by use of paid political advertising conceived to solicit funds foundered. The test campaign barely succeeded in stimulating enough giving to pay the costs of the advertising program. The failure may have been due to the timing of the venture. Midsummer television viewing is in a period of slump. Enthusiasm for politics must compete with vacation plans and outdoor recreation; and it is difficult to engender much enthusism for a national political party midway between national campaigns. At any rate, the campaign was dropped and the national committee was forced to look elsewhere for new resources.

But a CBS effort to furnish a format for the opposition party to state its case on national television also collapsed in a morass of legal technicalities. Democratic national committee chairman Lawrence O'Brien was granted time by CBS to open a series, called "Loyal Opposition." There were to be four "Loyal Opposition" programs during the course of each year. The first appearance was scheduled following a speech by President Nixon concerning the Vietnam war. Rather than confine himself to answering the President's message directly, O'Brien ranged through a number of issues. The Republican national committee promptly demanded time to reply, arguing that O'Brien was not responding to the president. The Federal Communications Commission ordered CBS to furnish time for a reply, whereupon "Loyal Opposition" was packed in moth balls.[10] CBS wouldn't see its way clear to furnishing opportunities for answers to answers ad infinitum.

It had been a summer of sound and fury, but as the off-year campaign of 1970 got under way in early September, the status quo prevailed. The events of the summer had, however, focused new attention on the problem, had suggested some possible methods for alleviating the discrepancies in party income and access to television facilities, but actual accomplishments were negligible. Perhaps most discouraging was the fact that all of this actually did nothing to alleviate financial disparities that develope during campaigns themselves.

One of the most frequently voiced suggestions is that television time be made available to legitimate party candidates on a free basis, that time be commandeered during the course of a political campaign for making appeals to voters. There is a worldwide precedent for free time for political campaigning.

During a British election campaign, which has a maximum running time of approximately three weeks, all appearances by representatives of the British parties on the two BBC networks and ITA facilities are given without charge. Parties have the freedom to produce their programming in any way they see fit, and the facilities are donated by the broadcasting concerns.[11]

The British system, however, is vastly different from the structure of broadcasting in the United States. The BBC's two networks are supported by license fees collected by the government and turned over to the corporation. There is no commercial support, and hence no loss of revenue occasioned by the preemption of commercially sponsored programs.

The Independent Television Network, on the other hand, does stand to lose advertising revenue, but the facilities used by the ITV Network are owned by the Independent Television Authority, a government corporation. Thus, in England more than the airwaves belong to the public—the facilities are likewise publicly owned.

Campaign time is likewise granted free for use of the facilities of the television networks in Scandinavia, Germany, France, Italy, and Japan. But as in the case of the United Kingdom, the structure of broadcasting is wholly unlike that of the United States. The German networks are supported in part by advertising, but all commercials are carried during the one-hour period from 7:00 to 8:00 P.M. Political broadcasts are normally accommodated during this hour, but they preempt program material and not commercials, which are separated from the programs.

Italian broadcasting is similar to German in that RAI-TV, the Italian state network, is only partially dependent on advertising support; the remainder derives from license fees. All commercials are carried, as in Germany, during a specified commercial segment of the evening, and there is no sponsorship as such. As a result, in Italy as in Germany the scheduling of the political broadcast does not necessitate the cancellation of a sponsored program.

In Japan's December 1969 election, both government operated NHK network, which is supported by license fees, and the commercial stations which are more comparable to the networks in the United States than to their European counterparts, carried political programs broadcast by candidates for the Japanese Diet. The government subsidized the campaign to the extent of paying for the time utilized on commercial stations.

If the government of the United States were to insist that time for political campaigning be made available free of charge to political candidates, the broadcasters would have every right to shout that they were being discriminated against. The argument is used that the airwaves belong to the people, and thus time and facilities should be free; but the fact is that studios, cameras, sets and props, lights, recording equipment, transmitters and antennas belong to private owners and not to the people. It is questionable whether the government has the right to insist on free usage of these facilities, particularly if broadcasting is to be singled out as the only institution or agency which makes such contributions. The airlines also use air which presumably belongs to the people and like broadcasting operate under government licensing, but the planes and ground facilities are private property. Should the airlines likewise be forced to make free travel available to political candidates and their staffs?

There are two possible means of reducing the cost of television time to the candidate or the party without undue discrimination against the broadcaster. One is to grant government subsidies which would pay part or all of the costs of a specified number of political broadcasts; the other would be to put into effect some kind of rate reduction which would reduce the time charges to a manageable level. The "Voter's Time" proposal of the Twentieth Century Fund suggests a combination of the two. Bills which have been introduced in Congress have called for making time available to political candidates either at the lowest rate granted to any advertiser for comparable time and facilities, or on the basis of a specified discount.

Broadcasters themselves have taken significant steps toward making the lowest rates given to any advertiser available to political candidates. It seems likely that by 1972 voluntary action will have accomplished substantial reductions in time charges. This, however, is by no means the whole answer to the problem. Production costs, which are made up of charges for creative talent and costs of film or tape, raw stock, camera work, editing, muscial scoring, writing and reproducing copies, in 1968 made up between 20 and 33 percent of the total cost of broadcast expenditures.[12]

It is not unlikely that if time costs are substantially reduced, candidates and their managers will simply utilize the savings to put more of their resources into production. The result would be only a redistribution of the expenditures. It seems inevitable that a candidate will spend whatever money he is able to obtain from his supporters. Reductions in time costs, thus, are unlikely to go far toward reducing the imbalance in expenditures between those candidates who have adequate funds and those who have to scrape the bottom of the barrel for every penny they are able to raise for the purchase of television time and facilities.

The granting of free time, selling at a discount, or government subsidies may alleviate the financial burden, but they fail to strike at the heart of the problem: the necessity for giving an even break to all candidates, whether strongly supported by substantial resources or operating on a financial shoestring. While furnishing some minimal aid to hard pressed candidates, they would require sacrifices from the television industry while imposing no burden on those other suppliers of required campaign services, such as office rent, communications, transportation, print advertising, and personnel. A more equitable solution seems in order, a solution which will not penalize one medium while making more resources available for the others.

There also remains the problem of the minority party. The American government is operated essentially on a two-party system, but third parties were significant factors in the 1912, 1924, 1948, and 1968 national elections, and have from time to time achieved substantial importance in state campaigns. Any restrictions in the United States regarding campaign expenditures or utilization of television time would have to furnish some support for such third or fourth parties as might achieve sufficient strength as to be considered legitimate factors in an election campaign if the traditional protection for minority interests is to be maintained.

The United States poses some curious additional problems in equitably distributing television time. A candidate for Congress in the fourth district of Connecticut, in order to reach the bulk of his voters, would have to obtain time from one of the New York metropolitan television stations since the closest station in Connecticut, located in New Haven, reaches only a small part of Fairfield County. There is not one single VHF television station in the entire state of New Jersey. In their recently fought campaign for the office of mayor of the city of Newark, the opposing candidates were forced to pay premium prices for New York City stations in order to reach Newark voters. Much of the signal was wasted on residents of New York City, Suffolk and Nassau Counties on Long Island, Westchester County, New York, and Fairfield County, Connecticut.

In the southern half of New Jersey a candidate for office, in order to use television, must buy his facilities in Philadelphia. Thus a good portion of his expenditures go to pay for coverage of Pennsylvania congressional districts, an utter waste from the point of view of winning election in New Jersey. The tenth congressional district of the state of Ohio poses more serious problems. There are no television stations in the tenth congressional district, which is composed of eight counties in the southeastern quadrant of the state. Four of the eight counties get some coverage from stations located in Columbus, and the other four get minimum coverage from stations located in the state of West Virginia. The costs for television campaigning for a candidate for Congress in the tenth Ohio district are thus magnified to levels far greater than for congressmen from the second district, for example, in the state of North Dakota. In North Dakota, Congressman Mark Andrews is able to reach his entire constituency with only minimal "wastage" of signal which drifts across the line into Montana, South Dakota, or Canada.

In the Ohio tenth approximately 90% of the coverage of the West Virginia stations which the candidate buys is in the state of West Virginia. This gives him a 10% efficiency factor on his purchase. In order to reach the other four countries in his constituency he has to go to Columbus, from which only about 4% of the total coverage reaches his district. Thus 96% of his purchase price is wasted in areas in which there are no voters to cast ballots for him. Any program adopted to equalize campaign expenditures and to create equal opportunities for major party candidates would have to take into consideration these discrepancies in coverage.

There is one possible future answer for this built-in obstacle to television usage. If community antenna television grows as rapidly as some experts now predict, the candidate will be able to select specific cable systems for campaign appeals, thus enabling him to campaign most vigorously where efforts are most productive and avoid wasting circulation. Such saturation coverage by cable will probably not be possible, however, in this decade even though its ultimate impact on campaigning may be substantial.

Cable systems have grown slowly since the first were built in the early 1950s. Growth, however, began to accelerate in the late 1960s; by early 1971 between 5,000,000 and 6,000,000 homes in the United States were subscribing to cable service. But the majority of these still remain in areas which, for physical reasons, are unable to obtain clean, clear television signal.

New technology in the meantime has made it possible for this kind of broadband communications system to deliver a variety of services in addition to a superior television signal. Some projections indicate that as many of 50% of all of the homes in the United States may be subscribers to cable service by 1980.

Cable services which started with a maximum of 12 channels —or simply enough to deliver improved pictures from established television stations—are now expanding to 20 channels and upwards. The FCC is in the process of making it mandatory that some local programming be added to the services available on cable vision; thus, at some time in the relatively near future facilities would be available for political broadcasting. It will be theoretically possible by the mid to late 1970s for a big-city candidate to block out a portion of a cable system which feeds into homes in his congressional district. He could then deliver his program directly to his constituents without wastage in adjacent areas. Candidates in the tenth congressional district in Ohio have already been making some use of CATV because of the high cost involved in using regular television and its built-in inefficiencies. If the proper steps are taken early, it is conceivable that the use of the cable might be made available free of charge to the legitimate candidate who is fully qualified by election law to run for public office. He would still have to face up to the costs of production if he intended to use film or videotape programs, but the savings on time charges should be adequate to enable him to devote much more of his resources to physical program production.

Network broadcasters who oppose free time suggestions generally regard Section 315 of the Federal Communications Act of 1954 as the main obstacle preventing inexpensive and widespread coverage of candidates.[13] Broadcasters have been reluctant while Section 315 is on the books to take any chances with its enforcement which might jeopardize their program schedules and force them to furnish broadcast time to minority party candidates who are of little interest to the normal station audience and of no significance whatsoever in the election campaign itself. They are fearful of being inundated by requests from candidates whose principal objective is obtaining television exposure. A number of FCC decisions over the years have increased the skittishness.

Section 315 bears directly on the question of campaign financing, to the extent that appearances by candidates for public office would probably be more frequent on both networks and individual stations if there were no requirements enabling hosts of inconsequential fringe candidates to demand equal time. The networks point out that, if they were to risk the enforcement against them of Section 315 by scheduling the major party candidates for free time, that the quota of fourteen to eighteen candidates who normally run for the presidency could quickly grow in multiples of two or four or even ten. It is a relatively simple matter to qualify on the presidential ballot in one state of the fifty.

There were no major obstacles to suspension of Section 315 for the 1960 presidential campaign because the incumbent president, General Eisenhower, remained neutral. In 1964, however, President Johnson, who had no intention of participating in debates, showed little enthusiasm for seeing Section 315 eliminated for that campaign. Whether he did or did not apply specific pressure on members of Congress to reject suspension, the fact remains that without the President's active leadership on matters affecting the White House, Congress is unlikely to move.

Members of Congress have shown equally little enthusiasm for eliminating the Section as it applies to Congressional races. The very simple reason is that they have no desire to give any advantage to opposition candidates. This same lack of enthusiasm for helping the opposition has also served to inhibit the passage of legislation which would limit the costs of campaigning and thus make it easier for an opposition candidate to achieve equal status with the incumbent.

There is one unfortunate aspect to the heavy flow of publicity generated by the Kennedy-Nixon debates which resulted from the 1960 suspension of Section 315. Many members of Congress are apparently inhibited from supporting permanent repeal because they associate repeal of 315 with debate. They have no desire to expose themselves to this risky brand of political contest.

Repeal of the rule, however, would not necessarily mean that candidates from one end of the country to the other would be forced to pair off on the rostrum before television cameras to argue their respective cases. It is just as likely that grants of time will be made to the candidates to use as they see fit: for formal talks, interviews, question-and-answer sessions, film biographies or short documentaries. Discretion to decide acceptable types of campaign programs would reside with station management.

None of the proposals made so far to solve the dilemma posed by rising costs of campaigning on the one hand and growing inequities between candidates on the other offers a fool-proof solution to the problem. All start from the same basic proposition: it would be a disaster for a democracy if one political party were to drift off into oblivion, or for a qualified and competent candidate to fail at election because of inadequate exposure resulting from a shortage of campaign funds. But none offers assurances that an efficient and equitable plan can be developed.

Essentially there are three possible routes that can be taken toward reducing the inequities. The first is to reduce the cost of the political campaign by making time on the air either less costly or free; the second, to create new sources of financing through government subsidies, tax incentives, or perhaps by removing the ceilings on contributions; the third, a combination of the first two.

The fallacy in the first alternative is that television time charges are only one element—although a major one—in the whole spectrum of campaign costs. It is conceivable that a candidate with substantial resources at his disposal would simply shift the savings in his time charges to more elaborate and more costly production. This could conceivably put the less affluent candidate at an even greater disadvantage, since it is unlikely that charges for creative talent, film processing and editing, and media placement, can be reduced by government order or by industry-wide agreement.

Government subventions would not necessarily narrow the gap, unless strict limitations were imposed on total expenditures. Subsidies, however, would raise the floor and enable all qualified candidates to achieve at least some minimum exposure. Greater tax incentives to contributors would serve the same purpose.

The most complete and detailed package that has been proposed with regard to national elections is the Twentieth Century Fund's "Voters' Time" proposal, as made by its Commission on Campaign Costs in the Electronic Era.

"Voters' Time" would call for government subsidies to buy time in specified amounts from all television networks and stations in the country at 50% of the applicable rate-card price. Presidential and vice-presidential candidates of major parties would participate in six half-hour programs during the last 35 days before an election campaign. These would be broadcast simultaneously on every broadcasting facility including community antenna television within the borders of the United States. The Commission does not specify formats except for the fact that it emphasizes that they must be "rational" discussions of issues.

The problem of adequate representation for minority parties is disposed of by setting up three categories of candidates for the presidential and vice-presidential offices. The first category would consist of candidates of parties that have placed first or second in two of the preceding presidential elections. They would be entitled to six prime-time 30-minute periods during the last 35 days prior to election day.

The second category would enable candidates of parties that received a "sizable vote" in the preceding election to utilize two prime-time 30-minute periods each. The Commission suggests that "sizable" be defined as one-eighth of the number of votes cast in the preceding election.

The third category would enable candidates of all parties that "show evidence of potential vote, but not necessarily a past electoral record of significance" one prime-time 30-minute period during the last 35 days before the election.

In order to qualify under the third category a candidate would have to appear on the ballot in at least three-fourths of the states, with the District of Columbia considered a state. It would be mandatory that these states represent a sufficient number of electoral votes to constitute a majority in the electoral college.

Under the terms of category two, Theodore Roosevelt would have qualified on the basis of the record of the Bull-Moose Party in 1912; Senator LaFollette with the Progressive Party in 1924; and George Wallace in 1968. Henry Wallace, in the 1948 election, would have failed, since he received only about two and four-tenths percent of the total electoral vote; but he would have qualified under category three in that he would have shown "evidence of potential vote." The Socialist Party, led by either Eugene V. Debs or Norman Thomas, would have qualified seven times under terms of category three. The institution of "Voters' Time" would in no way affect the amount of paid time to be purchased by the candidate or committee supporting him, whether such paid time would involve straight political speeches, interviews, or spot announcements of whatever duration.

The principal advantage of the commission's proposal is that all candidates of significance, irrespective of the resources in their treasuries, would be enabled to achieve a minimum amount of exposure on the nation's television facilities. Furthermore, they would appear at a time when no other programming could be scheduled to compete with them. This would not necessarily guarantee a high rating; but the viewer would have no other program to which to turn.

A subsequent report from the Twentieth Century Fund task force set up to deal with the financing of congressional campaigns suggested a broad program of reforms that would reduce inequities, enforce standards of honesty and fairness, and make more funds available for campaign purposes. The task force was hopeful that some action would be taken by the Congress prior to the 1970 elections; but Congress was reluctant to move, apparently, say the critics, because of the complexity of the problem and the congressmen's reluctance to do any favors for potential opponents. Committees of Congress did consider, however, during the 1970 session legislation enforcing lower rate charges by television operators, the repeal of Section 315, and the imposition of spending limits. The bill which resulted from these efforts was vetoed, however, by President Nixon.

The problem of limiting campaign expenditures poses a number of imponderable questions. Can you actually enforce a limitation? Should the limitation be applicable to all campaign expenditures, including staff, space, office supplies, travel and communications, or should it be limited to television alone? If it is limited to television, is it possible to equate $1,000 spent on one station with $1,000 spent on another with less audience reach, impact, ratings and share of audience?

Should the candidate whose television advertising achieves a high degree of appeal be reduced to the level of the less creative?

The British have had considerable experience with a limitation of expenditure of campaign funds, but only as they relate to the specific period of the campaign, which normally runs approximately 21 days. These restrictions apply only to expenditures within the constituency in question. Exposure on television in the United Kingdom is free, but generally not available to any candidates other than party leaders.

The Representation of the People Act of 1949, and an amended Representation of the People Act in 1969, established specific ceilings for expenditures in the constituencies. In a rural area a candidate is allowed to spend £1,800 plus one shilling, or 12¢, for every six voters in the constituency. In the urban areas the limit is £1,800 plus one shilling for each eight eligible voter. Since in the average constituency there are roughly 70,000 voters, the total sums available run from about £2,800 in the urban constituencies to about £3,200 in less populated rural areas, small sums compared to what is spent by the congressional candidate in the United States.[14]

There is no limit, however, on what central headquarters of the party can spend, except that it can't support individual candidates in specific constituencies. There is one other significant loophole: the restrictions apply only to the limited period of the campaign and are not applicable to the periods between campaigns. Since British elections are mandatory only every five years, the controls are applicable to only three weeks out of a maximum of 260.

Television time is furnished without charge. This relates to both time and facilities which are furnished by the BBC and the Independent Television Authority. Provisions have been made for regular appearances by party leaders, cabinet members, and members of the "shadow" cabinet. But the backbencher has little opportunity for exposure. Significantly there are no spot announcements, no political commercials, and no paid time. The party has an opportunity to select its own representatives for regular political broadcasts, but the selection of personnel to appear on current affairs programs is made entirely at the discretion of the BBC executives in charge and the producers of the programs. There is no Section 315 to inhibit invitations.

The system is admirably well-suited to a small country which operates on a parliamentary basis, but is hardly applicable to the much larger United States. The ties between national party headquarters and local constituencies are much looser here than in the United Kingdom.

It is also significant that there is no primary election in the British system. Candidates for election to Parliament in local constituencies are selected by the national party in contrast to the United States, where in some states the primary system prevails and in others candidates are selected in party conventions. The dependence on the primary system in the United States, with all of its variations from state-to-state, poses problems which makes regulation of expenditures difficult—if not virtually impossible.

But even allowing for built-in inefficiency and waste, it still should be possible to devise a national system of controls which would protect the right of the competent, public-service-minded, politically-oriented individual to run for public office with some hope of success, and at the same time control abuses which may arise out of the system. Some type of governmental subsidy to political campaigning seems to be an absolute necessity. Such a subsidy was suggested as early as the first decade of the twentieth century by President Theodore Roosevelt. If it is true, as Herbert Alexander of the Citizens Research Foundation insists, that our problem is not excessive spending, but rather making better use of the resources we have, a government subsidy would go a long way toward building a base upon which the less affluent candidate would have a chance to appeal to his constituents.

The second logical step would include a reduction in television time cost. This could be achieved by imposing a formula similar to that suggested by the Twentieth Century Fund commission in its "Voters' Time" proposal, or by suggestions before the Pastore committee of the U.S. Senate. The most logical solution would seem to be to make it mandatory that television management sell its time for political broadcasts during campaign periods on the basis of the lowest rate made available to any advertiser for a comparable time period. It might be possible to reduce this time charge further by giving discounts to political advertisers. The burden on the giver could be made easier by permitting income tax deductions for political contributions.

Thirdly, Section 315 of the Federal Communications Act should be repealed. Congress may not be enthusiastic about supporting such repeal because of the theoretical advantage repeal would provide for opposition candidates. But elimination of 315's restrictive provision would make it possible for broadcasters to open up their facilities to a variety of political programs which are now inhibited by the nuisance factors inherent in the equal time provision.

Some form of debate program could very well be encouraged. It need not be formal debate; it can be an approximation of the debate as has become widespread in Western Europe and Japan; programs in which representatives of all parties appear simultaneously on a single stage to discuss issues and answer questions or simply state points of view.

Minority parties can be protected by a system similar to the one proposed by the Twentieth Century Fund commission; or by the German or British systems in which a third party is given access to the air waves but on a reduced basis as compared to the major parties. Increased donations—particularly from smaller givers—should be encouraged. This can be done partly by tax incentives which would give credit for expenditures up to reasonable limits or by encouraging mass giving to political funds which could later be distributed among the parties on a proportional basis.

The totally unworkable system of imposing limitations on campaign donations which has led to the proliferation of campaign committees should be dispensed with and replaced by a system in which one committee and one only represents the candidate or party. In order to accomplish this step, it would be necessary to lift the ceiling on campaign contributions. If the ceiling were to be lifted and one committee made responsible for all receipts and disbursements, imposition of controls could be made much more effective. Surveillance over the activities of a single committee would be vastly easier than an attempt to keep up with the fifty, seventy-five, or one hundred committees which now solicit funds and make expenditures on behalf of a presidential candidate.

If ceilings on donations and solicitations are to be lifted, ceilings on expenditures should be similarly removed. The problem is not the amount of money spent, it is rather the manner in which it is spent. If the appropriate committee is obligated to report all of its receipts and all of its expenditures, at least the public will be enabled to know sources of funds and the manner in which they are allocated. Imbalances in total expenditures would be controlled in part by a combination of government subsidies for political advertising, less expensive television time, tax incentives for contributions and repeal of Section 315. Enforcement of reasonable restrictions on the expenditures of those funds could be expedited by a more rigorous application of the Corrupt Practices act. As Hubert Humphrey suggests, the Comptroller General of the United States might have the ultimate authority of enforcement.

In order to facilitate the solicitation of funds, television broadcasters should be encouraged to permit the placement by political parties or authorized committees of advertising messages requesting donations to the party or candidate. Parties and candidates alike should be encouraged to pay more attention to those features on the television broadcast schedule, including regular news broadcasts and regularly scheduled interviews which furnish free outlet for their ideas, attitudes, plans and programs. Attention to television news has significantly increased through the age of television and national candidates have generally acquired considerable skills in catering to the legitimate news requirements of both networks and stations. Some members of Congress, however, still have much to learn, particularly as to what constitutes news and what does not. Both networks and stations would undoubtedly be of assistance in furnishing suggestions, if not educational campaigns.

In order to counter in some measure the enormous powers accruing to the office holder, particularly the President of the United States, television broadcasters should be encouraged to establish procedures to institutionalize the granting of time to opposition leaders to respond. This should apply not only on the national level to messages from the White House, but similarly to speeches by governors, senators, and congressmen. On the national level, the Newton Minow suggestion that the opposition party annually select in convention an official party leader to voice its replies to the party in power might permit adoption of the British system.

The problem of imposing limitations on the television time to be used by candidates for office diminishes in importance as opportunities are furnished for the opposition to acquire at least a minimum opportunity. If it is felt necessary to impose time or expenditure limits on political advertising, it would seem more logical to place the limitation on the time used rather than on the money expended. Multiplying the minutes of time employed by the total number of households in a given market area would furnish a formula. Modern computer techniques would make the keeping of such records a less complicated matter than in previous years.

Within a relatively short span of years community antenna television, more properly described as cable vision or broad-band communications, will be available to substantial proportions of the total United States population. Since these broadband communications will furnish many more channels than are available now on the normal broadcast television receiver, it should be possible to allocate for the duration of political campaigns one or more such channels to political purposes. This could be done on a free basis, or at the most for out-of-pocket charges, since it is unlikely that the economics of broadband communications will demand that each and every channel be wholly self-supporting.

Attracting audiences to channels given over wholly to political broadcasting will not be easy. If one assumes, however, that the normal entertainment channels will be opened up to additional appearances by candidates, it follows that broadband communications can be used for appeals to the faithful supporters, those who regularly attend party rallies and devote time and effort to candidate support. Expert political tacticians regard the energizing of committed supporters as being one of the principal functions of the campaign effort. Broadband communications offer the opportunity for the campaign rally without hiring a hall.

It is entirely conceivable that some of the problems which perplex us in the early 1970s will diminish in importance by the end of the decade if broadband communications should come into as widespread usage as is now anticipated.

The only question which is apparently insoluble is the problem of production costs. It might be possible to impose limitations if reasonable yardsticks could be set up for expenditures on television production. But the imposition of such limitations would destroy a good deal of the initiative which now goes into the political campaign. It would certainly dull some of the incentives to vigorous and aggressive campaigning.

Perhaps there would be an advantage in limiting campaign appearances to what the Twentieth Century Fund's commission describes as "rational" performances. The one form of political advertising which could well be banned by law if rationality were to be a criterion is the spot announcement of ten, twenty, thirty or sixty seconds duration. Abuses of the technique were so widespread in the fall 1970 campaign that a wave of resentment swept the country and there is reason to think that some particularly aggressive users of the spot technique were beaten by the negative reaction. Perhaps a "rational" performance could be defined as one of five minutes duration or more.

No matter what steps are taken, what cost reductions are made, what additional opportunities are created, the man in office in any country will continue to have an advantage which can only be reduced or softened, but not eliminated. He can still command time and facilities to state his case under the most favorable circumstances; he can choose the time and place; he can enlist the support of the governmental unit he represents to help make his case. This is an advantage which can't be restricted by law. The necessity of appearing before the public on issues of national or state consequence is inherent in government. There will be abuses; there will be office holders on both state and national levels who will deliver political messages in the guise of the public interest. The only relief available under the law or within the political system is the privilege of response to those performances which can be interpreted as largely political in nature. Steps should be taken to guarantee such rights.

A democratic society needs to recognize the values of its political campaign; it needs to keep the channels open both for office holders and contestants for that office; it needs to devise a system to avoid penalizing an able and potentially useful candidate because he lacks resources; it needs to create opportunities for him to state his case, to project his personality or his image, to demonstrate his capabilities and to give the voters an opportunity to choose freely among candidates who have had equal opportunities to make their qualifications known.

THE NEXT DECADE
AND BEYOND

Only the boldest visionary would have dared to foretell in 1950 the shape of television as a political force only two decades later. Governor Thomas Dewey of New York, his press secretary James C. Hagerty, and his principal advisor, Herbert Brownell, supported by Bernard Duffy and his aides of the Batten, Barton, Durstine & Osborn Advertising Agency, must have had some inkling. Their usage of television in the 1950 campaign for the governorship indicated they were prepared for an entirely new medium for political campaigning. Senator William Benton of Connecticut, after having undergone a vigorous television-dominated campaign for the Senate in 1950, told a *New York Times* reporter in March 1951: "The potentialities of television are so great that they could revolutionize politics. The terrifying aspect is the high cost, the expense of which could well determine election or defeat."

Senator Benton was one of the few who had the prescience to anticipate that the little ten-inch screen which intrigued only a few daring political tacticians in 1950 would dominate political planning and spending less than a decade later. The viewers in seven million households who had begun to rearrange their furniture, change their meal hours, and give up going out to the movies in order not to miss Milton Berle, Sid Caesar, Imogene Coca, and Ed Sullivan in 1950 had grown in a decade to a mighty army, embracing nearly 100% of American homes. Candidate Dwight Eisenhower could theoretically have projected his fatherly image into approximately 20 million homes in his 1952 campaign, but the boyish appearing John F. Kennedy could reach three times as many in 1960. Candidates Kennedy and Nixon did in fact debate before between 70 and 80 million persons in September and October of that year.

The trickle of dollars finding their way into the mainstream of political campaigning by television in 1950 grew into a torrent by 1960 and was reaching tidal wave proportions by 1970. There is ample evidence to indicate that, as Senator Benton predicted, "the terrifying aspect" of "high cost" was in fact, in some cases, determining "election or defeat." A medium which in 1950 was a new toy to be tried by the daring had become a monstrous cyclops whose single hypnotic eye dominated the political process at all levels from county assessor to the presidency of the United States.

The question now is: what will the next two decades bring? Will television continue to grow in power, influence and cost, or will it be supplanted or supplemented by some new communications medium? Is cable television the new force that will begin to break broadcast television's stranglehold, or might it be direct broadcast from satellites, both of which are in reality television delivered by different communications technology? Or will the video cassette or disc become the dominant vehicle for delivering the political message to the home or office? Or will the long-heralded home communications center replace television, radio, newspaper, magazines, circulars, leaflets and broadsides?

Certainly dramatic changes will occur. Radio first made its appearance at a national political convention as recently as 1924. While radio never achieved the enormous impact that television was to demonstrate in the decades of the 1950s and

1960s, it could not be overlooked by campaign planners of the
'30s and '40s. It began during those years to reshape both political campaign strategy and governmental relations with the
public. In only twenty years, however, radio was relegated to a
secondary position as television forced its way into the center
of the campaign stage. The accelerating of technological change
makes one wonder whether television's center stage role will
begin to erode as quickly as did radio's when the new combined picture and sound technology began to shunt it aside.

The most likely usurper of broadcast television's dominant
position would appear now to be broadband communications,
more commonly known at this stage as cable television or
community antenna television (CATV). From an unobtrusive
beginning in the early 1950s in isolated mountain valleys that
broadcast television signals could not penetrate because of
unfavorable terrain, cable television has begun to break out
of its rural confinement and penetrate into the more intensively populated cities.

The man-made mountains and valleys of Manhattan Island
have proved nearly as inhospitable to television signals as the
Appalachian Mountains of Pennsylvania and West Virginia or
the Rockies of the mountain states. San Francisco and San
Diego are heavily dependent upon cable for delivery of television signals, and Chicago may soon be interlaced with cable.
An upsurge of cable installations in the late 1960s led to approximately a seven percent penetration of all American
homes by the end of the decade. Experts are now predicting
that between a third and a half of all American homes will be
wired by 1980—approximately the same degree of density that
prevailed in television at the time of political conventions and
election of 1956.

The advantages of cable to the political strategist and the
government public relations specialist are many and potentially
dramatic. Cable systems with from 20 up to 48 channels will
have an abundance of facilities available for new uses, including
political and governmental broadcasts. Just as the advertising

agency seeks to concentrate its commercial message in areas where sales are most likely, the campaign manager will theoretically be able to zero in on areas where his message will do the most good and avoid throwing away his money and his efforts where he cannot hope for votes.

The candidate for Governor of New Jersey, or Mayor of Newark, will no longer be forced to buy time on New York City stations whose rate cards reflect mass circulation in New York and Connecticut as well as New Jersey. The candidate for Congress for the tenth district in Ohio is already using cable because of the wastefulness of buying facilities from West Virginia or Central Ohio television stations, which reach only minimally into his territory. Other cable systems in such widely scattered points as Greesboro, North Carolina; Farmington, New Mexico; San Diego, California and Honolulu, Hawaii made facilities available in 1968 for congressional candidates and for aspirants to a wide variety of lesser offices.

The candidate for Congress in a New York City, Chicago or Los Angeles constituency will in all probability after cable develops further, be able to isolate out a channel covering his district and thus avoid paying a high price for coverage of all the remainder of New York City plus large portions of New York State, New Jersey and Connecticut.

There are other intriguing possibilities with cable. In the near future it is expected that cable systems will install a two-way facility that will permit a subscriber to send messages back to cable headquarters. At the very least it will be possible for the cable system management to keep a record on a minute by minute basis of households tuned in to any given channel; thus, the candidate will be able to identify viewers of his message. The imaginative candidate and his managers may be able to devise programs which will elicit responses from viewers on a "return path" facility. Even though in the earlier stages the "return path" may consist only of a narrow band limiting response to coded messages, it is conceivable that the creative political mind will be able to query potential voters and even set up a district wide question and answer conference with his constituents which in effect will provide a plebiscite.

As two-way communications become more sophisticated, a development which we can logically expect within the next two decades, a broad range of devices serving both the purposes of governmental communications to the electorate and candidate contact with voters appear a realistic possibility.

A national government channel might enable the administration in power to present its case and obtain reactions in a national referendum. Members of Congress who now have little opportunity for national exposure and even restricted opportunities to reach their own constituents would be enabled to maintain a give-and-take relationship with their own districts in which they can obtain immediate reaction to policy statements. Pre-recorded messages on given issues could be called up by viewers on demand from computer storage facilities by the use of a device which will probably resemble a touch-tone telephone.

Opportunities for more personalized appeals aimed directly at voters' interests during campaign periods are an even more significant potentiality for some time within the next two decades. It is conceivable that the candidate could query voters on topics in which they are interested before beginning a campaign speech. The man-in-the-street device, used so successfully by Governor Dewey in his 1950 campaign, could involve a larger cross section of the electorate. The John F. Kennedy speech to the Houston Ministerial Union in 1960 could be made available for retrieval by coded message in all parts of the country where the Kennedy campaign managers saw fit to distribute it. The Richard Nixon arena programs of 1968 could involve whole communities rather than small studio audiences, if campaign managers were willing to relax some of the tight controls they maintained over those programs. The election eve broadcasts of both President Nixon and Hubert Humphrey could have eliminated the battery of telephone operators who accepted telephoned questions and relayed them to the candidates. The device could also have widened the base of national participation.

Advertising agencies may be able to use cable for copy testing purposes, thus eliminating such devices as the use of the *Reader's Digest* mailing list in 1952 to arrive at the "Eisenhower, Man of Peace" theme used for spot announcements in that year. Money raising efforts could be expanded, simplified and the commitment to donate funds speeded by using the device of the telethon with voters requested to make contributions immediately by pushing buttons on two-way cable devices. At some time in the future it appears that facsimile printout devices will be attached to householders' cable terminals. At such time the voter will be able to call up from a storage point entire speeches, significant quotes or such factual information regarding candidates, platforms or voter records as he may desire.

The most significant result may well be to eliminate some of the frustration which arises out of the present one-way mass audience approach. The average voter may not have an opportunity to debate with his elected representatives, but he will have a device to make his attitudes known, obtain instant responses, and achieve a closer personal relationship which should serve to alleviate some of his feelings of detachment from governmental and political activity.

Cable undoubtedly will open up new opportunities and enable cost savings, but it will not necessarily solve all the problems which are being generated by television.

Because there will be an additional number of channels available, the political candidate and his supporters will have to compete even more vigorously for attention. This may put even a greater premium on production techniques and creativity. If cable becomes the workhorse for political campaigning, it is entirely possible that the regular broadcast television networks will be used only for major campaign efforts and the local stations by-passed in favor of less expensive, more controllable cable.

This presupposes that network television will not be affected by the growth of cablevision; a highly speculative assumption. It is conceivable that the entire structure of broadcasting may be so altered at the end of the two decades that conventional television will no longer have the charm to the politician and the influence on the voter that it has as the 1970s begin.

The knottiest problem campaign planners must solve is how to get viewers to watch their cable channel when their candidate is performing or when his message is being transmitted over a 24 or 36 or 48 channel system. They run the risk that the program will be lost in an avalanche of education, entertainment, information and miscellaneous services. In such a vast proliferation of programming, the political campaign appeal runs the risk of being inundated in an ocean of competition. Of course some of that competition exists in television now. The only completely safe bet to trap the viewer is the short commercial spot inserted between highly rated programs. Perhaps outlawing the broadcast television "spot" and the application of some ingenuity to promotion of cable programs, combined with creating attractive political messages, will enable cable to replace broadcast television as a prime outlet. The cost saving should be sufficient to attract the best minds in political campaign techniques to turn their efforts in that direction.

It is unlikely that cable will serve as a direct replacement for the mass media campaign performance. It is questionable whether it will frequently, if ever, duplicate the size of the audience that can be attracted to a televised political rally. But it can enlarge the size of a campaign meeting in the supermarket parking lot, the county fair grounds or the high school auditorium, at the same time maintaining a similar degree of personal contact. The absence of the candidate in the flesh can be counteracted by the opportunity for pushbutton queries and responses. Large numbers of interested voters now undergo the inconvenience of leaving the comfort of home and traveling to such rallies. It stands to reason that more would participate if it were unnecessary to leave the easy-chair in the living room.

Cable may offer another technological innovation that will test the creative talents of campaign managers, the facsimile or hardcopy printout. It is quite conceivable, according to experts, that one adjunct to the cable-fed television receiver will be a device comparable to the present facsimile machine, which will print in the living room messages transmitted from the cable's head-end. It is fascinating to contemplate how a candidate might combine his message to voters with printed questions and answers, attitudes and opinions delivered directly to the viewer by cable. The hardcopy could include quotes from previous speeches, statistics, slogans, still pictures or even quotes from his opponent with appropriate replies. There is no reason full speeches, voting records or biographical data could not be stored in computer memory for release on call.

Abandonment of microwave relay facilities in favor of city-to-city satellite transmission will probably result in a dramatic reduction in distribution costs for national or regional television programs. The national cable network could thus become a comparatively inexpensive achievement for delivering the political message. While it seems unlikely that the direct-to-home satellite broadcast will be developed for use in the United States because of the existence of our considerable network of earth-bound facilities, it still must be considered a possibility. If such a system were ever to be put into use, the President of the United States could address all the people of the nation simultaneously without the use of co-axial cables, microwave relays, or television antennas and transmitters. One transmitter and antenna would relay the signal to a satellite stationed 22,300 miles over the equator at a point due south of Omaha. The satellite would receive the signal, amplify it, and return it. Rooftop antennas connected to television sets in the home would receive the signal and project it onto a screen or by a process of amplification of light onto a living room wall.

The video cassette or disc could introduce an entirely new dimension. Marketing of video playback equipment, which will project program materials onto the television screen, began in mid 1971. Some analysts predict that video playback technology will be making a significant impact by the late 1970s. It is possible to visualize the candidate and his manager recording their programs in cassette or disc form for circulating among their constituents. The cassette or disc may be too costly for personalized distribution, but circulation by what television distributors call the "bicycling" process could make it possible for the cassette or disc to be the center of attention at a neighborhood coffee party or cocktail rally, after which a campaign worker could take the cassette on to the next gathering of campaign supporters. A combination of broadband communications with cassette playback would enable cable to serve as the distribution mechanism, thus eliminating the necessity for hand-carrying the cassette from rally to rally.

It doesn't seem very likely that the picture phone will play a significant role in local campaigns, but it may become an invaluable tool for presidential campaign organizations. A conference call link-up among campaign executives and the candidate could eliminate some of the expensive and time-consuming travel to central points for mid-campaign strategy sessions. The picture phone will permit examination of documents, statistics, charts, and perhaps, most importantly from the campaign point of view, new campaign materials prior to their release to the general public.

The advantages accruing to political campaigning from new technology will not be lost on government. Cable channels can be dedicated to extended live coverage of congress, state legislatures, school boards and city councils. There will be ample cable space available for regular reports to constituents by elected officials. A full-time weather channel has been suggested. Government agencies and departments on national, state, and local levels will have new opportunities to deliver reports and new information to the public. The Department of Agriculture will have a device for reporting on new developments of interest to farmers and gardeners, the Department of Commerce on business and scientific information, and the Department of Health, Education and Welfare on developments of wide public interest in these fields. The Pentagon and NASA too will have a new communications channel to test the skills of their highly publicized public information departments.

President Lyndon B. Johnson in his speech accompanying the signing of the Public Broadcast Act in 1968 said that our problem now is not "making miracles, but managing them." That will be the problem of campaign managers and government officials alike, as the age of television broadens out into the age of television plus cables, cassettes, picture phones, communication satellites and other technologies still on the drawing boards.

The revolution begun by television in 1950 has already created profound changes in the political process, but the revolution has only begun. The accelerating pace of technological discovery and the capability of society to adapt suggest that the drama of the 1950s and 1960s will be repeated many times over. No one could have anticipated in 1948 that nearly every home in the United States would be able within twenty years to watch at the moment they take place a political convention, the counting of ballots on election night, the inauguration of a president, or a debate between two presidential candidates.

If television as we know it could grow so swiftly, why couldn't some new technology grow with an equally rapid pace? Television has furnished many opportunities for more effective government and more effective political campaigning. It has likewise posed many new problems—problems of campaign expenditures, image making, news management, harnessing the medium in the most effective way and of curbing excesses. Perhaps our concern with these problems is already outdated. Perhaps rather than debating efforts to make our obsolescent device better serve our electoral processes, we should be preparing for the next step in communications technology. At the very least while learning how better to cope with television as we know it now, it is essential to keep one eye on the future. As early as the 1972 national election, broadband communications and video cassettes may be on the market in sufficient volume to make them political communications devices of significance.

The American political system has survived nearly 200 years of newspapers, more than 50 years of radio, more than 20 years of television; and where television may have in its shorter span of time had the most profound impact, political communications, except for the new technology, are just about what they were before. Oratorical styles have changed, the spot announcement has become a dominant campaign device, interviews and question-and-answer programs of the arena style are largely replacing old-style oratory, advertising agencies and public relations firms are playing a much greater role, but the basic elements remain constant: the candidate, his organization, and his attitude on the issues of the day. Television has simply accelerated communications among and between these various elements and made them more personal and more graphic. Television has served to quicken the pace, enlarge the contacts, personalize the leadership and increase the budget, but it has not changed the basic essentials of the governing and political processes, nor has it provided an opportunity for direct participation by masses of voters.

The obligation on the part of the public and its leaders the world over is to be more ready to adapt to change than we were when television suddenly burst upon us in the 1950s. By being better prepared, we can avoid some of the traps that television set in the last twenty years. By anticipating in advance what technology may bring in the future, we can avoid the "tyranny of small decision." We can harness modern technology rather than letting it call the tune. We can avoid the excesses which have tarnished television's remarkable record.

ACKNOWLEDGMENTS

The account of the complicated relationships between television on the one hand and politics and government on the other which follows in this volume could not have been constructed without the warm and enthusiastic cooperation of a mumber of persons who played significant roles in the maturation of the "electric mirror" during the past two decades.

Particularly helpful were James C. Hagerty, who figures prominently in the book as Press Secretary first to Governor Dewey, then to President Eisenhower and finally as an ABC executive; Robert R. Mullen, who was deeply involved in the early pre-convention Eisenhower movement; Carroll Newton of Batten, Barton, Durstine & Osborn, who was the first advertising agency professional in the art of blending politics and television; Reggie Schuebel, the veteran time buyer, who was always in the front ranks when the National Democratic Party campaigned on television or radio in the 1950s and early 1960s; Allan Gardner and Barry Nova, who planned and placed the advertising for Hubert Humphrey in his campaign for the presidency in 1968 and almost pulled out an unexpected victory; Bill Connell, John Stewart and Ted Van Dyk of Humphrey's staff and Humphrey himself who was not bashful in describing his reactions to the 1968 convention and campaign.

Also from the political arena helpful information was furnished by Robert Smalley, now executive assistant to the Secretary of Commerce, who managed vice-presidential campaigns for both William J. Miller in 1964 and Spiro T. Agnew in 1968 and a senatorial campaign for Robert Griffin of Michigan in 1966; by Howard Gamser, staff director of the committee set up by the Democrats at their 1968 convention to recommend changes in convention procedures and the committee's chairman, Congressman James C. O'Hara of Michigan.

Robert Strauss, Treasurer of the Democratic National Committee, filled in some gaps. It is also impossible to overlook a rich lode of political experience shared by GOP chairman William Miller of the Republican National Committee in 1964, by arrangements committee vice chairman Robert Pierce, subcommittee heads Robert Snodgrass and Mrs. Ike Kampmann, party officers Fred Scribner and Mrs. C. Douglass Buck, Jr. and and convention manager Robert Knowles.

Among representatives of the media particularly helpful were Theodore F. Koop, who was my eyes and ears in Washington for the decade of the 1950s as director of CBS News operations in Washington; Elmer Lower, who was then the CBS News specialist in convention and election coverage and went on to the presidency of ABC News; Julian Goodman, now president of NBC, but previously the second in command at NBC News; Louis G. Cowan, who has worked both sides of the street as advisor to candidates and as network television president at CBS; J. W. (Bill) Roberts, chief of the Time-Life Broadcast News Bureau in Washington, who filled in the story of the regional and local broadcast bureaus in Washington, and Robert Menaugh, the veteran head of the House Radio and Television Gallery. Izzy Siegal, head of the CBS photo section, was particularly helpful in combing through his picture files for a graphic record of significant episodes in television's history in political and governmental affairs.

Information concerning the functioning of the "electric mirror" outside the United States was obtained from experienced and knowledgeable experts in a variety of countries. In the United Kingdom, Sir Geoffrey Cox, former editor of Independent Television News, and Nigel Ryan, its present editor; John Grist, head of Current Affairs for the BBC; E. R. Thompson, formerly Deputy Head of News for the BBC; Robert McKenzie, Professor at the London School of Economics and expert political broadcaster for the BBC, and James D. Halloran, head of the Communications Research Center at the University of Leicester, were particularly helpful.

Similar roles were played in Germany by Peter von Zahn, independent film and television producer and television advisor to the CDU, and Professor Erwin Scheuch of the University of Cologne; in Sweden by Olof Rydbeck, now Swedish Ambassador to the United Nations, and formerly Director General of the Swedish Broadcasting Corporation, and by Edward Ploman, then Director of International Relations for Swedish Broadcasting Corporation, but now Executive Director of the International Broadcast Institute; in Italy by Luigi Barzini, author, columnist and member of the Italian Parliament; and in Japan by Tadamasa Hashimoto, Director of International Relations for NHK, the Japanese Broadcasting Corporation, and formerly NHK News Director, and by Hiroshi Sakomoto, formerly Deputy Director of the IBI, who has now returned to NHK in Tokyo as an executive in its International Affairs Division.

On the logistical side an invaluable contribution was made by Lloyd Morrisett, president of the Markle Foundation, who furnished office space, a skilled secretary-typist in Mrs. Margarete Hicinbotham, and a helpful office manager in Mrs. Virgina Dunlap.

At the Encyclopaedia Britannica Educational Corporation, Renate Moser typed an edited manuscript including the illegible scrawls, and Donna Carrick, in addition to carefully checking facts, was also a perceptive critic of style.

Special thanks are due to Helen Anderson, who kept a full and orderly file as my secretary both at CBS and Time, Inc., in addition to being an interested observer of the development of the "electric mirror."

There is another source of particular inspiration and satisfaction that should not be overlooked. A special medal of commendation should some day be struck for that gallant undermanned contingent of inexperienced CBS News television troups who confidently set out in Chicago in 1952 to whip the opposition and set the pattern for political coverage in subsequent years. When the medals are finally struck, they should go among others to Don

Hewitt, Fritz Littlejohn, David Zellmer, Perry Wolff, Walter Cronkite, Tommy Thompson and a host of others, who worked sixteen hours a day or more, because they wanted to cover the story and were satisfied with a job well done as an adequate reward.

NOTES

CHAPTER 1

1. "Benn Demands TV Programs for Trade Unions," *Daily Telegraph* (London), May 3, 1971, p. 5.
2. "The Selling of the Pentagon" was initially broadcast February 23, 1971 and repeated March 23, 1971.
3. Crater, Rufus, "What the Shooting Was All About," *Broadcasting,* July 1971, pp. 20–22.
4. The full House membership, rejecting the recommendation of its Commerce Committee, voted 226 to 81 to recommit a proposed citation to the committee.
5. Gould, Jack, "Cautions on Interpreting Vote on Stanton," *The New York Times,* July 27, 1971, p. 55.

CHAPTER 2

1. Hamilton, W.S., "The Information Jungle," *EBU Review,* May 1969, pp. 16–22.
2. Morgan, Thomas B., "The People Machine," *Harper's Magazine,* January 1961, pp. 53–57.
3. Lang, Kurt and Gladys, *Politics and Television,* Chicago, Quadrangle Books, 1968, pp. 36–77.
4. Ibid., pp. 78–149.

CHAPTER 3

1. Alexander, Herbert E. and Meyers, Harold B., *Fortune,* March 1970, p. 104; and Heard, Alexander, *The Costs of Democracy,* Chapel Hill, University of North Carolina Press, 1960, pp. 7–8.

2. Bendiner, Robert, *New York Times Magazine,* November 2, 1952, p. 13.

3. Alexander and Meyers, op. cit., p. 189. Former FCC Chairman Newton Minow, writing in *TV Guide* of March 7, 1970, page 9, suggests that of the approximately $200 million dollars spent on television, about three-fourths went into the production and placing of spot announcements.

4. McGinniss, Joe, *The Selling of the President 1968,* New York, Trident Press, 1968.

5. White, Theodore H., *The Making of the President 1968,* New York, Atheneum, 1969, p. 334.

6. Schneider, John G., *The Golden Kazoo,* New York, Rinehart & Co., 1956.

7. Morgan, Thomas B., op. cit., p. 54.

8. Donnelly, Richard, "How TV Turned A Race Around," *Television Magazine,* December 1966, pp. 38–41, 63–65.

CHAPTER 4

1. An unpublished mansuscript reporting on a study made by ABC News in 1968 shows virtually no change in voting patterns as a result of early election projections.

CHAPTER 5

1. Alexander and Meyers, op. cit., p. 104.

2. McGinniss, Joe, *op. cit.* McGinniss, quoting memoranda from members of the Nixon entourage, and citing his own experiences touring with the Nixon group, furnishes detailed descriptions of the methods used, as McGinniss describes it, to create the Nixon "image." For a description of the contribution made to creating the first spot announcement campaign in a televised presidential campaign, see Mayer, Martin, *Madison Avenue, USA,* New York, Harper & Row, 1958, pp. 293–297.

3. Alexander and Meyers, op. cit.

4. Chester, Lewis, Hodgson, Godfrey and Page, Bruce, *An American Melodrama,* New York, The Viking Press, 1969, p. 640.

CHAPTER 7

1. Clay T. Whitehead, director of the Office of Telecomunications Policy of the White House, called for the elimination of the fairness doctrine in a speech to the International Radio and Television Society in New York on October 6, 1971. Whitehead argued that the fairness doctrine should be replaced by an act providing assurances that the public at large will have adequate coverage of public issues. Such a right, said Whitehead, should be enforced through the courts rather than through the Federal Communications Commission.

2. Gould, Jack, "CBS Offers Free Time to Critics of White House," *New York Times,* June 23, 1970, p. 1. A further description can be found

in *Broadcasting* on June 29, 1970, pp. 32–34, under the title "Opening TV to Political Outs."
3. Anon., "CBS Takes 'Opposition' Off the Air," *Broadcasting*, August 24, 1970, p. 34.

CHAPTER 8

1. "People's Platform," CBS Radio Network, Broadcast July 22, 1952. The text of the Moody statement can be found in *Freedom of Information Center Publication No. 67, The Great Debates*, written by Robert E. Sanders and published by the University of Missouri School of Journalism, Columbia, Missouri, in November 1961.
2. Frank Stanton, president of CBS, wrote Senator Moody on August 6, 1952, endorsing Senator Moody's proposal.
3. The Kennedy wire accepting the invitation to debate was addressed to President Stanton of CBS dated July 29, 1960. The Nixon wire of acceptance was dated July 31.
4. Those attending the meeting included four Nixon supporters: Fred Scribner, Ted Rogers, Herbert Klein and Caroll Newton; one Kennedy representative, Leonard Reinsch, and one delegate each for the four networks: John Charles Daly for ABC, Lester Bernstein for NBC, Joseph Keating for MBS and the writer for CBS.
5. The network delegation was unchanged from the August 9, except that William R. McAndrew, NBC's executive vice president in charge of news, had replaced Lester Bernstein.
6. There was one notable exception. Jim Hagerty told Lou Shollenberger of CBS News on December 22, 1960, "You can bet your bottom dollar that no incumbent president will ever enage in any such debate or joint appearance in the future."
7. An excellent summary of opinions and statistical surveys may be found in Sanders, Robert E., op. cit., pp. 20–22.
8. One sentence from Nixon's telegram of acceptance, filed July 31, 1960, specified that ". . . joint appearances would be conducted as full and free exchange of views without prepared texts or notes and without interruption."
9. A detailed description of this confrontation may be found in Chester, Lewis, et al., op. cit., pp. 337–349.

CHAPTER 9

1. Oulihan, Richard, *The Man Who*, New York, The Dial Press, 1971. This book describes the 1932 Democratic Convention in detail.
2. The text of the code may be found in a mansucript written by Charles A. H. Thompson of the Brookings Institution in Washington, entitled "The Politics of National Party Conventions," p. 15.
3. This analysis exists in memo form in the CBS News files.
4. During the 1968 National Convention, the Democratic Party established a commission on rules chaired by Congressman James G. O'Hara of Michigan. The commission has made a thorough study of conven-

tion procedures and has submitted recommendations to the National Committee that would radically alter the convention process; but it seems unlikely that tradition can be lightly brushed aside and the full O'Hara program adopted.

CHAPTER 10

1. Twentieth Century Fund Commission on Campaign Costs in the Electronic Era, *Voters Time,* New York, The Twentieth Century Fund, 1969, p. 12.
2. Donnelly, op. cit.
3. Stone, Richard, *Wall Street Journal,* August 14, 1970, p. 1.
4. Alexander and Meyers, op. cit.
5. Ibid.
6. Federal Communications data quoted by Alexander and Meyers, op. cit., p. 189. Alexander and Meyers estimate that "the total bill for putting political messages on the air" for all candidates and parties, including production and other costs was approximately 90 million dollars or "nearly a third of all money spent on campaigning that year."
7. Report of the Twentieth Century Fund Commission on Campaign Costs in the Electronic Era, op. cit., p. 16.
8. Alexander and Meyer, op. cit.
9. Gould, Jack, op. cit., *Broadcasting,* June 29, 1970, pp. 32–34.
10. *Broadcasting,* op. cit., August 24, 1970, p. 34.
11. Two unpublished manuscripts, circulated by the Alicia Patterson Fund and written by William V. Shannon, furnish a detailed and colorful description of the British election process, particularly as it relates to financing. One entitled "How Does One Become an M.P.?" was distributed in December 1969 and the other "Money in Politics" in February 1970.
12. Newton Minnow used these figures in testifying before the Pastore Committee.
13. For a detailed examination of the Section 315 problem excellent analyses are furnished by Richard S. Salant in a pamphlet entitled "Political Campaigns and The Broadcaster," published by Harvard College in Boston in 1958 and by Charles A. H. Thompson in "Television, Politics and Public Policy," published by the Brookings Institution in May 1958.
14. Shannon, William V., op. cit.

BIBLIOGRAPHY

Academy of Television Arts and Science. *TV and Politics: A Forum,* Academy of TV Arts and Sciences, 1968.

Alexander, Herbert E. and Meyers, Harold B. "A Financial Landslide for the GOP," *Fortune,* March 1970, pp. 104–105, 186–189.

Alexander, Herbert E. "Political Broadcasting: What is its Impact on Elections?" Center for Information on America, 1964.

The American Institute for Political Communication. "Evolution of Public Attitudes Toward The Mass Media During An Election Year," Washington D. C., The American Institute for Political Communications, 1969.

The American Political Science Association. Report of the Commission on Presidential Campaign Debates, Washington D. C., The American Political Science Association, 1964.

Anon. "Television and Politics" *Television Magazine,* July 1960, pp. 46–49.

Anon. "TV's $20,000,000 Gift to the Presidential Campaign," *Sponsor,* November 7, 1960, pp. 29–32.

Arlen, Michael. *Living Room War,* New York, Viking Press, 1969.

Barrett, Marvin, Editor. *Survey of Broadcast Journalism 1969–1970,* New York, Grosset & Dunlop, 1970.

Barrett, Marvin, Ed. *Survey of Broadcast Journalism 1968–69,* New York, Grosset & Dunlop, 1969.

Bendiner, Robert. "How Much Has TV Changed Campaigning?" *New York Times Magazine,* Nov. 2, 1952, pp. 13+.

Berelson, Bernard R., Lazarfeld, Paul F. and McPhee, William N. *Voting —A Study of Opinion Formation in a Presidential Campaign,* Chicago, University of Chicago Press, 1954.

Bogardus, E. S. "Television and the Political Conventions," *Sociology and Social Research,* September-October, 1952, pp. 115–121.

289

Bogart, Leo. "Changing News Interests and the News Media," *The Public Opinion Quarterly,* Winter 1968–69, pp. 560–574.

Bogart, Leo. *The Age of Television,* New York, Frederick Unger Publishing Co., 1958, Chapter V, "The Political Effects of Television."

Bagdikian, Ben H. *The Information Machines,* Harper & Row, New York, 1971.

Bagdikian, Ben H. "Television—'the President's Medium'?" *Columbia Journalism Review,* Summer 1962, pp. 34–38.

Barnouw, Erik. *The Image Empire,* New York, Oxford University Press, 1970.

Brucker, Herbert. "What's Wrong With Objectivity?" *Saturday Review,* October 11, 1969, pp. 77–79.

Burdick, Eugene and Brodbeck, Arthur J. *American Voting Behavior* Glencoe, Illinois, The Free Press, 1959.

Burns, James MacGregor. "Despite the Hoopla, it's the Best System," *New York Times Magazine,* April 26, 1964, pp. 11–12.

Campbell, Angus. "Has Television Reshaped Politics?" *Columbia Journalism Review,* Fall 1962, pp. 10–13.

Campbell, Angus; Converse, Philip E.; Miller, Warren E.; Stokes, Donald E. *The American Voter,* New York, John Wiley & Sons, 1960.

Campbell, Angus; Gurin, Gerald; and Miller, Warren E. "Television and the Election," *Scientific American,* May 1953, pp. 46–48.

Cannon, Clarence. *Democratic Manual: for the Democratic National Convention of 1960,* Democratic National Committee, 1960.

Cannon, James E., Editor. *Politics USA,* New York, Doubleday, 1960.

Carney, Francis M. and Way, H. Frank, Jr. *Politics 1960,* San Francisco, Wadsworth, 1960.

Cater, Douglass. *The Fourth Branch of Government,* Boston, Houghton Mifflin, 1959.

Center for the Study of Democratic Institutions. *The Great Debates,* Santa Barbara, Center for the Study of Democratic Institutions, 1962.

Chester, Lewis; Hodgson, Godfrey and Page, Bruce. *An American Melodrama: The Presidential Campaign of 1968,* New York, Viking Press, 1969.

Christenson, Reo M. and McWilliams, Robert O. *Voice of the People: Readings in Public Opinion and Propaganda,* New York, McGraw Hill, 1962.

CBS Television. *The Blue Conventions,* New York, CBS Television, 1956.

CBS Television Technical Operations Department. *TV Industry Pool: 1952 Political Convention Coverage,* New York, CBS Television, October 27, 1952.

Cone, Fairfax M. "Memo to Tomorrow's Madison Avenue," *Saturday Review,* October 11, 1969, pp. 71–74.

Crosby, John. *Quadrennial Madness, New York Herald Tribune,* July 7, 1952.

Cunningham and Walsh. *Television and the Political Candidate,* Cunningham and Walsh, New York, March 1959.

David, Paul T.; Goldman, Ralph M.; and Bain, Richard C. *The Politics of National Party Conventions,* Washington, D.C., Brookings Institution 1960.

David, Paul T. Editor. *The Presidential Election and Transition, 1960–1961,* Washington, D.C. Brookings Institution, 1961.

Donnelly, Richard. "How TV Turned A Race Around," *Television Magazine,* December 1966, pp. 38–41+.

Elliott, William Y. *Television's Impact on American Culture,* East Lansing, Michigan State University Press, 1956.

English, David. *Divided They Stand,* Englewood Cliffs, New Jersey, Prentice Hall, 1969.

Frost, David. *The Presidential Debate, 1968,* New York, Stein & Day, 1968.

Gelman, Morris J. "TV and Politics: '62," *Television Magazine,* October 1962, pp. 64–67+.

Glick, Edward M. *The Federal Government—Daily Press Relationship,* Washington, D. C., The American Institute for Political Communication, 1967.

Glick, Edward M., Editor. *The New Methodology: A Study of Political Strategy and Tactics,* Washington, D. C., American Institute for Political Communication, 1967.

Gould, Jack. "Why Should Mr. Nixon Have The Show All To Himself?" *New York Times,* February 8, 1970.

Grafton, Samuel. "TV and the GOP Candidates," *TV Guide,* May 30, 1964, pp. 24–27.

Halloran, James D; Elliott, Philip and Murdock, Graham. *Demonstration and Communication: A Case Study,* Harmondsworth, Penguin Books, 1970.

Halloran, James W. Editor. *The Effects of Television,* London, Panther Books, 1970.

Hamilton, W. S. "The Information Jungle," *EBU Review,* May 1969, pp. 16–22.

Heard, Alexander. *The Costs of Democracy,* Chapel Hill, University of North Carolina Press, 1960.

Higbie, Charles E. "1960 Election Studies Show Broad Approach, New Methods," *Journalism Quarterly,* Spring 1961, pp. 164–70.

Hornberger, Michael. "How TV Covers D. C.," *Television Magazine,* Jan. 1967, pp. 41+.

Hughes, Emmet John. "52,000,000 TV Sets—How Many Votes," *New York Times Magazine,* Sept. 25, 1960, pp. 23+.

Huntley, Chet; Brinkley, David and the Staff of NBC News. *Somehow It Works: A Candid Portrait of the 1964 Presidential Election,* New York, Doubleday, 1965.

International Business Machines. *The Fastest Reported Election,* New York, IBM, 1960.

James, Edwin H. "The Trouble $2,475,000 Can Buy," *Television Magazine,* December 1964, pp. 72–86.

Jenkins, Peter. "The Political Screen," *Contrast,* Autumn 1963, pp. 25–29.

Johns, James T. "Television and Politics '64," *The Beam,* June 1964, pp. 6–11.

Katz, Elihu and Lazarsfeld, Paul F. *Personal Influence, The Part Played By People In the Flow of Mass Communication,* New York, The Free Press, 1955.

Kelley, Stanley, Jr. *Professional Public Relations and Political Power*, Baltimore, Johns Hopkins Press, 1956.

Kennedy, John F. "A Force That Has Changed The Political Scene," Reprint from *TV Guide*, Nov. 14, 1960.

Kenworthy, E. W. "Campaign Special: TV or Train?" *New York Times Magazine*, April 29, 1956, pp. 13+.

Ketchum, McLeod and Grove. *The Effects of Political Convention and Campaign Television Coverage upon Politics in the United States*, Pittsburgh, Ketchum, MacLeod and Grove, 1960.

Klapper, Joseph T. *The Effects of Mass Communications*, Glencoe, Illinois, The Free Press of Glencoe Illinois, 1960.

Kraus, Sidney, Editor. *The Great Debates*, Bloomington, Indiana University Press, 1962.

Land, Herman. "Television and Elections," *Television Magazine*, April 1956, pp. 47–49+.

Lang, Kurt and Lang, Gladys. *Politics and Television*, Chicago, Quadrangle Books, 1968.

Lawrence, William H. "Presidential Press Conference," *TV Guide*, May 4, 1963, pp. 4–7.

Lerner, Max. "Television the Fourth Branch of Government," *TV Guide*, Nov. 28, 1970, pp. 6–9.

Luce, Clare Boothe. "Without Portfolio," *McCall's*, July 1960.

MacNeil, Robert. *The People Machine*, Harper & Row, New York, 1968.

Mannes, Marya. *Subverse: Rhymes For Our Times*, reprinted by permission of George Braziller Inc. and Harld Ober Associates.

Martin, Ralph G. *Ballots and Bandwagons*, New York, Rand McNally, 1964.

Mayer, Martin. *Madison Avenue, USA*, New York, Harper & Brothers, 1958.

McGinniss, Joe. *The Selling of the President 1968*, New York, Trident Press, 1969.

Merrill, J. R. and Proctor, C. H. *Political Persuasion by Television: Partisan and Public Affairs Broadcasts in the 1956 General Election*, East Lansing, Michigan State University, 1959.

Miami University, Department of Marketing. *The Influence of Television on the Election of 1952*, Oxford Research Associates, December 1954.

Minow, Newton. *TV Guide*, March 7, 1970, pp. 9–10.

Mitgang, Herbert. *Freedom to See: The Khrushchev Broadcast and Its Meaning for Television*, The Fund for the Republic, 1958.

Morgan, Thomas B. "The People Machine," *Harper's*, January 1961, pp. 53–57.

Morin, Relman. *The Associated Press Story of the Election, 1968*, New York, Pocket Books, 1968.

Murrow, Edward R. and other CBS News Correspondents, *Watch: The Television Guide of the 1956 Convention, the Campaign and the Election*, New York, Maco, 1956.

National Broadcasting Company. *The Longest Night*, New York, National Broadcasting Company, February 1963.

The New York Times. "What TV Is Doing To Us: A Survey of the Effects of Television on American Life," (Seven articles by the *NY*

Times radio and television editor, Jack Gould, based on nationwide reports from more than 100 *Times* correspondents), June 24, 1951 through June 30, 1951.

Novak, Robert D. *The Agony of the GOP, 1964,* New York, MacMillan, 1965.

Ogden, Daniel M. Jr. and Peterson, Arthur L. *Electing the President: 1964,* Chandler Publishing Co. 1964.

Oulihan, Richard. *The Man Who,* New York, Dial Press, 1971.

Paley, William S. "Television and the Presidential Campaign," An Address by William S. Paley, Chairman of the Board, Columbia Broadcasting System, Inc., delivered before the Poor Richard Club of Philadelphia, Jan. 17, 1953.

Pulse, Inc. "How Viewers Vote: A Special Pulse Study Checks Before and After Effects of TV on Attitudes Toward Candidates," *Television Age,* April, 1956, pp. 54–57.

RTNDA Bulletin. "Shakespeare Sees 'Liberal' Bias Suggests Balancing Ideological Make-Up of Staff," *RTNDA Bulletin,* Dec. 1969, pp. 11–12+.

Reddick, DeWitt C., Editor. *The Role of the Mass Media In A Democratic Society,* Papers and Descriptions from a Conference at the University of Texas, February 6 and 7, 1961, Austin, 1961, A University of Texas Public Affairs Publication.

Republican National Committee. *How To Use TV In a Political Campaign,* New York, Doyle Printing and Offset Co., 1962.

Anon. "Reshaping Teddy's Image," *Esquire,* June 1970, pp. 87–99.

Roper, Elmo. *You and Your Leaders,* New York, William Morrow & Co., 1957.

Royster, Vermont. "Presidential Press Conferences?" *The Quill,* February 1971, pp. 9–11.

Salant, Richard S. "Political Campaigns and The Broadcaster," Reprinted from *Public Policy: A Yearbook of the Graduate School of Public Administration,* Vol. VIII, 1958, Copyright 1958 by the Presidential Fellows of Harvard College.

Salant, Richard S. *The 1960 Campaign and Television,* Publication No. 66, Freedom of Information Center, University of Missouri, Columbia, October 1961.

Schneider, John G. *The Golden Kazoo,* New York, Rinehart & Co., 1956.

Sevareid, Eric. "In Defense of TV News," *TV Guide,* March 14, 1970, pp. 6–11.

Sevareid, Eric. *Candidates 1960,* New York, Basic Books Inc. 1959.

Shabecoff, Philip B. "Press and Television Coverage of the 1956 National Political Conventions," *Studies in Public Communications,* Summer 1959, pp. 40–46.

Shadegg, Stephen. *What Happened to Goldwater?* New York, Holt, Rinehart & Winston, 1965.

Shaffer, Helen B. "Television and the 1956 Campaign," Washington, D. C., *Editorial Research Reports,* 1955.

Shannon, William V. *Afterthoughts on a General Election,* Alicia Patterson Fund, July 1970.

Shannon, William V. *How Does One Become An M.P.?* The Alicia Patterson Fund, December 1969.

Shannon, William V. *Money and Politics,* The Alicia Patterson Fund, February 1970.

Simon, Herbert A. and Stern, Frederick, "The Effect of Television Upon Voting Behaviour in Iowa in the 1952 Presidential Election," *American Political Science Review,* June 1955, pp. 470–77.

Small, William. "To Kill A Messenger," New York, Hastings House 1970.

Spencer, Walter Troy. "The Agency Knack of Political Packaging," *Television Magazine,* August 1968, pp. 76–79.

Stanton, Frank. "An Appeal to the American People," *TV Guide,* Jan. 14, 1961, pp. 10+.

Steiner, Gary. *The People Look at Television, A Study of Audience Attitudes,* New York, Knopf, 1963.

Anon. "Television and Politics," Reprint from *Television Magazine,* July 1960.

Television Magazine. "The Schizoid Roles of TV In An Election Year," February 1968, pp. 28+. (Anon.)

Thompson, Charles A. H. *Television, Politics and Public Policy,* Reprint No. 25, Brookings Institution, May 1958.

Thompson, Charles A. H. *Television and Presidential Politics: The Experience in 1952 and the Problem Ahead,* Washington, D. C., Brookings Institution, 1956.

Thompson, Charles A. H. and Shattuck, Frances, M. *The 1956 Presidential Campaign,* Washington, D. C., The Brookings Institution, 1960.

Trenaman, Joseph & McQuail, Denis. *Television and the Political Image,* London, Methuen, 1961.

The Twentieth Century Fund Task Force on Financing Congressional Campaigns. *Electing Congress,* New York, The Twentieth Century Fund, 1970.

The Twentieth Century Fund Commission on Campaign Costs in the Electronic Era. *Voters' Time,* New York, The Twentieth Century Fund, 1969.

Wallace, David. *First Tuesday,* New York, Doubleday, 1964.

Ways, Max. "What's Wrong With News? It Isn't New Enough" *Fortune,* October 1969, pp. 110–113+.

Weisberger, Bernard. "How To Get Elected," *American Heritage,* August 1964, pp. 62–77.

Whale, John. *The Half Shut Eye: Television and Politics in Britain and America,* London, MacMillan & Co., 1969.

White, Theodore H. *The Making of the President 1960,* New York, Atheneum, 1961.

White, Theodore H. *The Making of the President 1964,* New York, Atheneum, 1965.

White, Theodore H. *The Making of the President 1968,* New York, Atheneum, 1969.

Wicker, Tom F. "Q's and A's about the Press Conference," *New York Times Magazine,* Sept. 18, 1963, pp. 24–25.

Wolff, Perry. *A Tour of the White House with Mrs. John F. Kennedy,* New York, Doubleday, 1962.

Wykoff, Gene. *The Image Candidates,* New York, MacMillan, 1968.

Wylie, Max. *Clear Channels,* New York, Funk & Wagnalls, 1955.

INDEX

ABC (American Broadcasting Company), 87
  Kennedy-Nixon Debates coverage, 198, 203
  1952 presidential election coverage, 222, 226
Adams, Sherman, 172
Advertising agencies. *See also specific agency.*
  in England, 146
  in Japan, 148
  role of, in television campaigning, 47, 57-63, 76-79, 108
Agnew, Spiro T., 5, 31, 155
  Des Moines speech, viii, 4, 5, 7-8, 164-65, 166, 167
Alexander, Herbert, 88, 244, 264
American Telephone and Telegraph Company, v
Andrews, Mark, 182, 256
AP (Associated Press), 81, 86
ARD (Arbeitsgemeinschaft der oeffentlichrechtlichen Rundfunkanstalten der Bundesrepublik Deutschland), 120, 128
Army-McCarthy hearings, 13
Arrowsmith, Martin, 173
Australia, television in, 141

Barrett, Edward W., 18
Bassett, James, 198
Batten, Barton, Durstine & Osborn agency, 47, 80, 92, 93, 94, 101, 104, 115, 196, 270. *See also* George H. Batten Company.
BBC (British Broadcasting Corporation), 120, 122, 123, 124, 125, 126, 128, 132-33, 252
Benn, Anthony Wedgewood, 4
Benton, William, 1, 270, 271
Berelson, Bernard, 83
Bernstein, Sidney, 147

Brandt, Willy, 142
  1969 election campaign, 39-41
Brinkley, David, 157, 158, 191
Broadcasting, 5
Broadcasting structure. *See* Networks, television.
Brownell, Herbert, 92, 270
Bryan, William Jennings, 74
Buchanan, Patrick, 91
Burns, John, 72
Butler, Paul, 3

Cable television systems
  and election campaigns, 256-57
  growth of, 272-73, 275-77
Califano, Joseph, 250
Canadian Broadcasting System, 31
Cantwell, Al, 92, 101
Carson, Johnny, 111, 181
Cavett, Dick, 111, 181
CBS (Columbia Broadcasting System), 2, 3, 33, 42, 81, 89
  coverage
    election campaigns, 96-97
    election returns, 82-83
    Kennedy-Nixon Debates, 197-98, 200, 203
    political conventions, 222, 226
  policy
    political fund-raising commercials, 246-47, 250
    spot announcements, 104
  programming
    "CBS News," 41, 112, 154
    "CBS Reports," 3
    "Face the Nation," 3, 29, 111, 181
    "Loyal Opposition," 168, 251
    "March of Time," 41-42
    "Meet the Press," 29, 111, 181
    "Person to Person," 42, 201
    "Pot Party," 3
    "See It Now," 13, 42
    "Selling of the Pentagon," 5-6, 186

HE
8700.7
.P6
M53

Mickelson, Sig.

The electric
mirror: politics
in an age of
television

DATE		
NOV 9 1976		
OCT. 11 1977		
NOV 2 9 1977		

CARD REMOVED